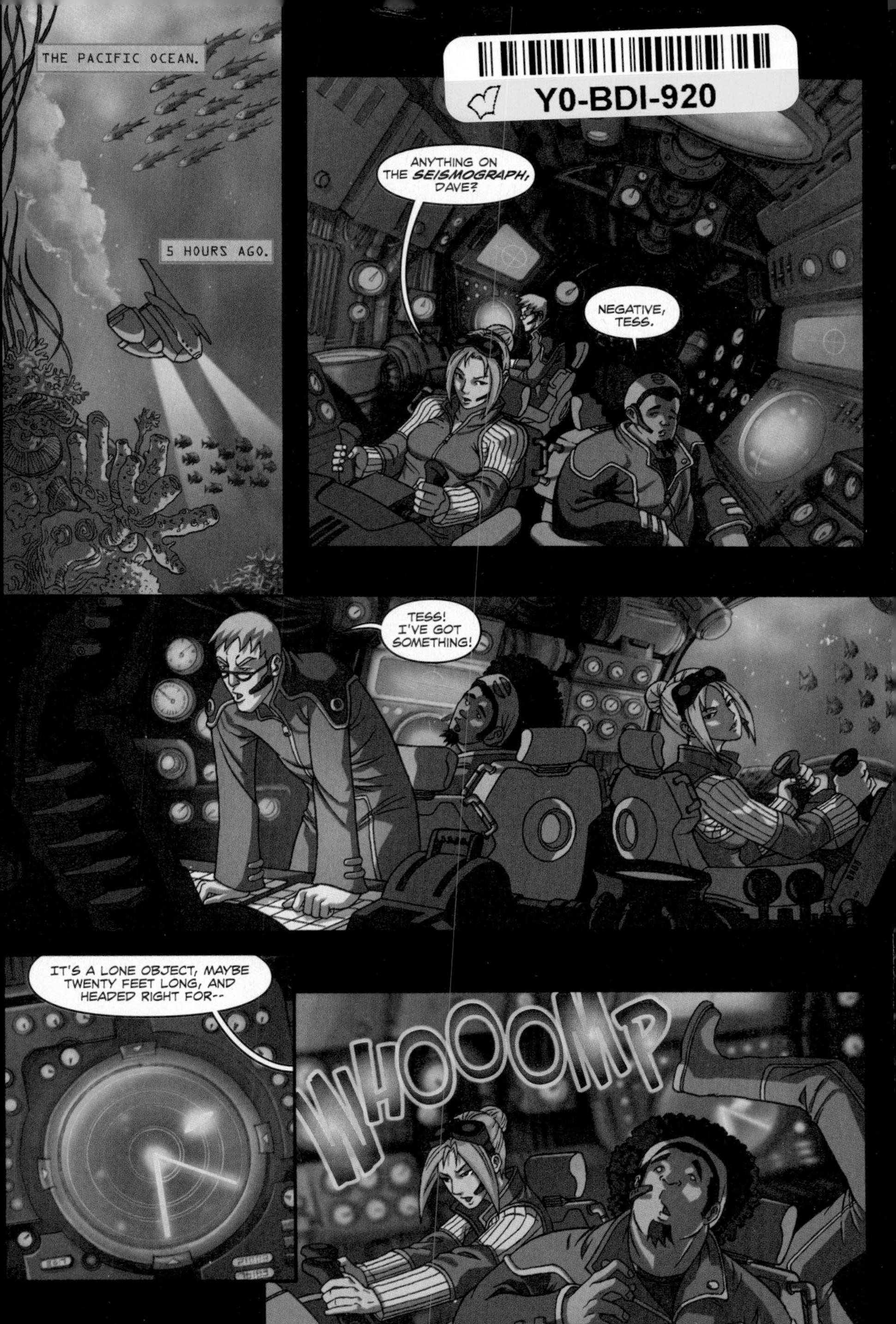
THE PACIFIC OCEAN.
5 HOURS AGO.
ANYTHING ON THE SEISMOGRAPH, DAVE?
NEGATIVE, TESS.
TESS! I'VE GOT SOMETHING!
IT'S A LONE OBJECT, MAYBE TWENTY FEET LONG, AND HEADED RIGHT FOR--
WHOOOOMP

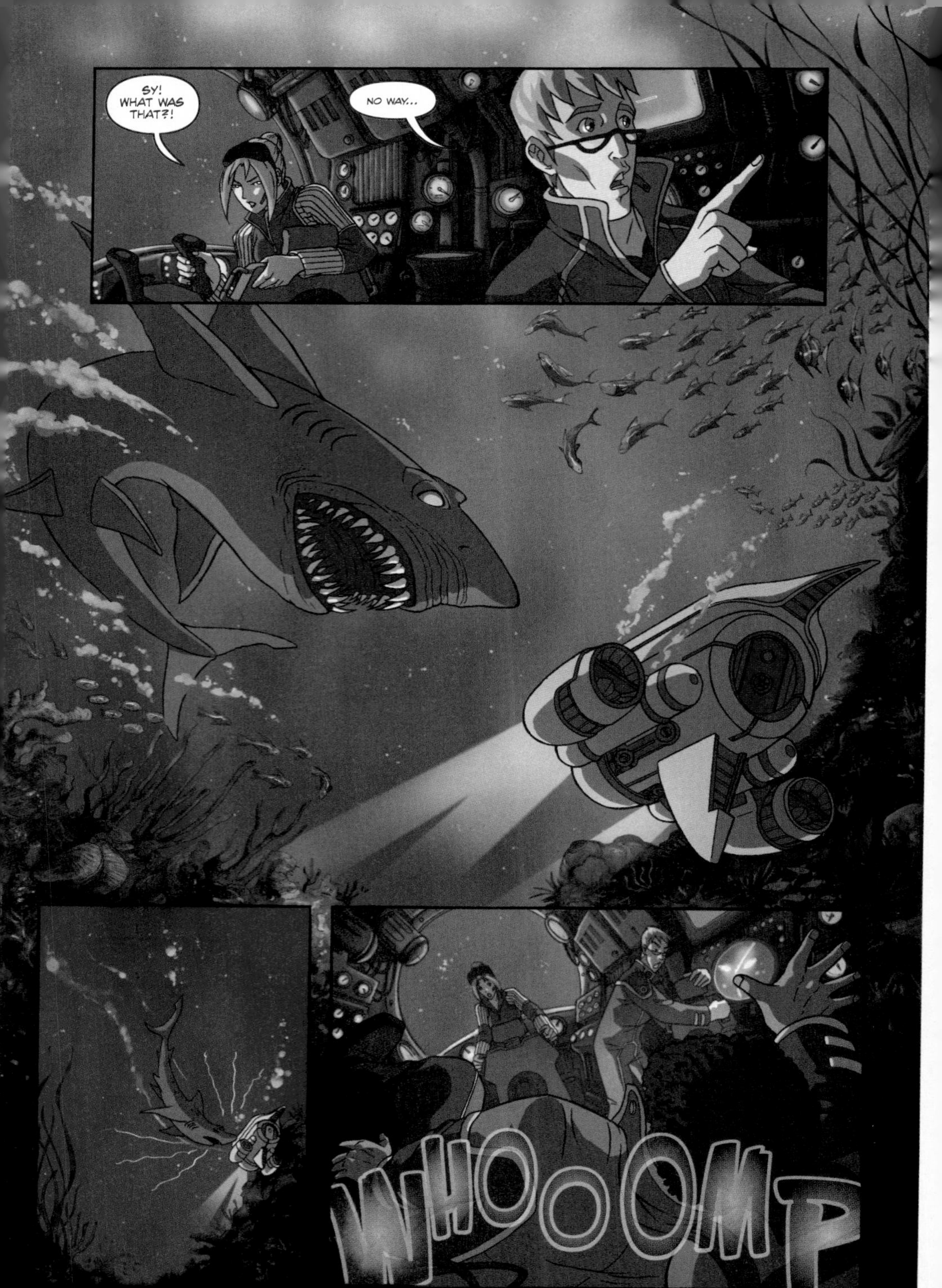
SY! WHAT WAS THAT?!
NO WAY...
WHOOOOMP

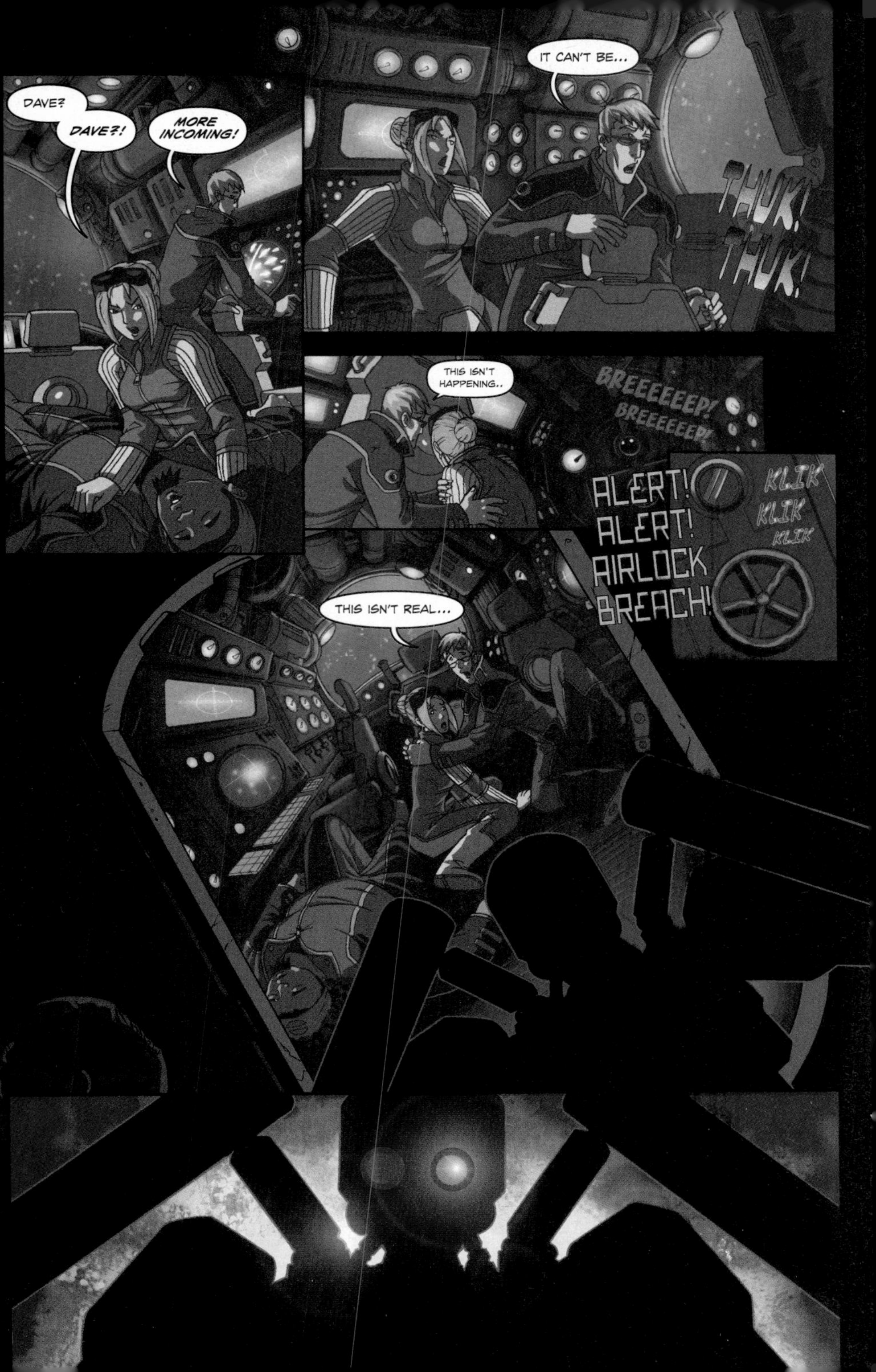
DAVE?
DAVE?!
MORE INCOMING!
IT CAN'T BE...
THUK! THUK!
THIS ISN'T HAPPENING..
BREEEEEEP! BREEEEEEP!
ALERT! ALERT! AIRLOCK BREACH!
KLIK KLIK KLIK
THIS ISN'T REAL...

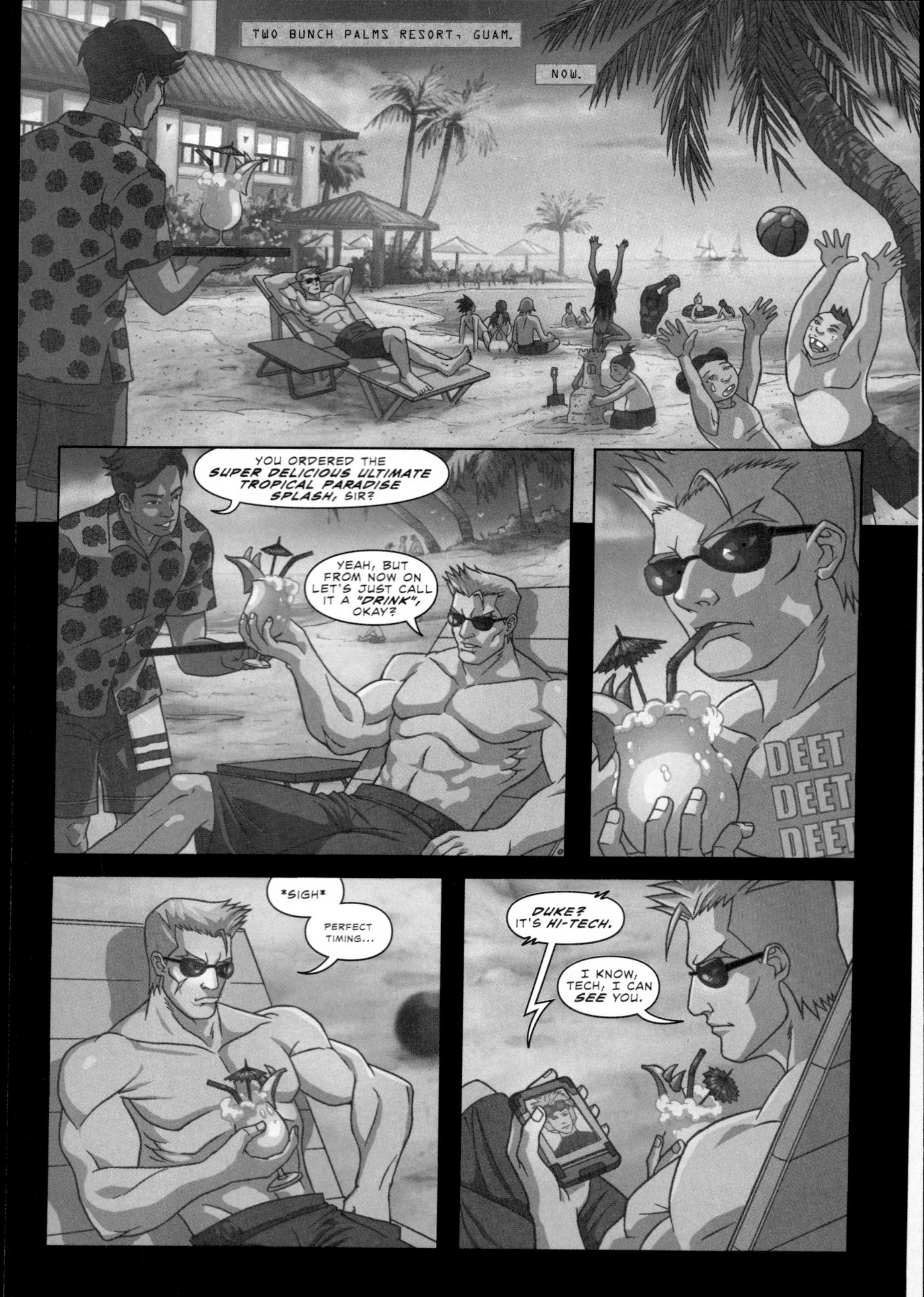
TWO BUNCH PALMS RESORT, GUAM.
NOW.
YOU ORDERED THE SUPER DELICIOUS ULTIMATE TROPICAL PARADISE SPLASH, SIR?
YEAH, BUT FROM NOW ON LET'S JUST CALL IT A "DRINK", OKAY?
DEET DEET DEET
SIGH
PERFECT TIMING...
DUKE? IT'S HI-TECH.
I KNOW, TECH, I CAN SEE YOU.

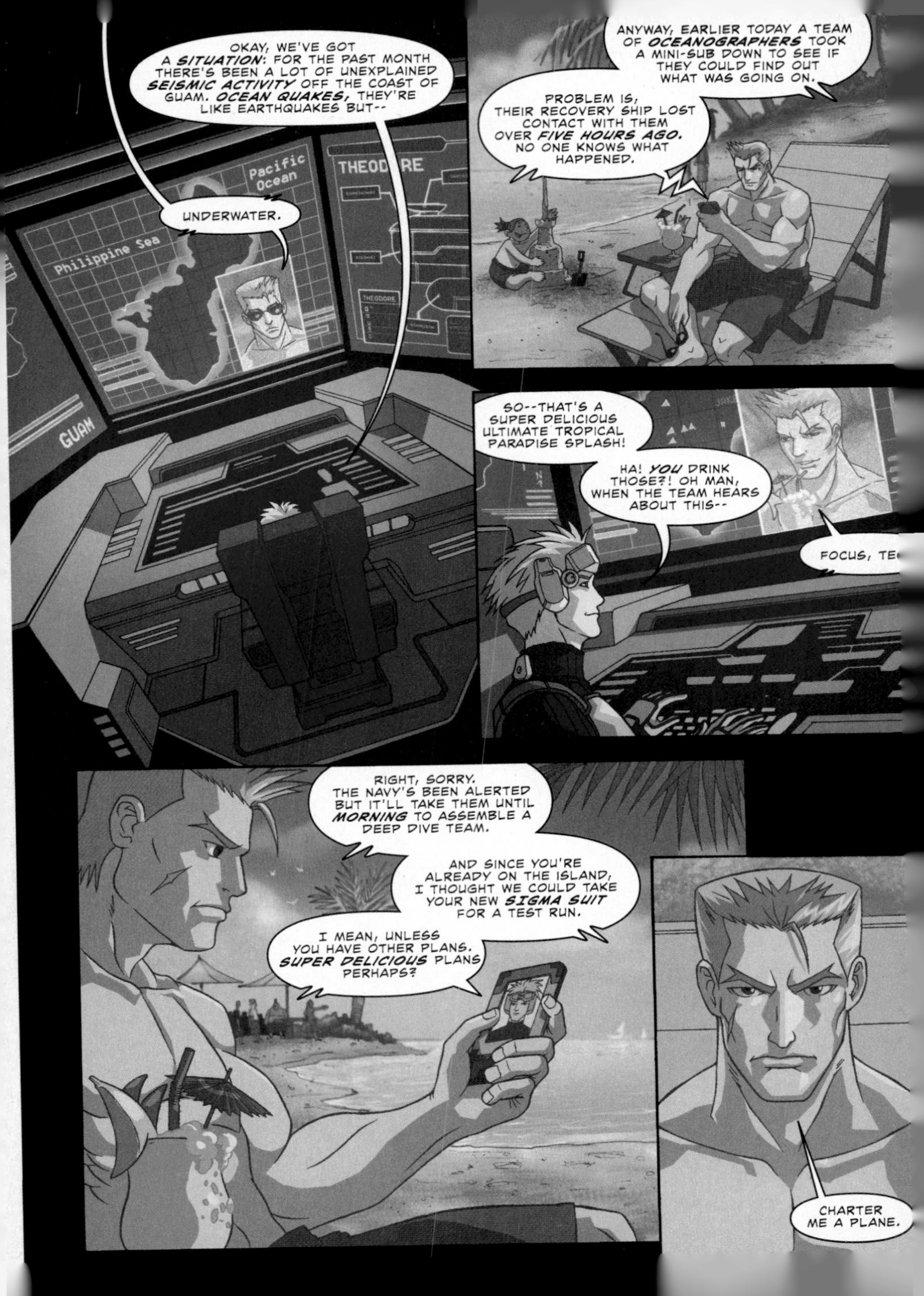
OKAY, WE'VE GOT A SITUATION: FOR THE PAST MONTH THERE'S BEEN A LOT OF UNEXPLAINED SEISMIC ACTIVITY OFF THE COAST OF GUAM. OCEAN QUAKES, THEY'RE LIKE EARTHQUAKES BUT--
Pacific Ocean
THEODORE
Philippine Sea
GUAM
UNDERWATER.
ANYWAY, EARLIER TODAY A TEAM OF OCEANOGRAPHERS TOOK A MINI-SUB DOWN TO SEE IF THEY COULD FIND OUT WHAT WAS GOING ON.
PROBLEM IS, THEIR RECOVERY SHIP LOST CONTACT WITH THEM OVER FIVE HOURS AGO. NO ONE KNOWS WHAT HAPPENED.
SO--THAT'S A SUPER DELICIOUS ULTIMATE TROPICAL PARADISE SPLASH!
HA! YOU DRINK THOSE?! OH MAN, WHEN THE TEAM HEARS ABOUT THIS--
FOCUS, TE
RIGHT, SORRY. THE NAVY'S BEEN ALERTED BUT IT'LL TAKE THEM UNTIL MORNING TO ASSEMBLE A DEEP DIVE TEAM.
AND SINCE YOU'RE ALREADY ON THE ISLAND, I THOUGHT WE COULD TAKE YOUR NEW SIGMA SUIT FOR A TEST RUN.
I MEAN, UNLESS YOU HAVE OTHER PLANS. SUPER DELICIOUS PLANS PERHAPS?
CHARTER ME A PLANE.

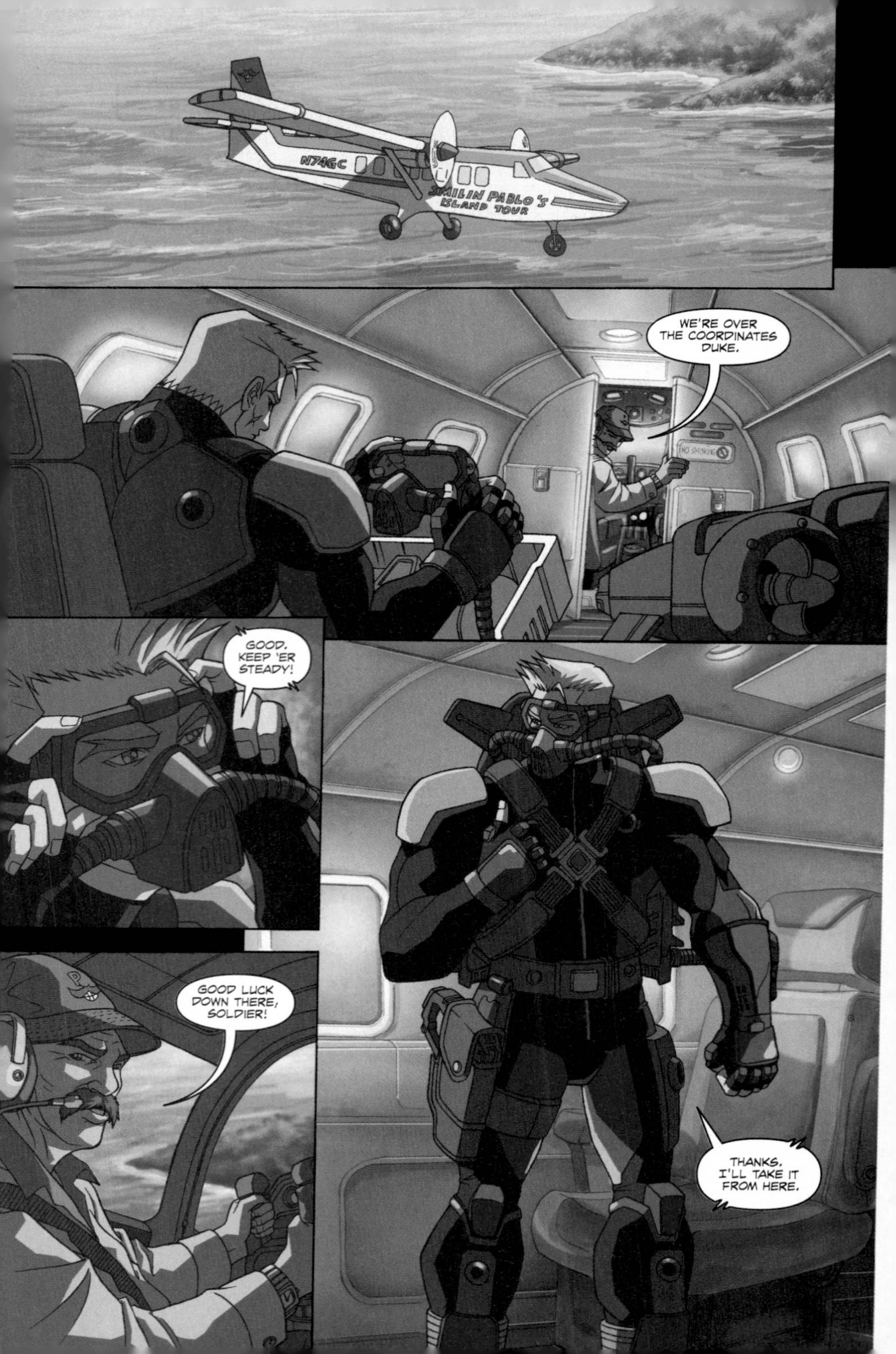
N74GC
SMILIN PABLO'S ISLAND TOUR
WE'RE OVER THE COORDINATES DUKE.
NO SMOKING
GOOD. KEEP 'ER STEADY!
GOOD LUCK DOWN THERE, SOLDIER!
THANKS. I'LL TAKE IT FROM HERE.

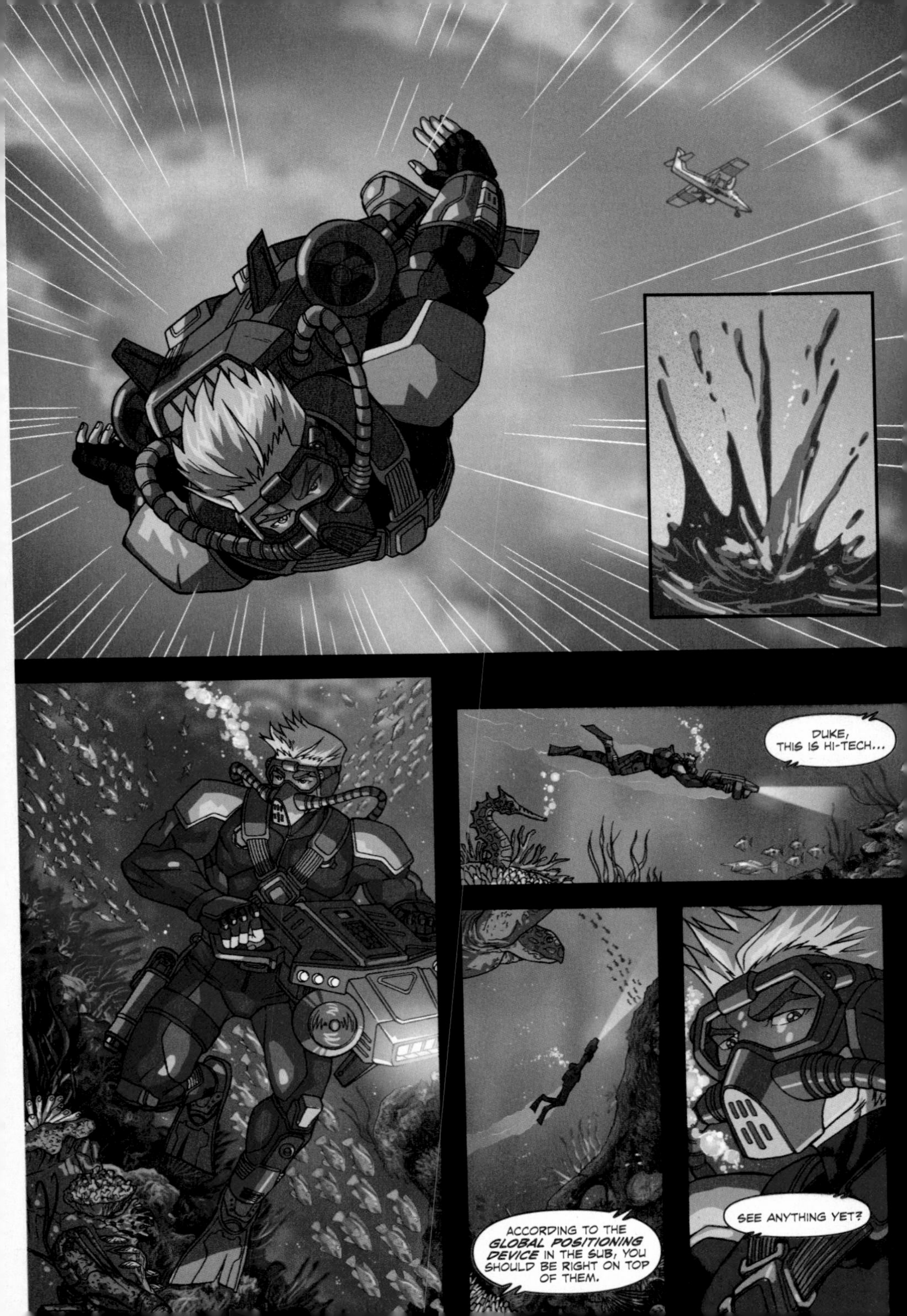
DUKE,
THIS IS HI-TECH...
ACCORDING TO THE GLOBAL POSITIONING DEVICE IN THE SUB, YOU SHOULD BE RIGHT ON TOP OF THEM.
SEE ANYTHING YET?

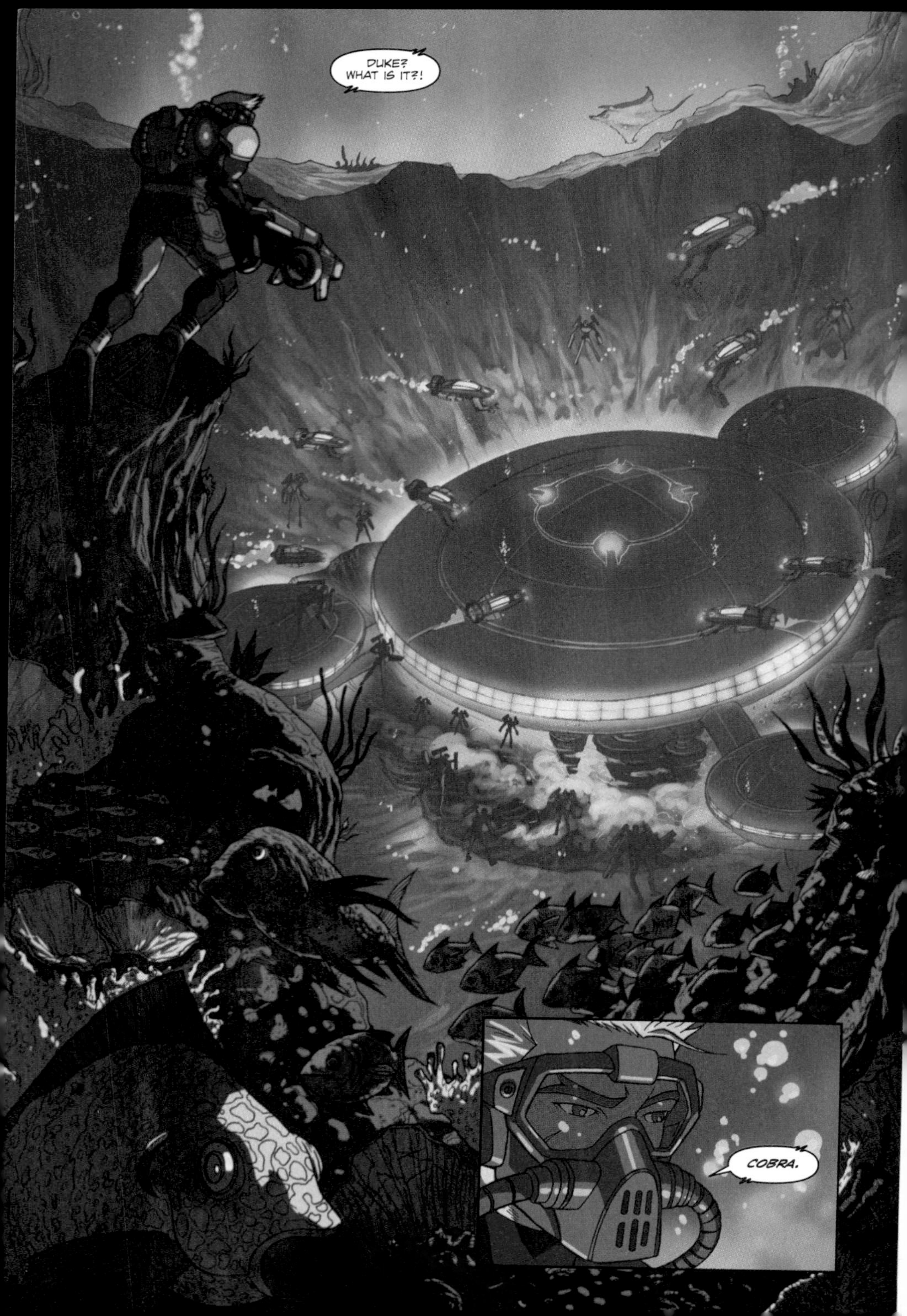
DUKE?
WHAT IS IT?!
COBRA.

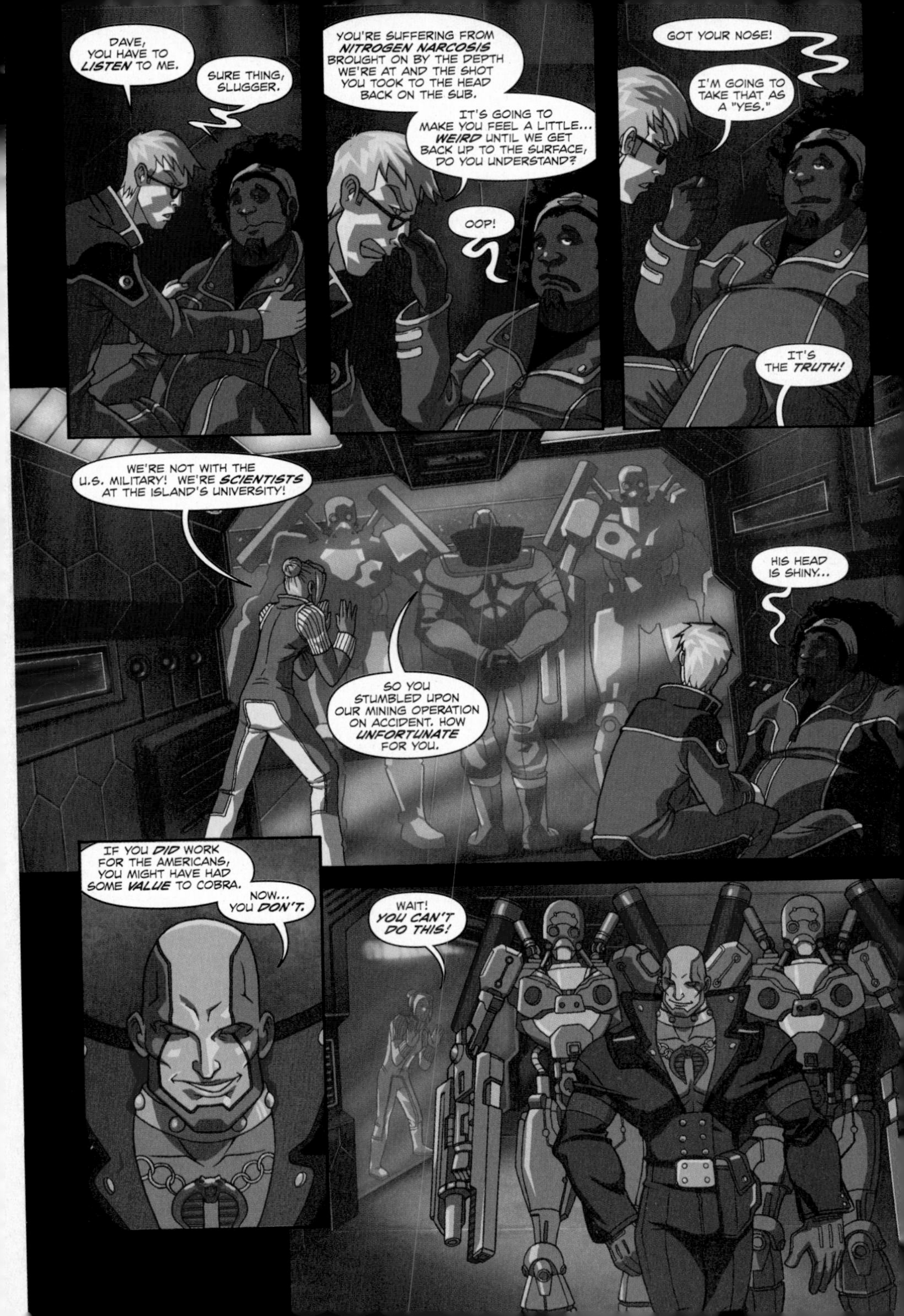
DAVE, YOU HAVE TO *LISTEN* TO ME.
SURE THING, SLUGGER.
YOU'RE SUFFERING FROM *NITROGEN NARCOSIS* BROUGHT ON BY THE DEPTH WE'RE AT AND THE SHOT YOU TOOK TO THE HEAD BACK ON THE SUB.
IT'S GOING TO MAKE YOU FEEL A LITTLE... *WEIRD* UNTIL WE GET BACK UP TO THE SURFACE, DO YOU UNDERSTAND?
OOP!
GOT YOUR NOSE!
I'M GOING TO TAKE THAT AS A "YES."
IT'S THE *TRUTH!*
WE'RE NOT WITH THE U.S. MILITARY! WE'RE *SCIENTISTS* AT THE ISLAND'S UNIVERSITY!
HIS HEAD IS SHINY...
SO YOU STUMBLED UPON OUR MINING OPERATION ON ACCIDENT. HOW *UNFORTUNATE* FOR YOU.
IF YOU *DID* WORK FOR THE AMERICANS, YOU MIGHT HAVE HAD SOME *VALUE* TO COBRA.
NOW... YOU *DON'T.*
WAIT! *YOU CAN'T DO THIS!*

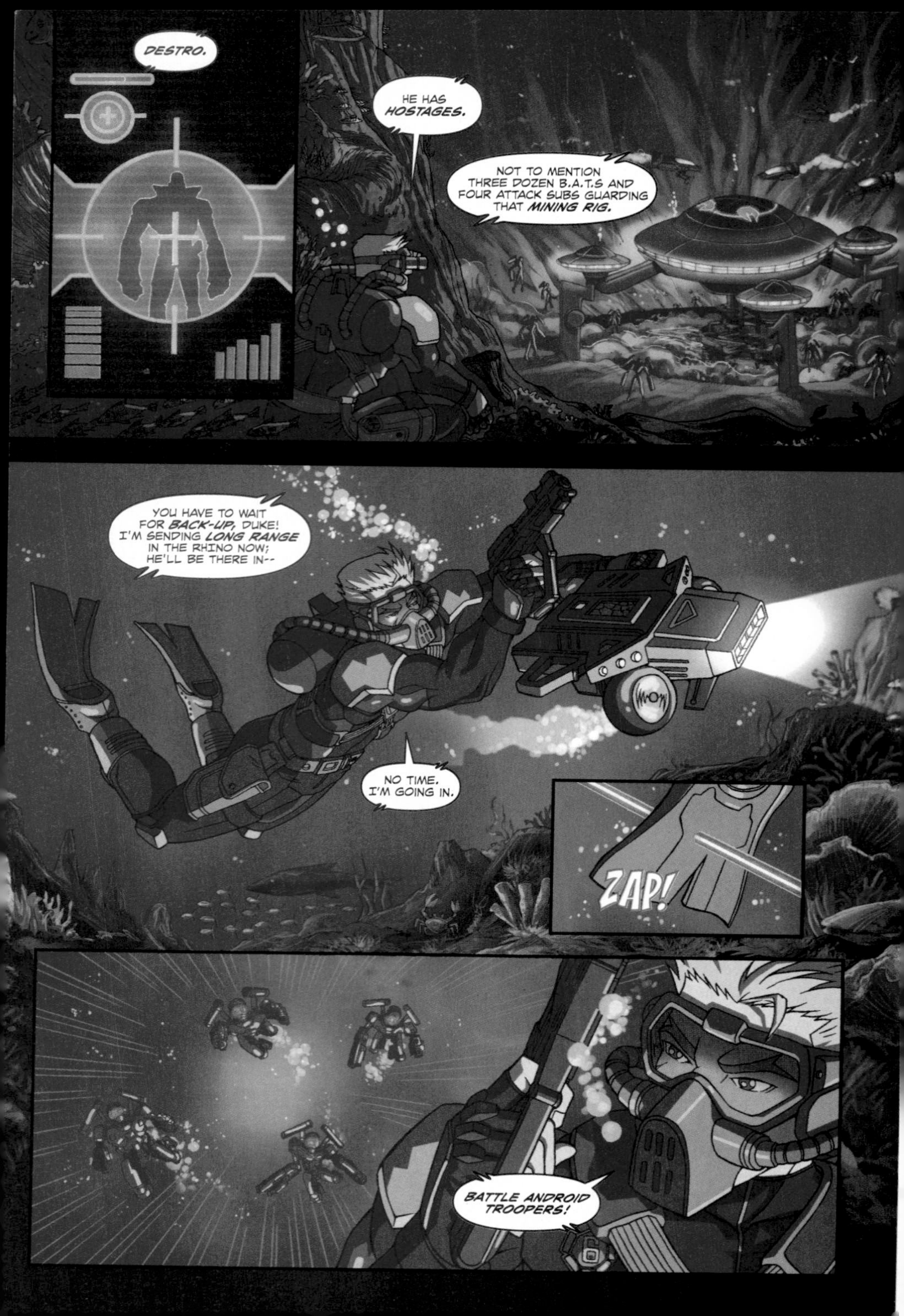
DESTRO.
HE HAS HOSTAGES.
NOT TO MENTION THREE DOZEN B.A.T.S AND FOUR ATTACK SUBS GUARDING THAT MINING RIG.
YOU HAVE TO WAIT FOR BACK-UP, DUKE! I'M SENDING LONG RANGE IN THE RHINO NOW; HE'LL BE THERE IN--
NO TIME. I'M GOING IN.
ZAP!
BATTLE ANDROID TROOPERS!

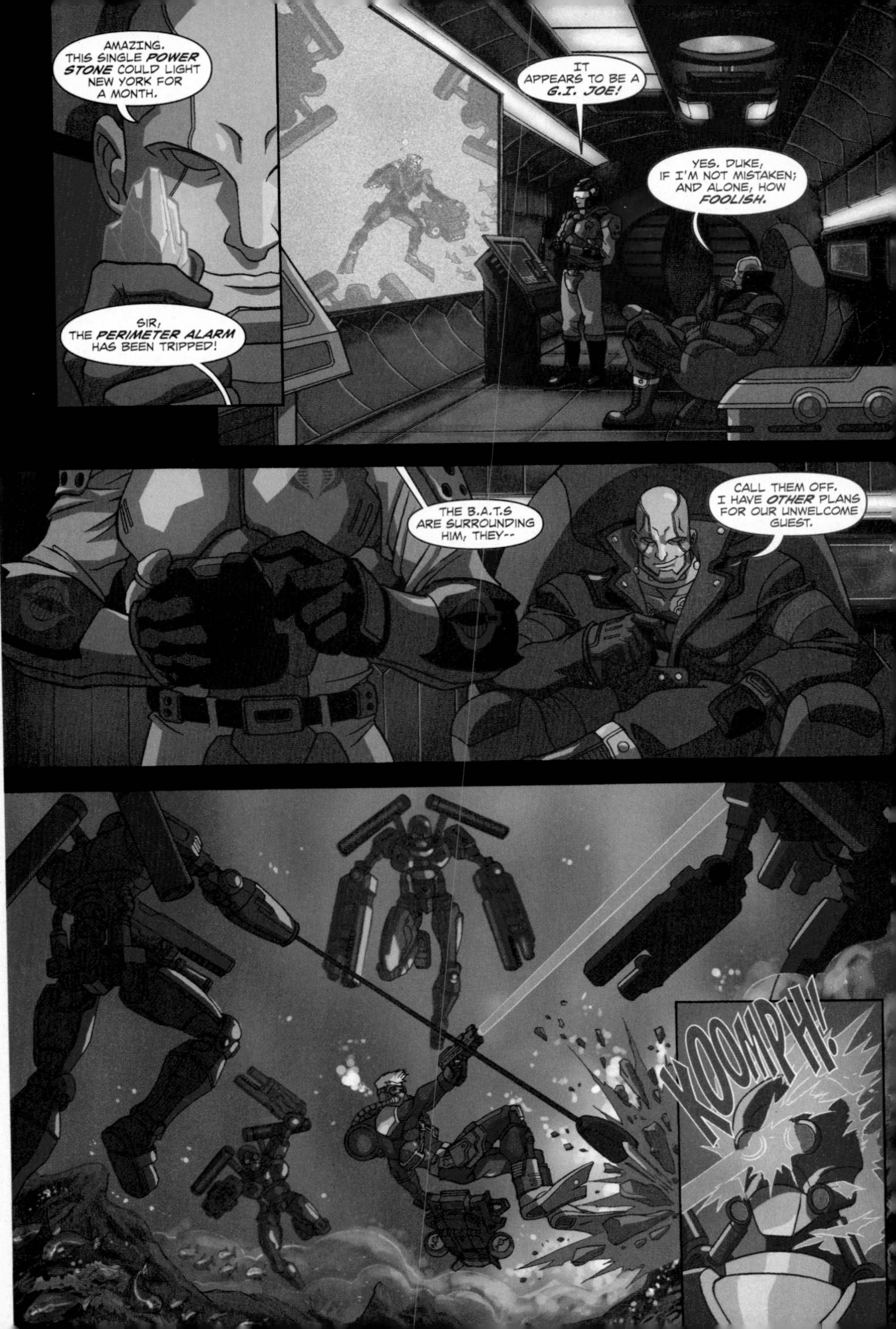
AMAZING. THIS SINGLE POWER STONE COULD LIGHT NEW YORK FOR A MONTH.
SIR, THE PERIMETER ALARM HAS BEEN TRIPPED!
IT APPEARS TO BE A G.I. JOE!
YES. DUKE, IF I'M NOT MISTAKEN; AND ALONE, HOW FOOLISH.
THE B.A.T.S ARE SURROUNDING HIM, THEY--
CALL THEM OFF. I HAVE OTHER PLANS FOR OUR UNWELCOME GUEST.
KOOMPH!

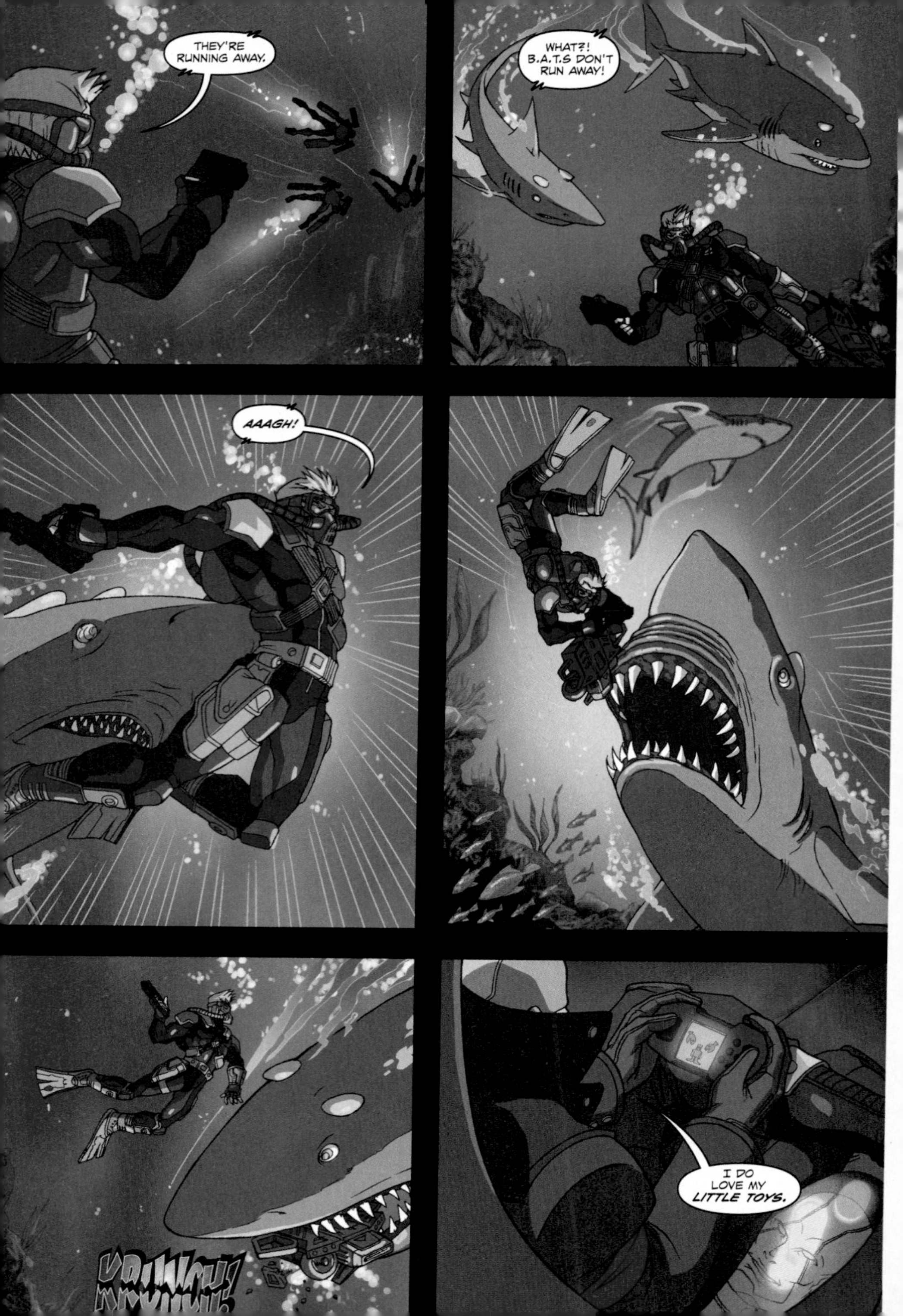
THEY'RE RUNNING AWAY.
WHAT?! B.A.T.S DON'T RUN AWAY!
AAAGH!
KRUNCH!
I DO LOVE MY LITTLE TOYS.

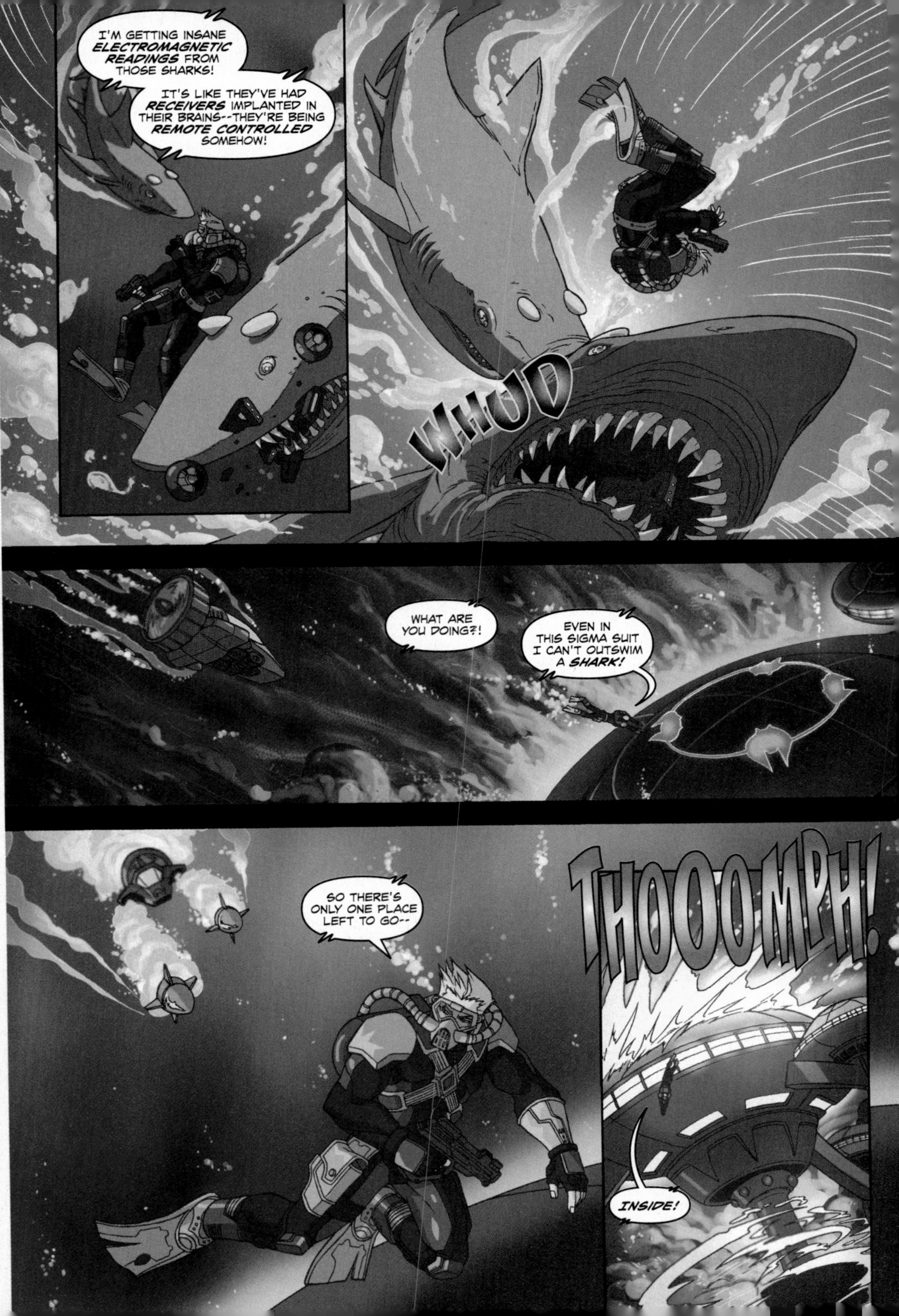
I'M GETTING INSANE ELECTROMAGNETIC READINGS FROM THOSE SHARKS!
IT'S LIKE THEY'VE HAD RECEIVERS IMPLANTED IN THEIR BRAINS--THEY'RE BEING REMOTE CONTROLLED SOMEHOW!
WHUD
WHAT ARE YOU DOING?!
EVEN IN THIS SIGMA SUIT I CAN'T OUTSWIM A SHARK!
SO THERE'S ONLY ONE PLACE LEFT TO GO--
THOOOMPH!
INSIDE!

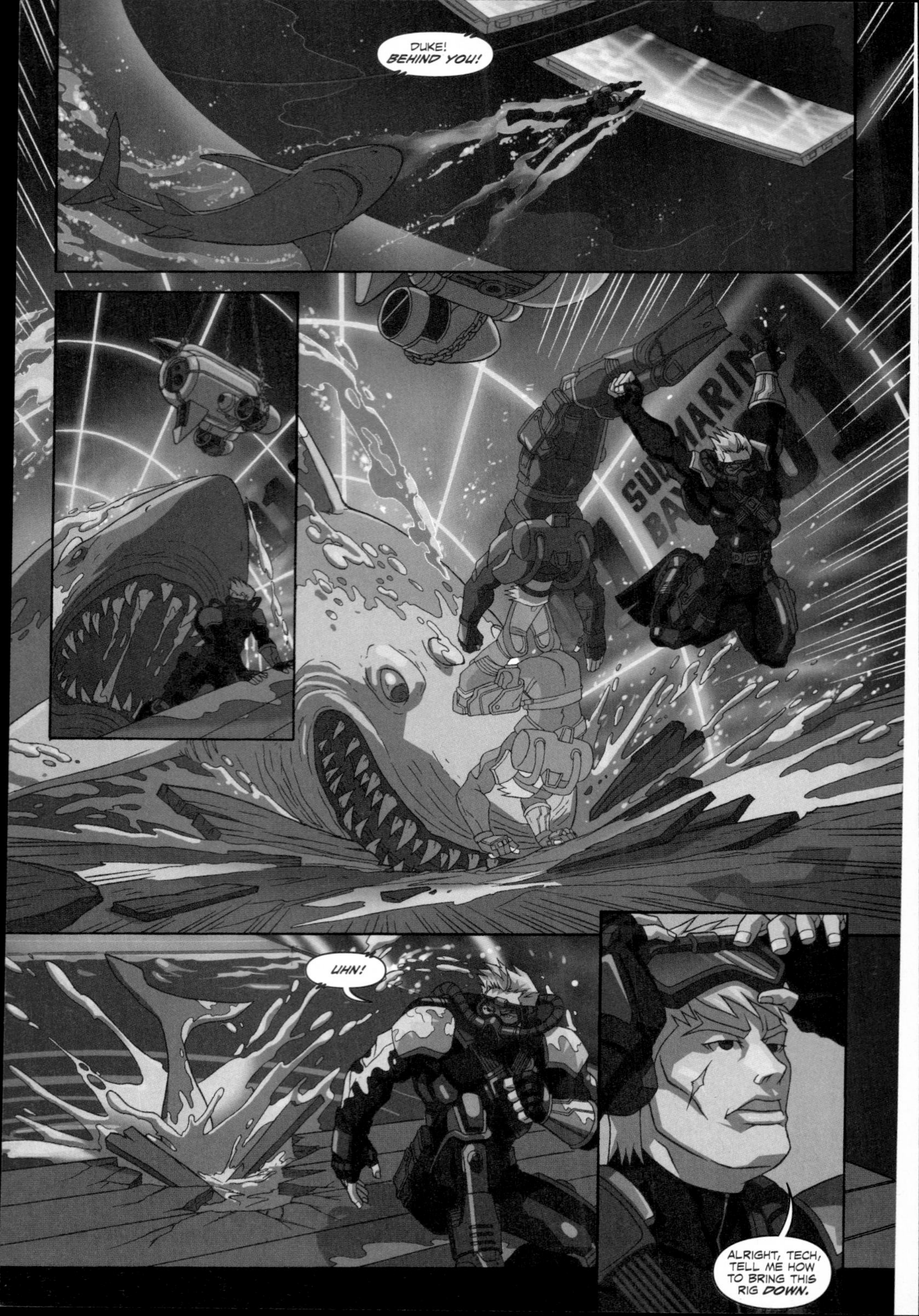
DUKE!
BEHIND YOU!
UHN!
ALRIGHT, TECH, TELL ME HOW TO BRING THIS RIG DOWN.

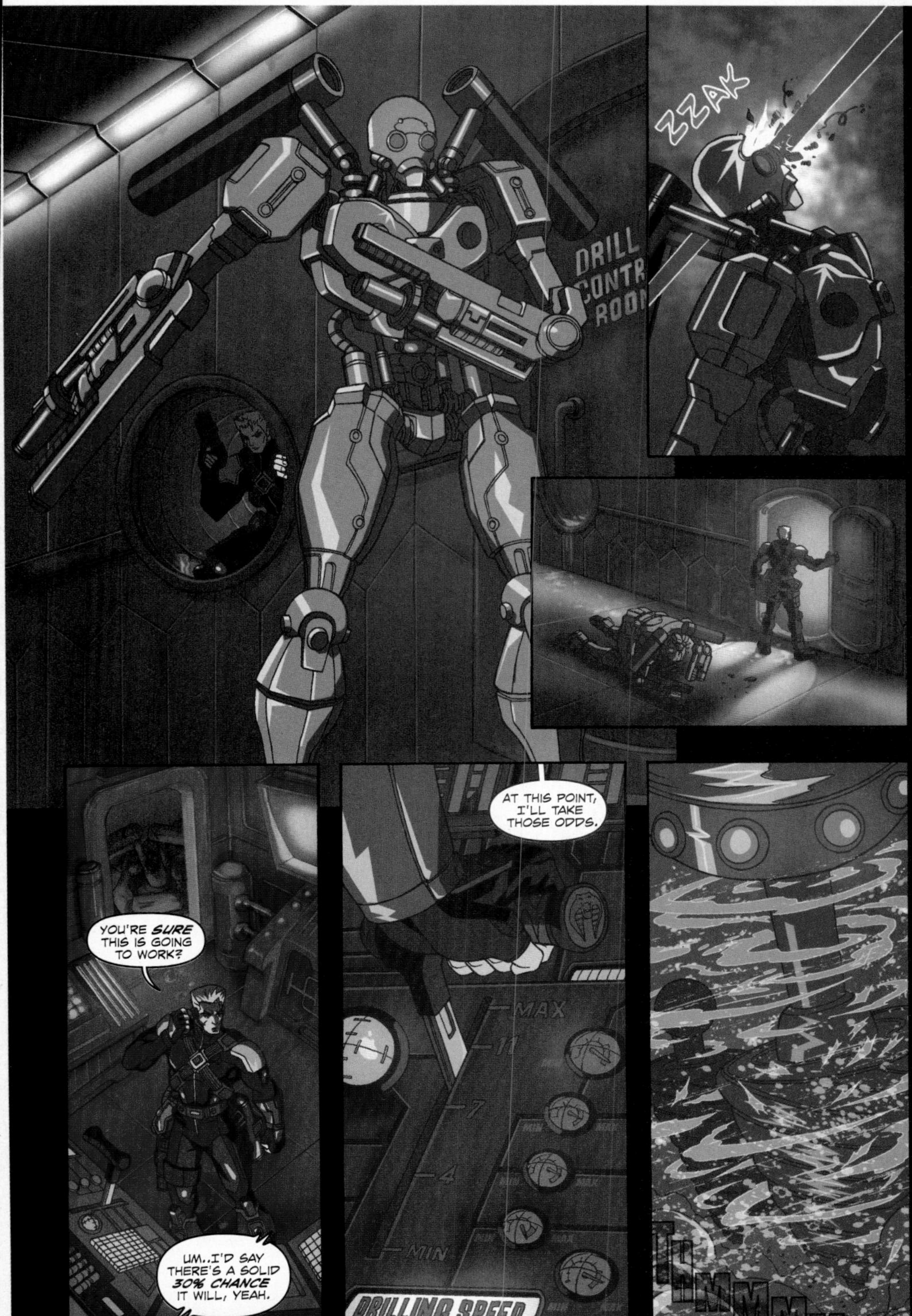
DRILL CONTR ROOM
ZZAK
YOU'RE SURE THIS IS GOING TO WORK?
UM..I'D SAY THERE'S A SOLID 30% CHANCE IT WILL, YEAH.
AT THIS POINT, I'LL TAKE THOSE ODDS.
MAX
MIN
DRILLING SPEED
THMMMM

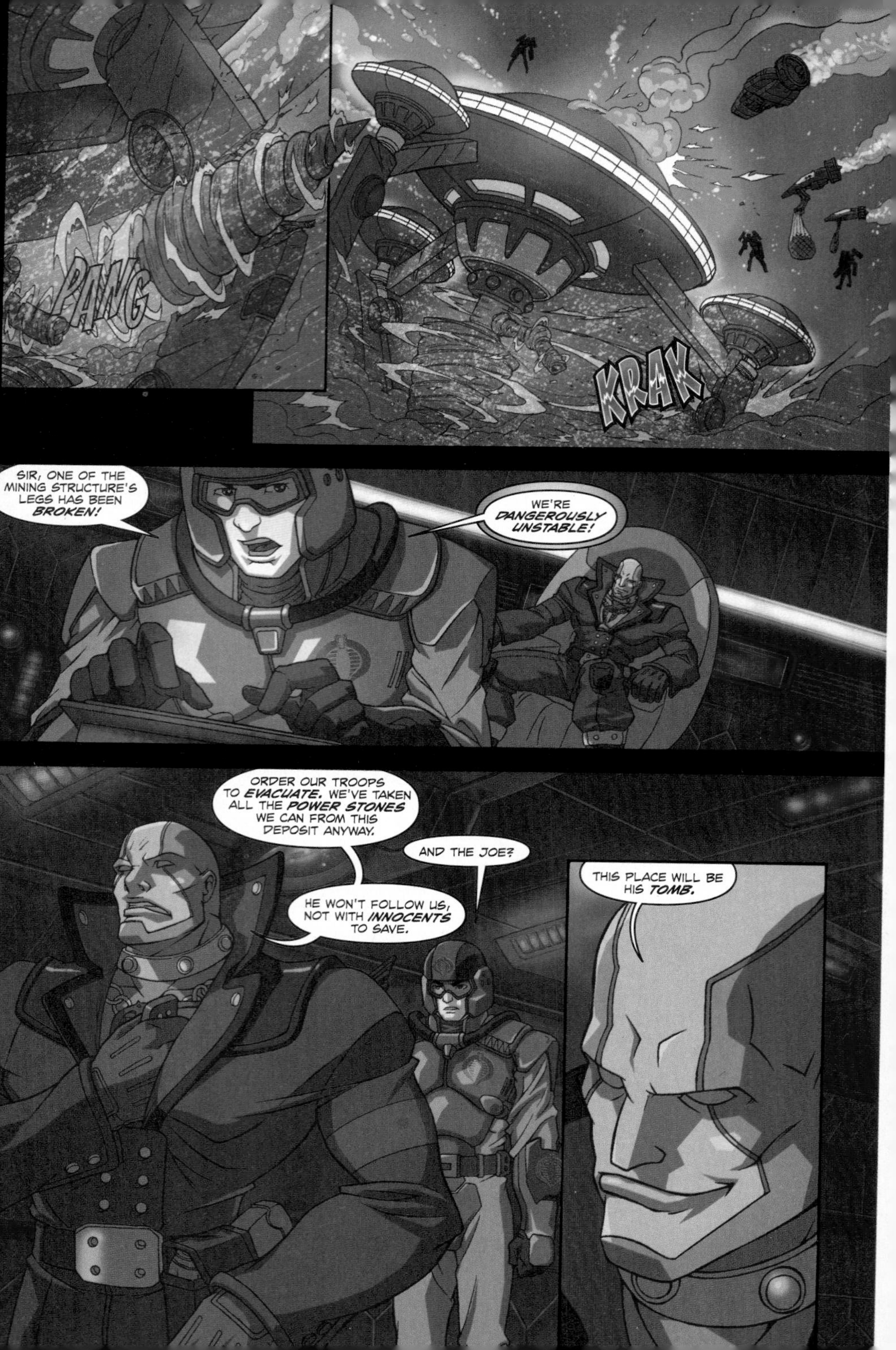
PANG
KRAK
SIR, ONE OF THE MINING STRUCTURE'S LEGS HAS BEEN BROKEN!
WE'RE DANGEROUSLY UNSTABLE!
ORDER OUR TROOPS TO EVACUATE. WE'VE TAKEN ALL THE POWER STONES WE CAN FROM THIS DEPOSIT ANYWAY.
AND THE JOE?
HE WON'T FOLLOW US, NOT WITH INNOCENTS TO SAVE.
THIS PLACE WILL BE HIS TOMB.

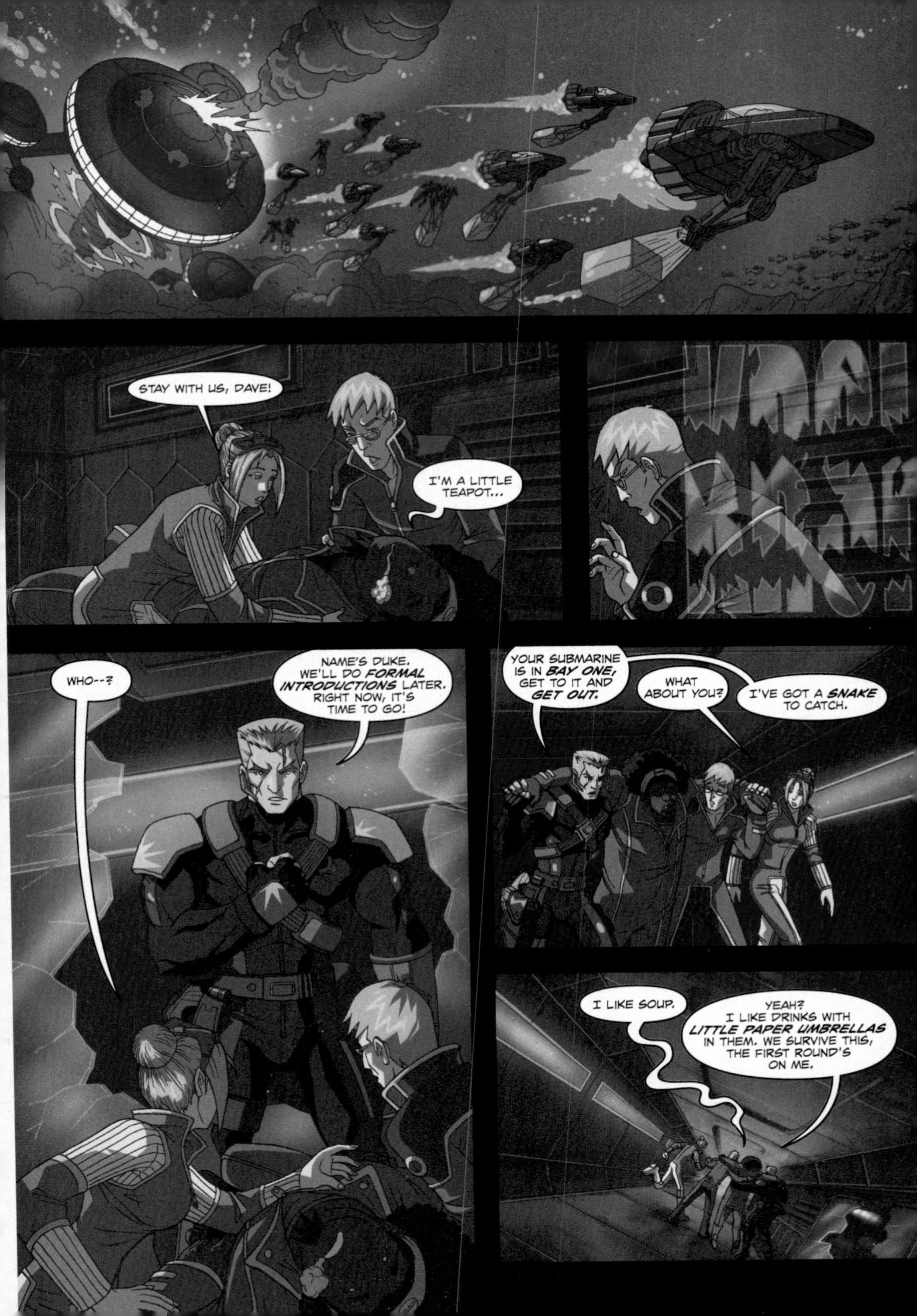
STAY WITH US, DAVE!
I'M A LITTLE TEAPOT...
WHO--?
NAME'S DUKE. WE'LL DO FORMAL INTRODUCTIONS LATER. RIGHT NOW, IT'S TIME TO GO!
YOUR SUBMARINE IS IN BAY ONE; GET TO IT AND GET OUT.
WHAT ABOUT YOU?
I'VE GOT A SNAKE TO CATCH.
I LIKE SOUP.
YEAH? I LIKE DRINKS WITH LITTLE PAPER UMBRELLAS IN THEM. WE SURVIVE THIS, THE FIRST ROUND'S ON ME.

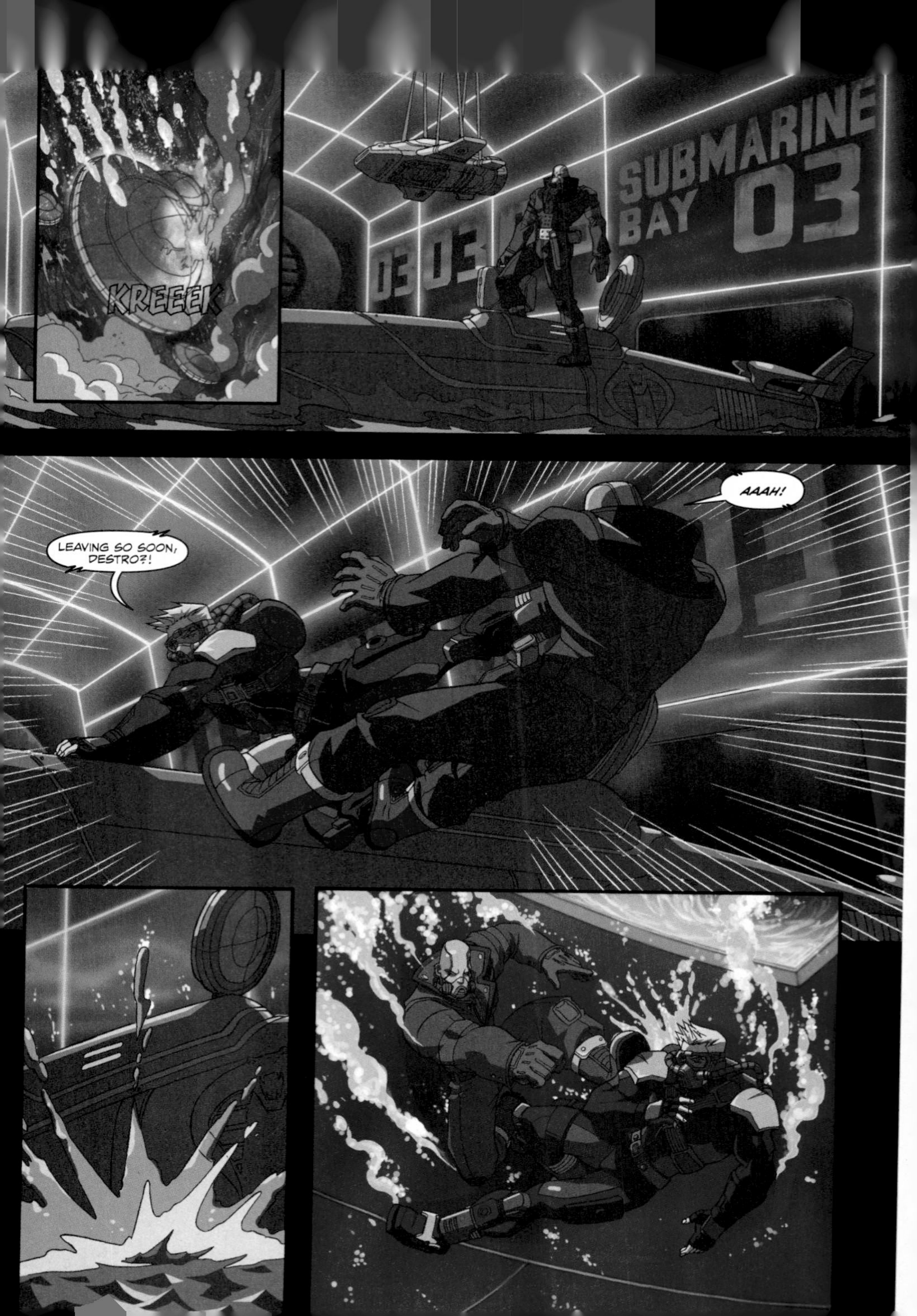
KREEEK
SUBMARINE BAY 03
0303
LEAVING SO SOON, DESTRO?!
AAAH!

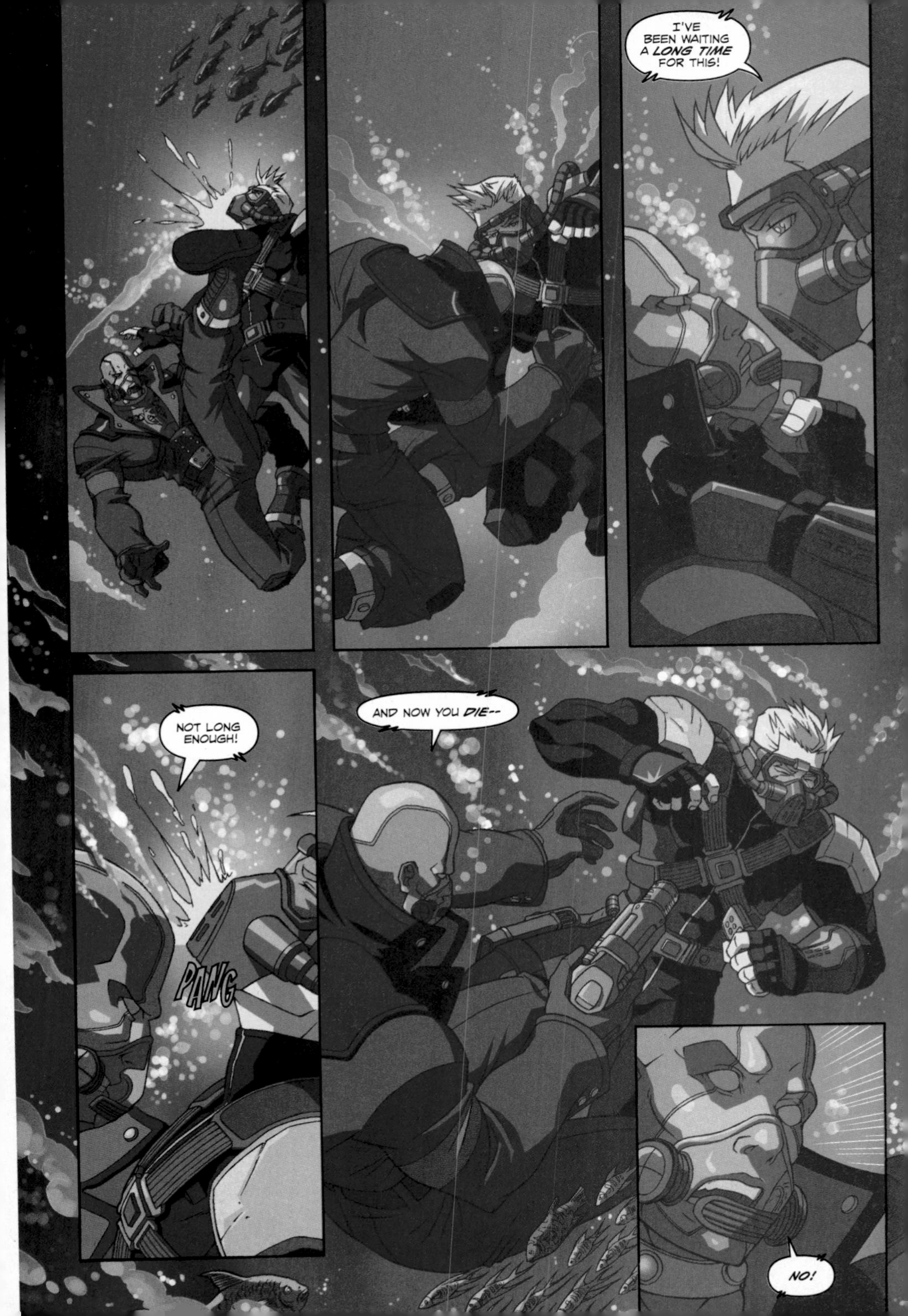

I'VE BEEN WAITING A *LONG TIME* FOR THIS!
NOT LONG ENOUGH!
AND NOW YOU *DIE*--
PANG
NO!

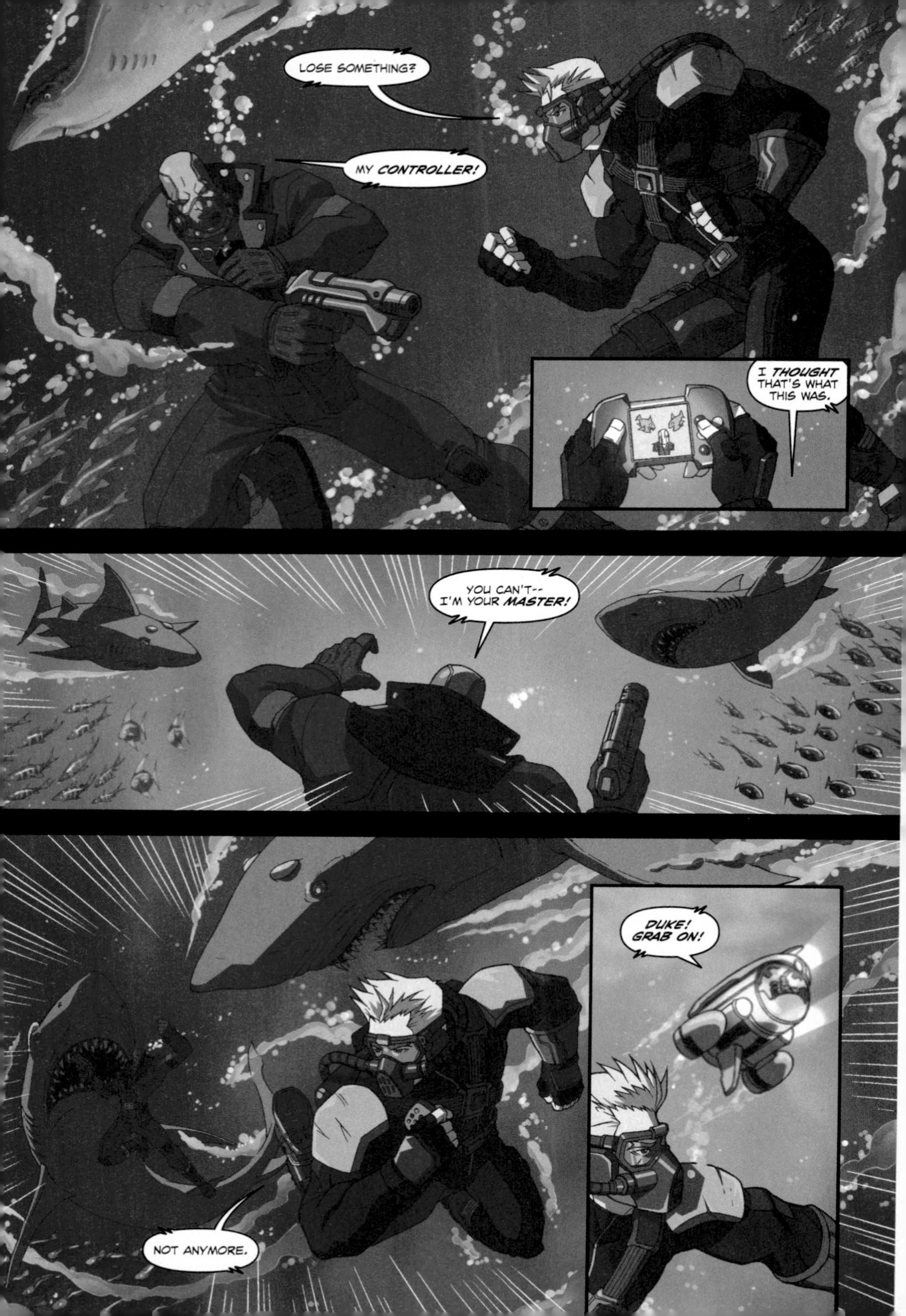

LOSE SOMETHING?
MY *CONTROLLER!*
I *THOUGHT* THAT'S WHAT THIS WAS.
YOU CAN'T-- I'M YOUR *MASTER!*
NOT ANYMORE.
DUKE! GRAB ON!

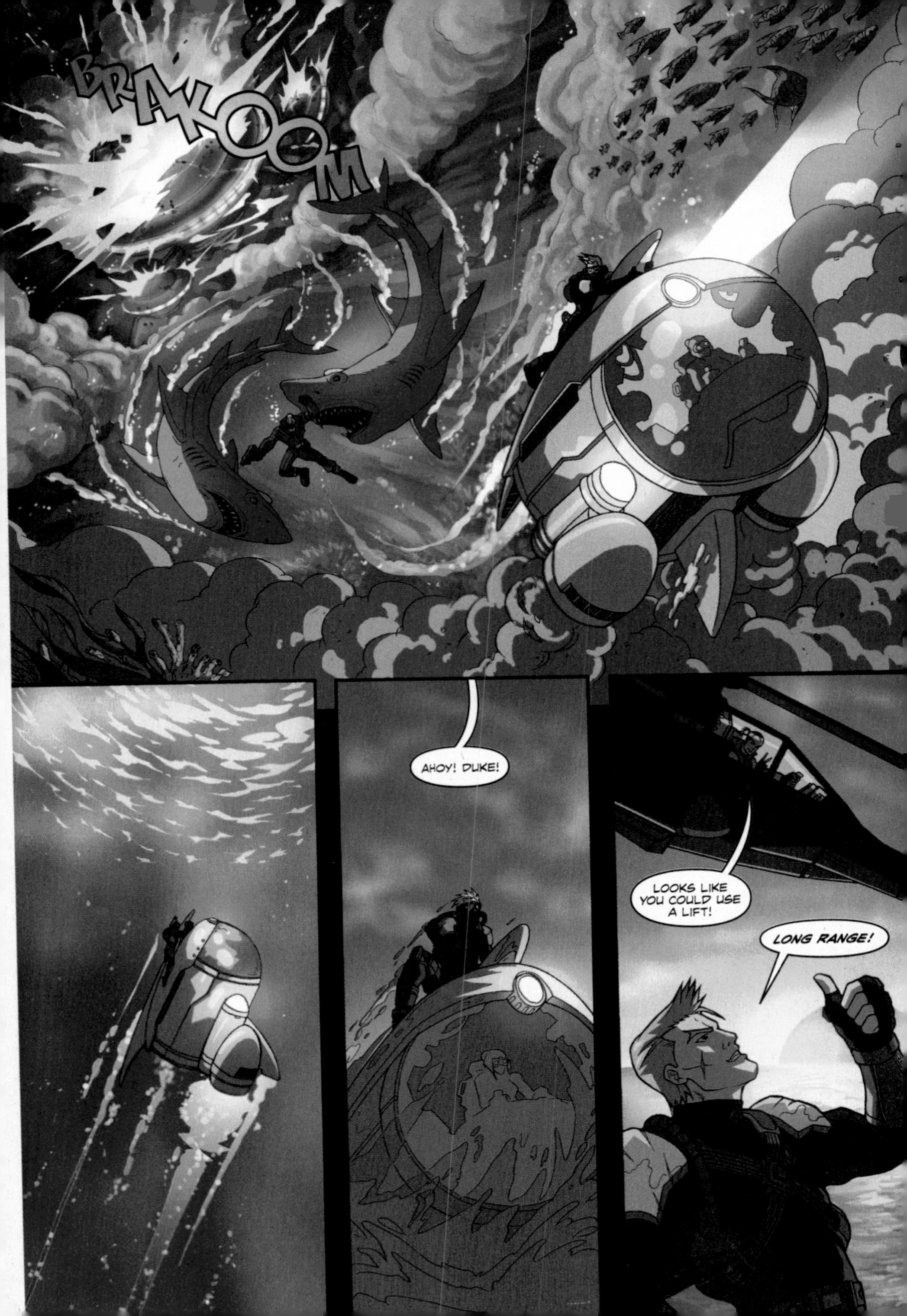
BRAKOOOM
AHOY! DUKE!
LOOKS LIKE YOU COULD USE A LIFT!
LONG RANGE!

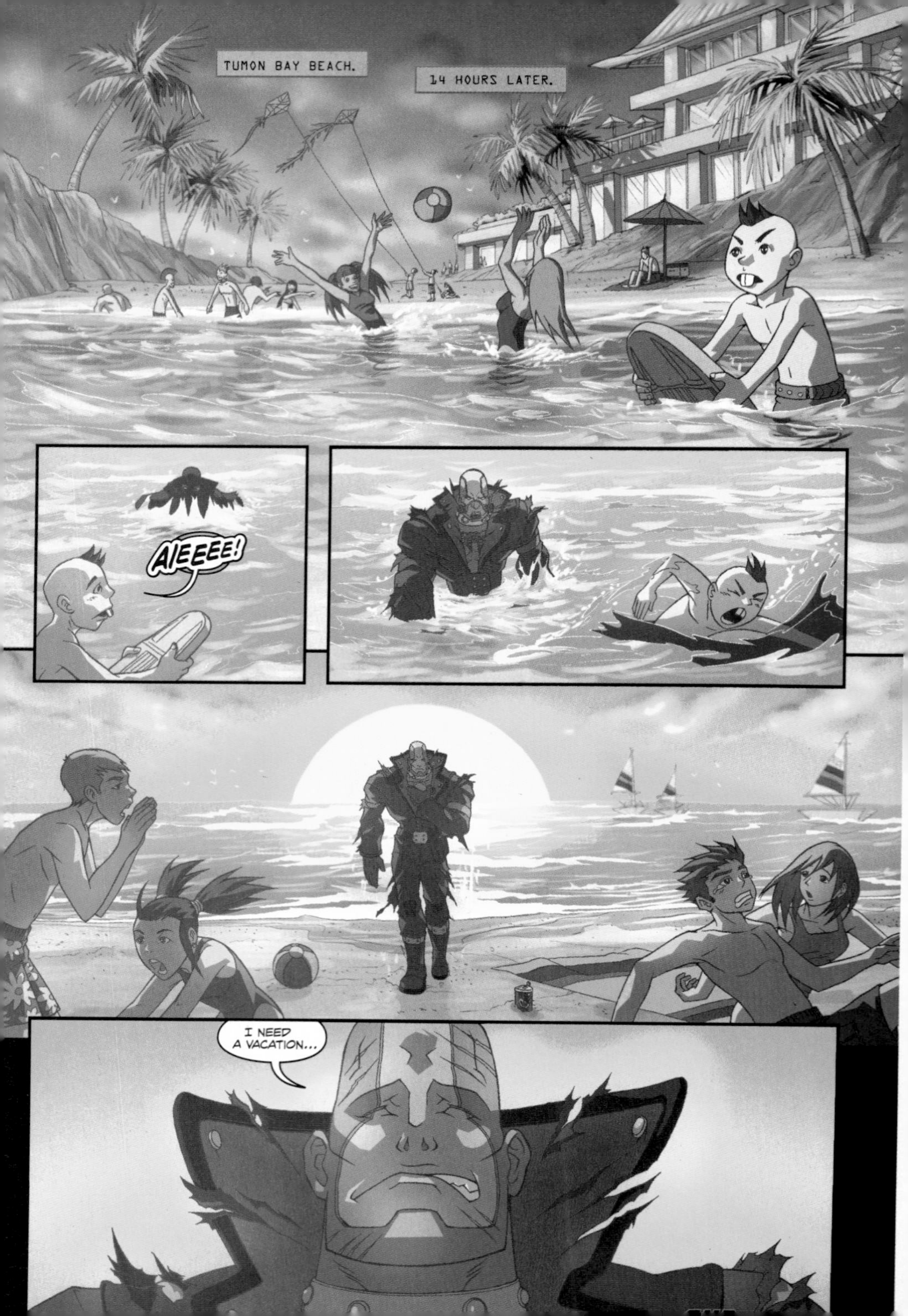
TUMON BAY BEACH.
14 HOURS LATER.
AIEEEE!
I NEED A VACATION...

SIGMA 6 is the code name for a new group of covert G.I. JOE operatives with highly specialized capabilities. They use innovative technology and gear designed exclusively for each of their missions. Working against them is the evil COBRA organization, whose goal is to take control of the world by sabotage, espionage and outright destruction. SIGMA 6 fights them at every turn and provides a swift solution to critical situations around the globe.

CLASSIFIED: AUTHORIZED PERSONNEL ONLY

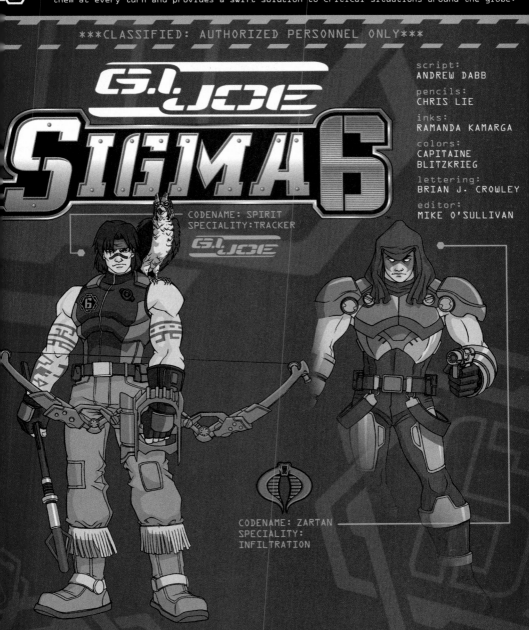

G.I. JOE SIGMA 6

script:
ANDREW DABB

pencils:
CHRIS LIE

inks:
RAMANDA KAMARGA

colors:
CAPITAINE BLITZKRIEG

lettering:
BRIAN J. CROWLEY

editor:
MIKE O'SULLIVAN

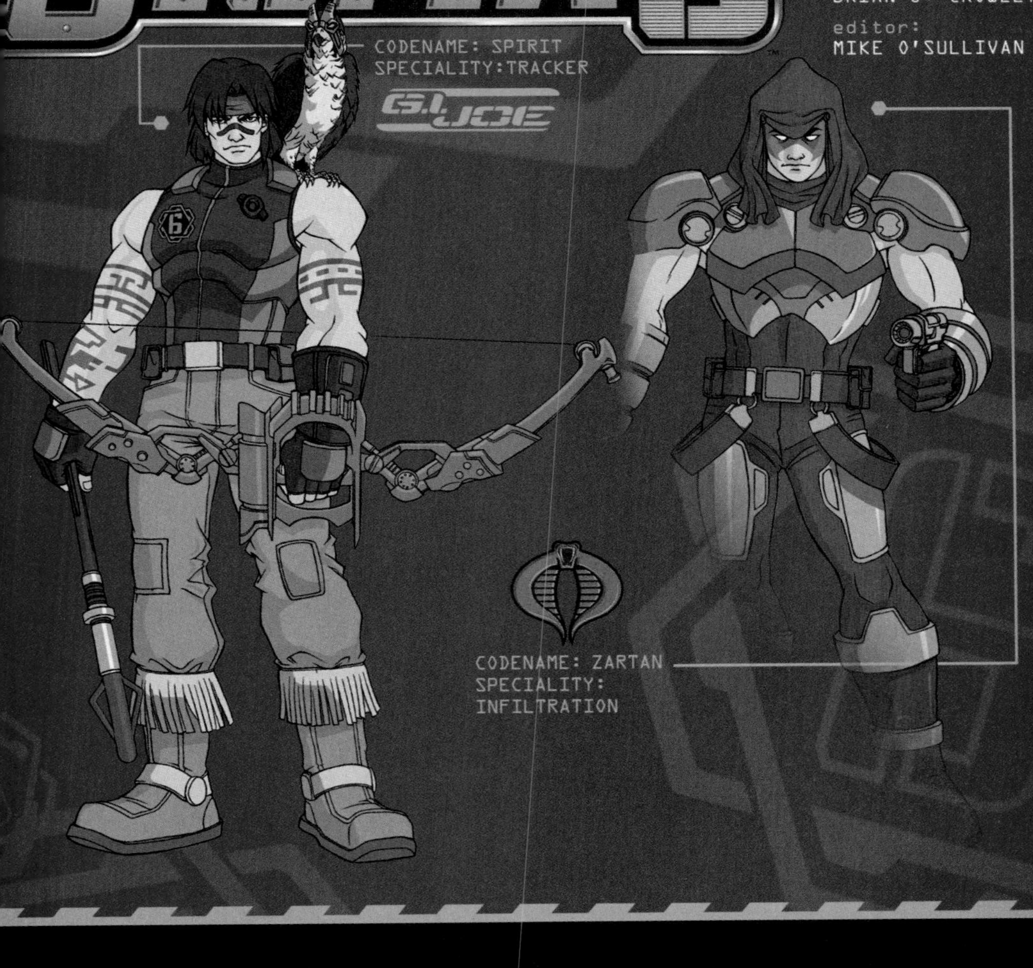
CODENAME: SPIRIT
SPECIALITY: TRACKER
G.I. JOE
CODENAME: ZARTAN
SPECIALITY: INFILTRATION

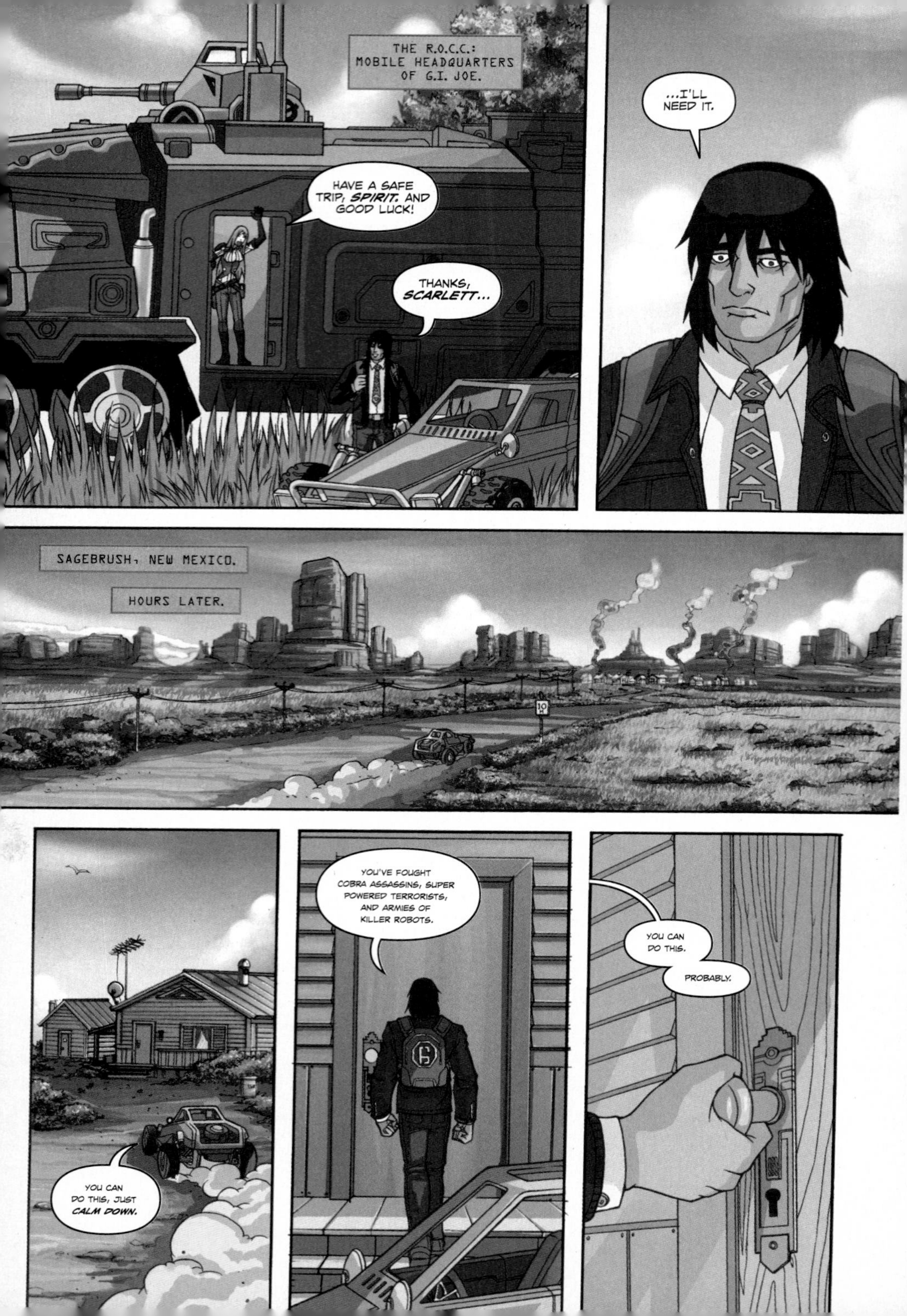
THE R.O.C.C.: MOBILE HEADQUARTERS OF G.I. JOE.
HAVE A SAFE TRIP, SPIRIT. AND GOOD LUCK!
THANKS, SCARLETT...
...I'LL NEED IT.
SAGEBRUSH, NEW MEXICO.
HOURS LATER.
10
YOU CAN DO THIS, JUST CALM DOWN.
YOU'VE FOUGHT COBRA ASSASSINS, SUPER POWERED TERRORISTS, AND ARMIES OF KILLER ROBOTS.
YOU CAN DO THIS.
PROBABLY.

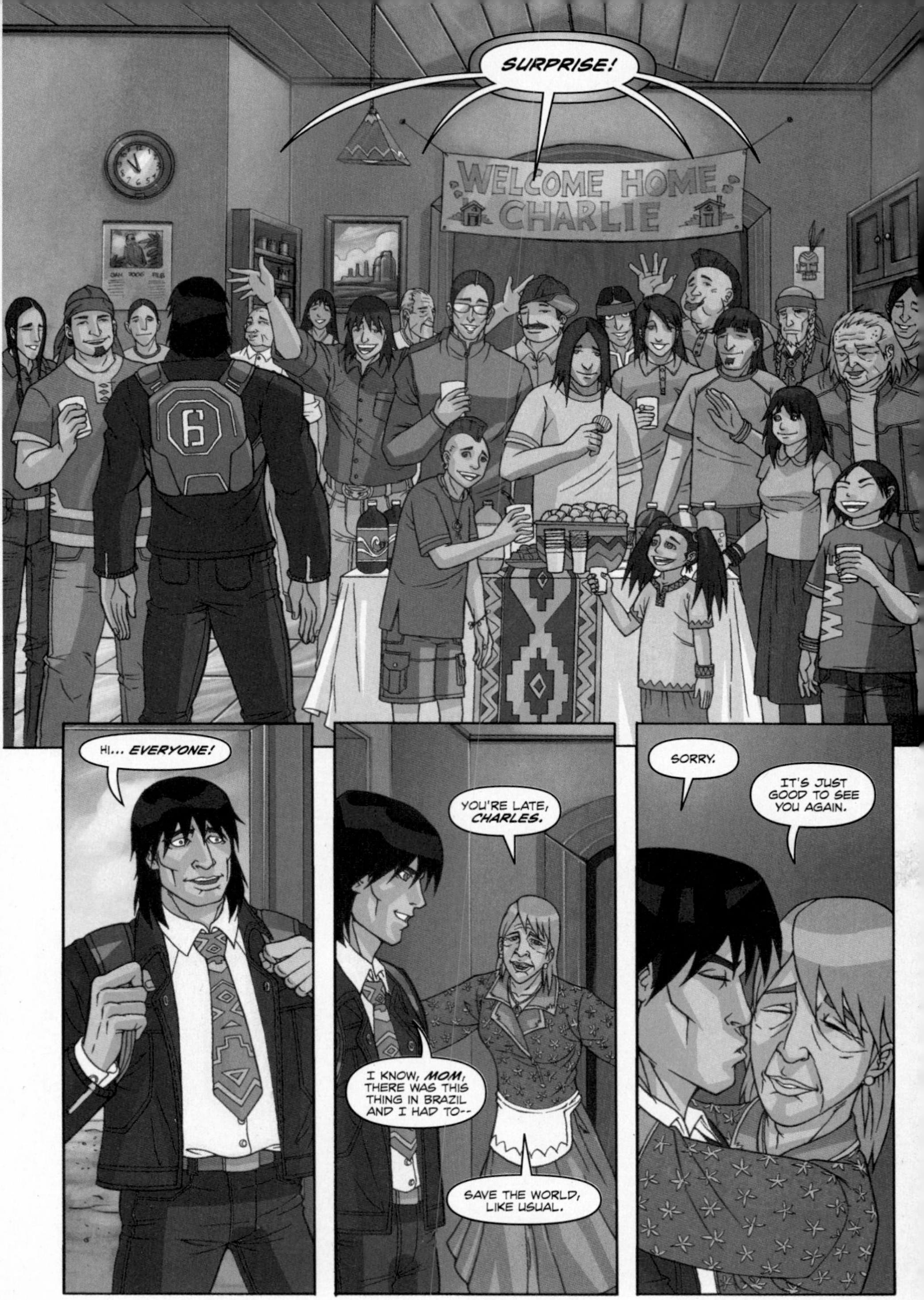
SURPRISE!
WELCOME HOME CHARLIE
HI... EVERYONE!
YOU'RE LATE, CHARLES.
I KNOW, MOM, THERE WAS THIS THING IN BRAZIL AND I HAD TO--
SAVE THE WORLD, LIKE USUAL.
SORRY.
IT'S JUST GOOD TO SEE YOU AGAIN.

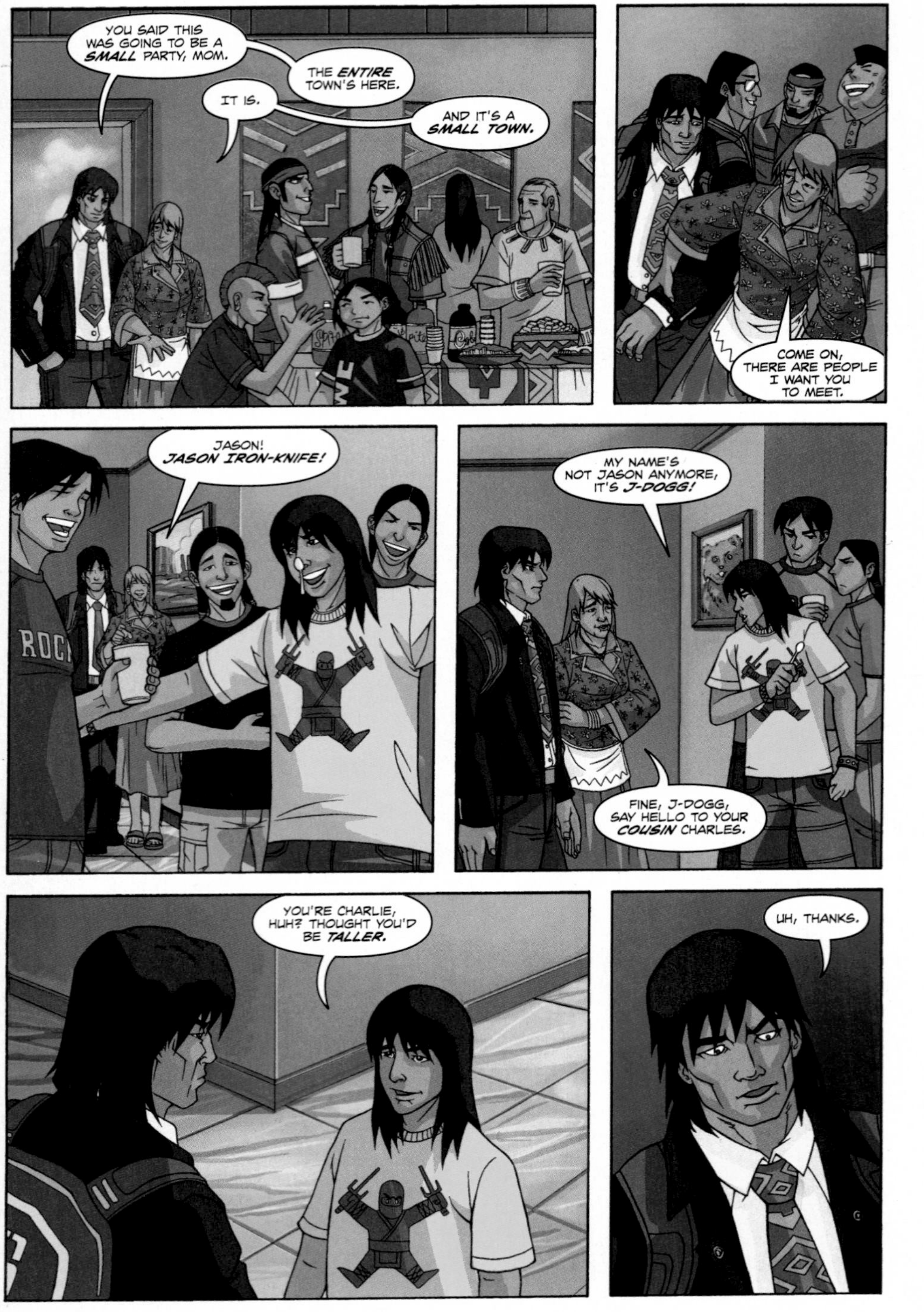
YOU SAID THIS WAS GOING TO BE A SMALL PARTY, MOM.
THE ENTIRE TOWN'S HERE.
IT IS.
AND IT'S A SMALL TOWN.
COME ON, THERE ARE PEOPLE I WANT YOU TO MEET.
JASON! JASON IRON-KNIFE!
ROCK
MY NAME'S NOT JASON ANYMORE, IT'S J-DOGG!
FINE, J-DOGG, SAY HELLO TO YOUR COUSIN CHARLES.
YOU'RE CHARLIE, HUH? THOUGHT YOU'D BE TALLER.
UH, THANKS.

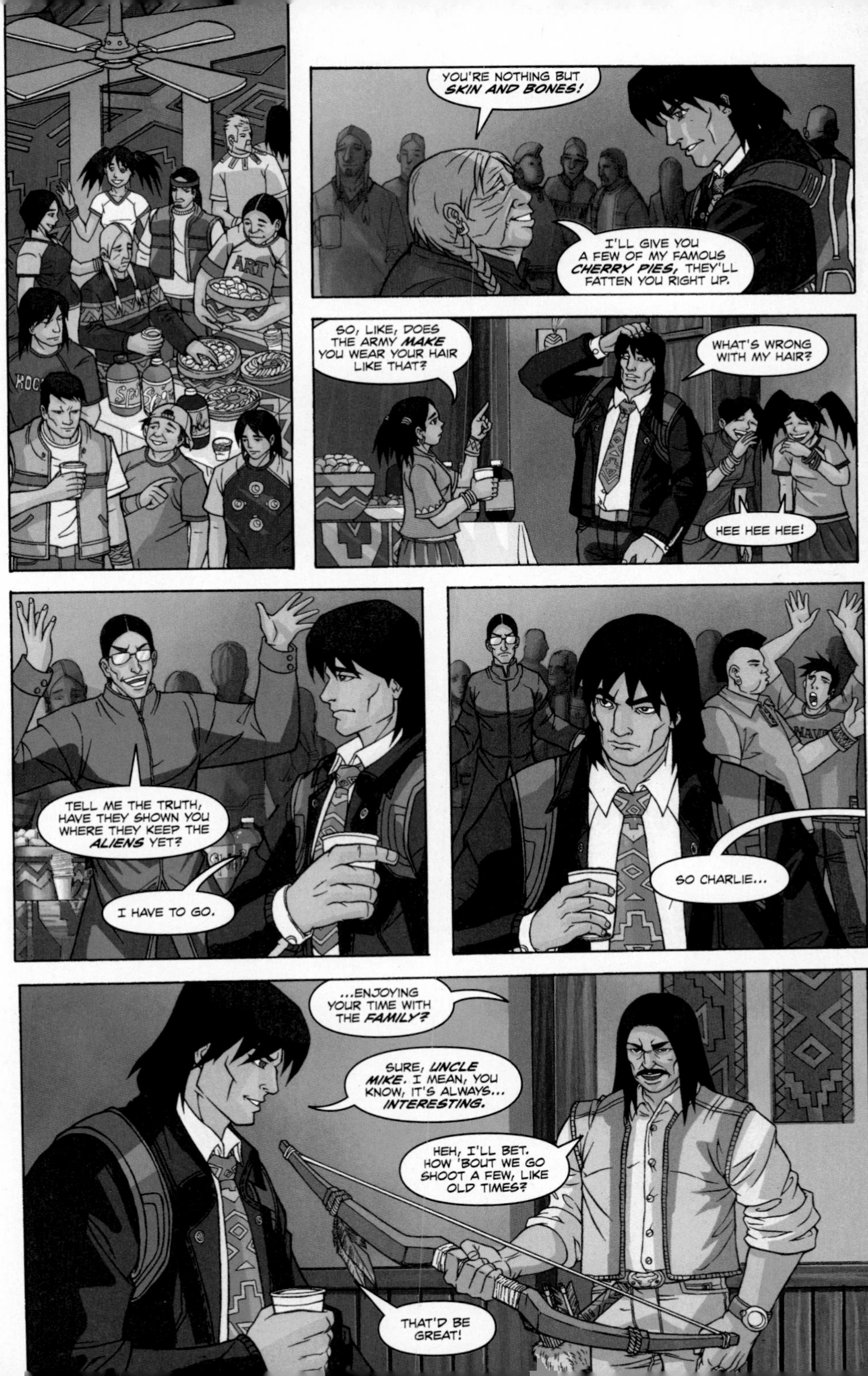
YOU'RE NOTHING BUT SKIN AND BONES!
I'LL GIVE YOU A FEW OF MY FAMOUS CHERRY PIES, THEY'LL FATTEN YOU RIGHT UP.
SO, LIKE, DOES THE ARMY MAKE YOU WEAR YOUR HAIR LIKE THAT?
WHAT'S WRONG WITH MY HAIR?
HEE HEE HEE!
TELL ME THE TRUTH, HAVE THEY SHOWN YOU WHERE THEY KEEP THE ALIENS YET?
I HAVE TO GO.
SO CHARLIE...
...ENJOYING YOUR TIME WITH THE FAMILY?
SURE, UNCLE MIKE. I MEAN, YOU KNOW, IT'S ALWAYS... INTERESTING.
HEH, I'LL BET. HOW 'BOUT WE GO SHOOT A FEW, LIKE OLD TIMES?
THAT'D BE GREAT!

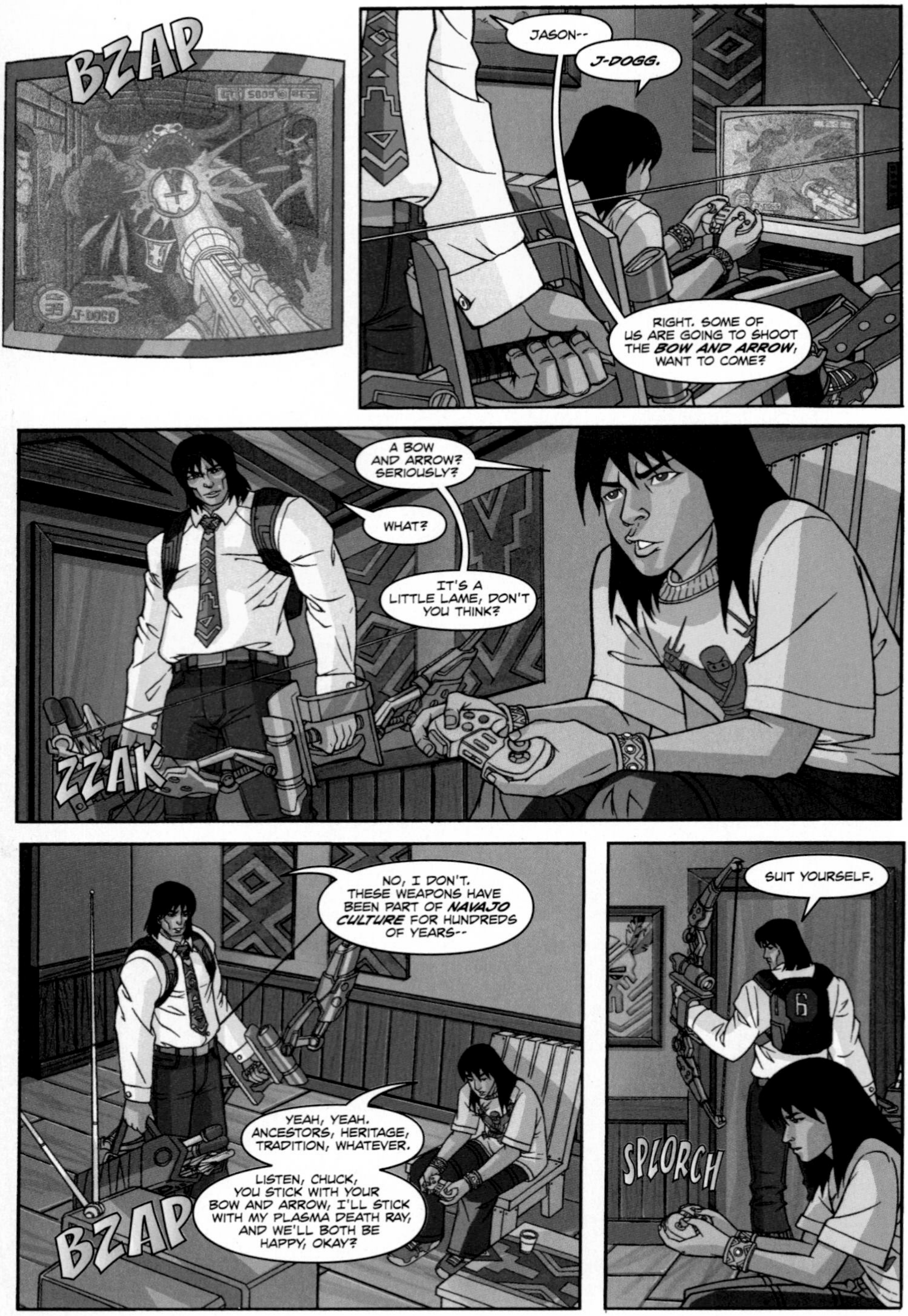
BZAP
J-DOGG
JASON--
J-DOGG.
RIGHT. SOME OF US ARE GOING TO SHOOT THE BOW AND ARROW, WANT TO COME?
A BOW AND ARROW? SERIOUSLY?
WHAT?
IT'S A LITTLE LAME, DON'T YOU THINK?
ZZAK
NO, I DON'T. THESE WEAPONS HAVE BEEN PART OF NAVAJO CULTURE FOR HUNDREDS OF YEARS--
YEAH, YEAH. ANCESTORS, HERITAGE, TRADITION, WHATEVER.
LISTEN, CHUCK, YOU STICK WITH YOUR BOW AND ARROW, I'LL STICK WITH MY PLASMA DEATH RAY, AND WE'LL BOTH BE HAPPY, OKAY?
BZAP
SUIT YOURSELF.
SPLORCH

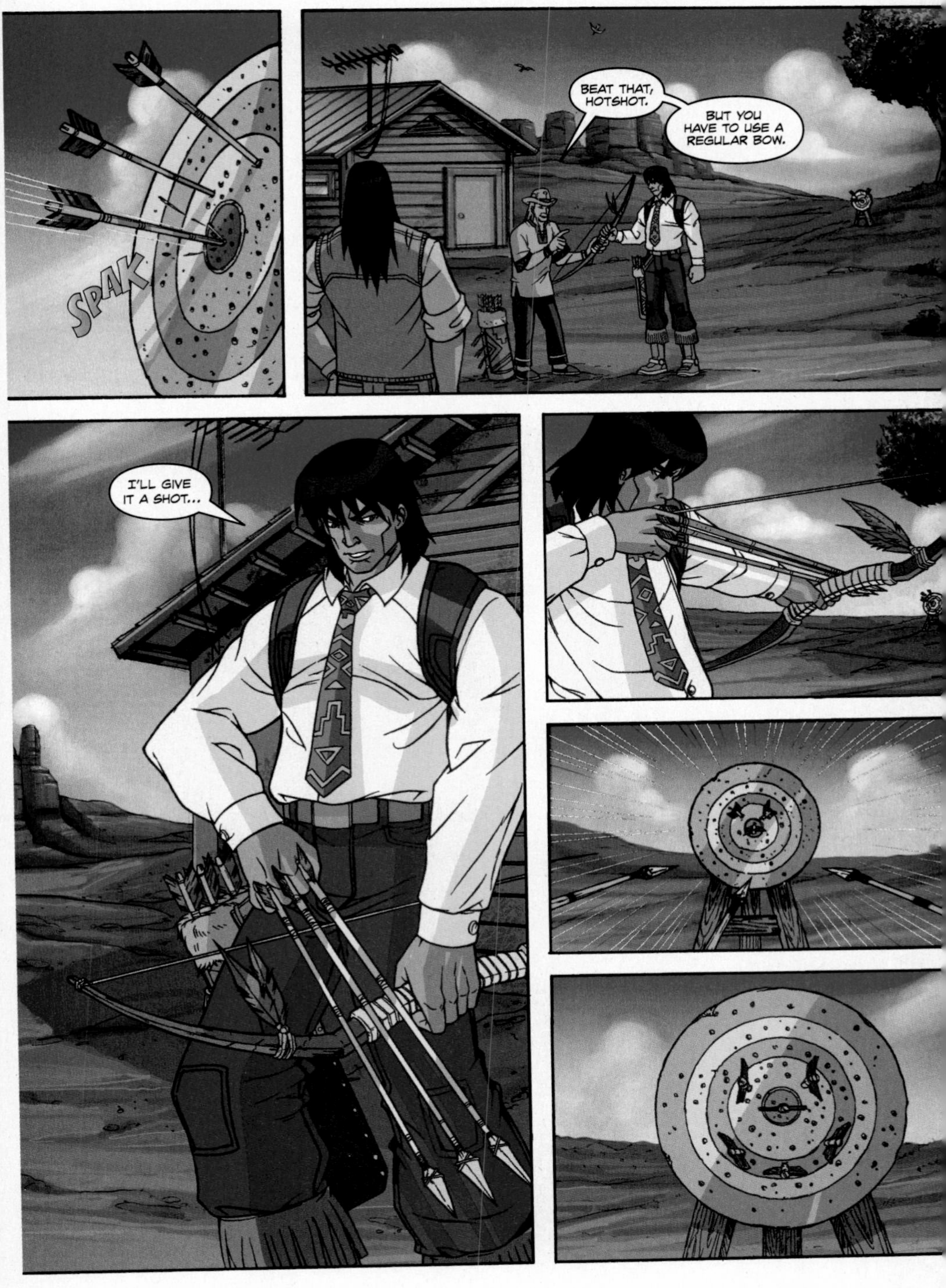
SPAK
BEAT THAT, HOTSHOT.
BUT YOU HAVE TO USE A REGULAR BOW.
I'LL GIVE IT A SHOT...

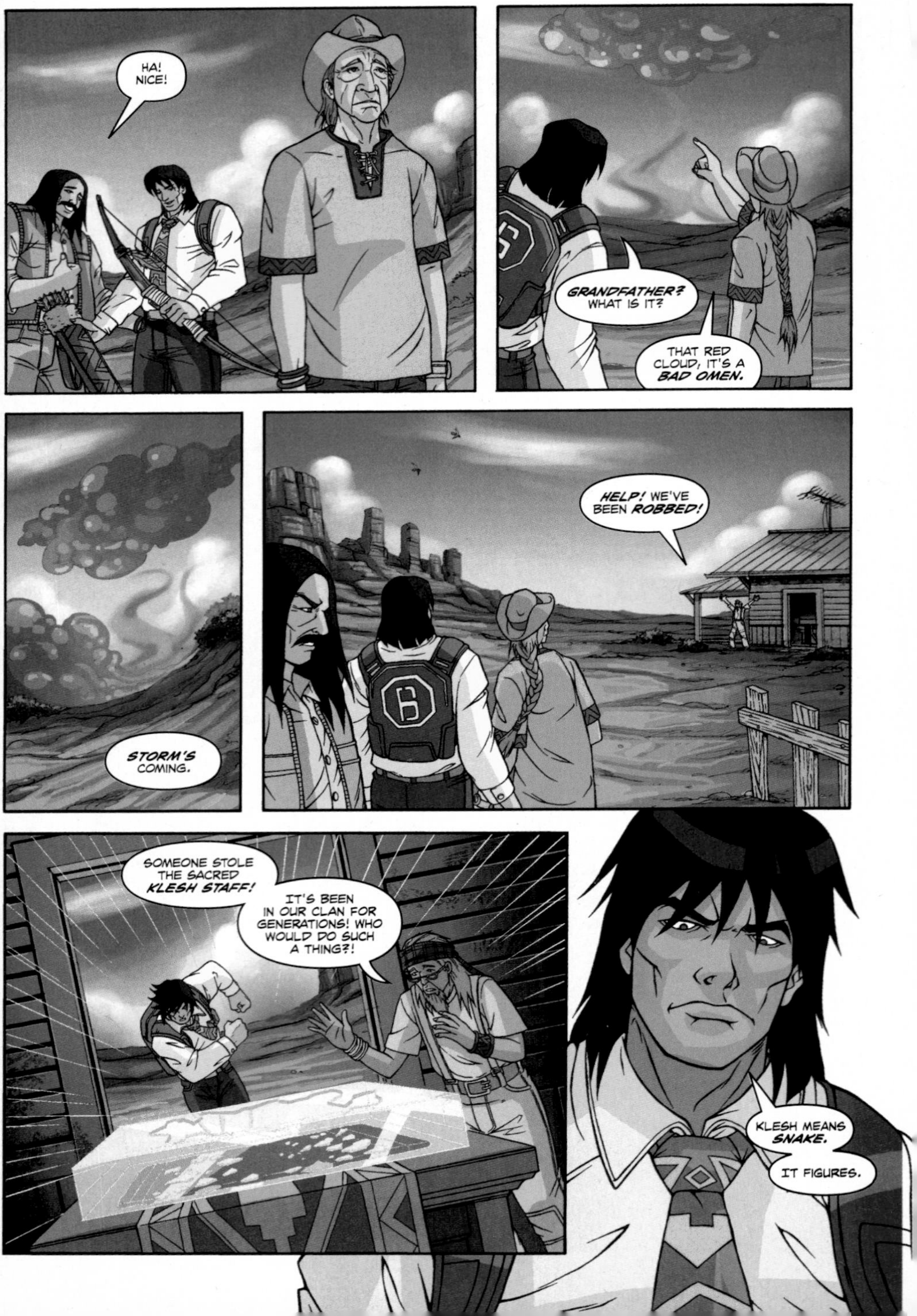
HA! NICE!
GRANDFATHER? WHAT IS IT?
THAT RED CLOUD, IT'S A BAD OMEN.
STORM'S COMING.
HELP! WE'VE BEEN ROBBED!
SOMEONE STOLE THE SACRED KLESH STAFF!
IT'S BEEN IN OUR CLAN FOR GENERATIONS! WHO WOULD DO SUCH A THING?!
KLESH MEANS SNAKE.
IT FIGURES.

CHARLIE!

I'VE CALLED THE POLICE, BUT THEIR NEAREST OFFICER IS ALMOST *SIXTY MILES* AWAY.

IN THE MEANTIME, A FEW OF US ARE FORMING A *POSSE*, AND I THOUGHT--

NO.

THESE TIRE TRACKS ARE AT LEAST AN HOUR OLD, AND THERE ARE NO FRESH FOOTPRINTS LEADING FROM THE VILLAGE.

WHOEVER STOLE THE STAFF IS STILL *IN TOWN*.

BUT THAT'S IMPOSSIBLE, NO ONE IN THE TRIBE WOULD TAKE IT, AND WE'RE THE *ONLY ONES* HERE.

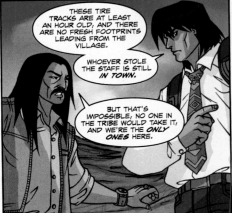

MAYBE. MAYBE NOT.

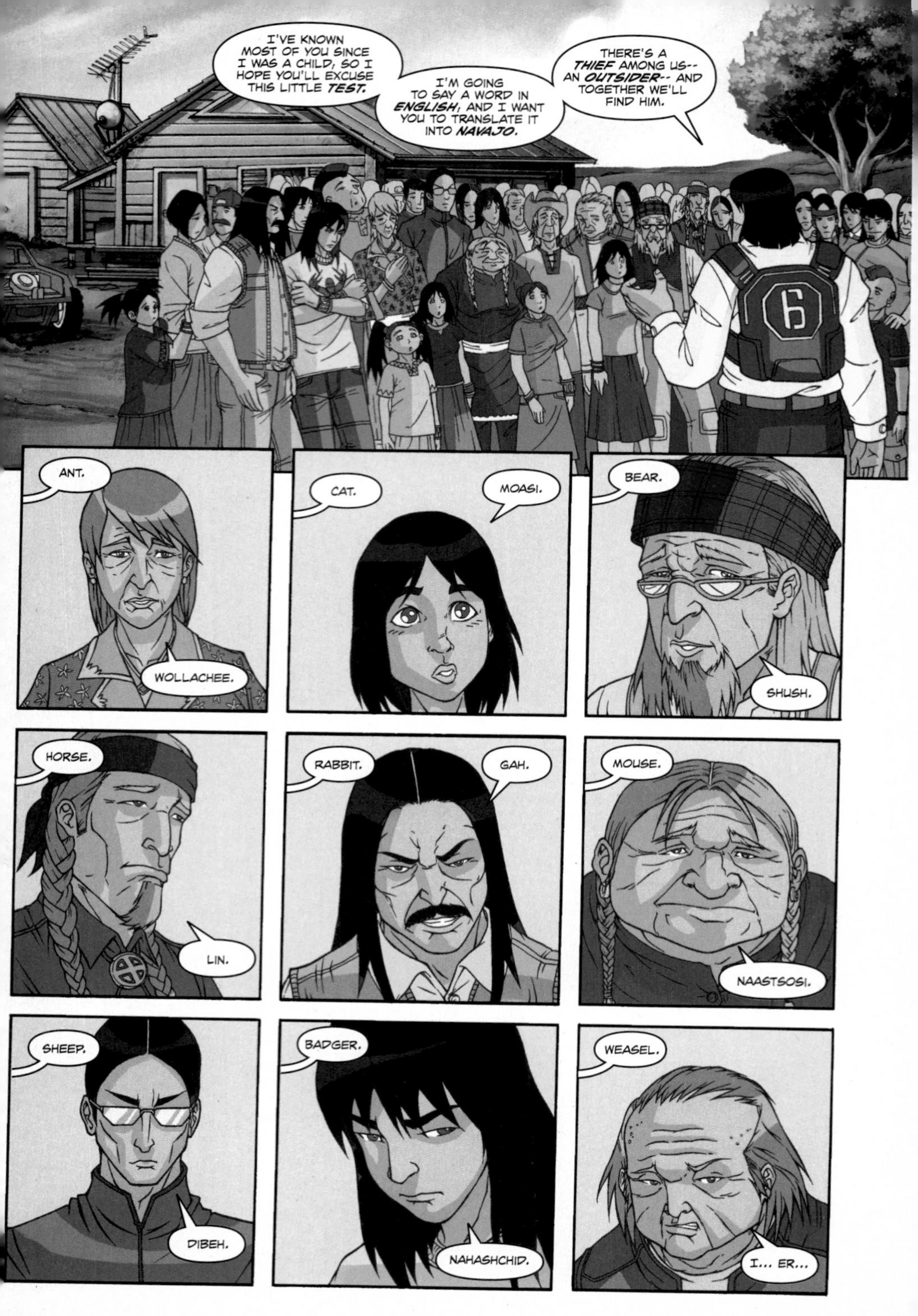
I'VE KNOWN MOST OF YOU SINCE I WAS A CHILD, SO I HOPE YOU'LL EXCUSE THIS LITTLE TEST.
I'M GOING TO SAY A WORD IN ENGLISH, AND I WANT YOU TO TRANSLATE IT INTO NAVAJO.
THERE'S A THIEF AMONG US-- AN OUTSIDER-- AND TOGETHER WE'LL FIND HIM.
ANT.
WOLLACHEE.
CAT.
MOASI.
BEAR.
SHUSH.
HORSE.
LIN.
RABBIT.
GAH.
MOUSE.
NAASTSOSI.
SHEEP.
DIBEH.
BADGER.
NAHASHCHID.
WEASEL.
I... ER...

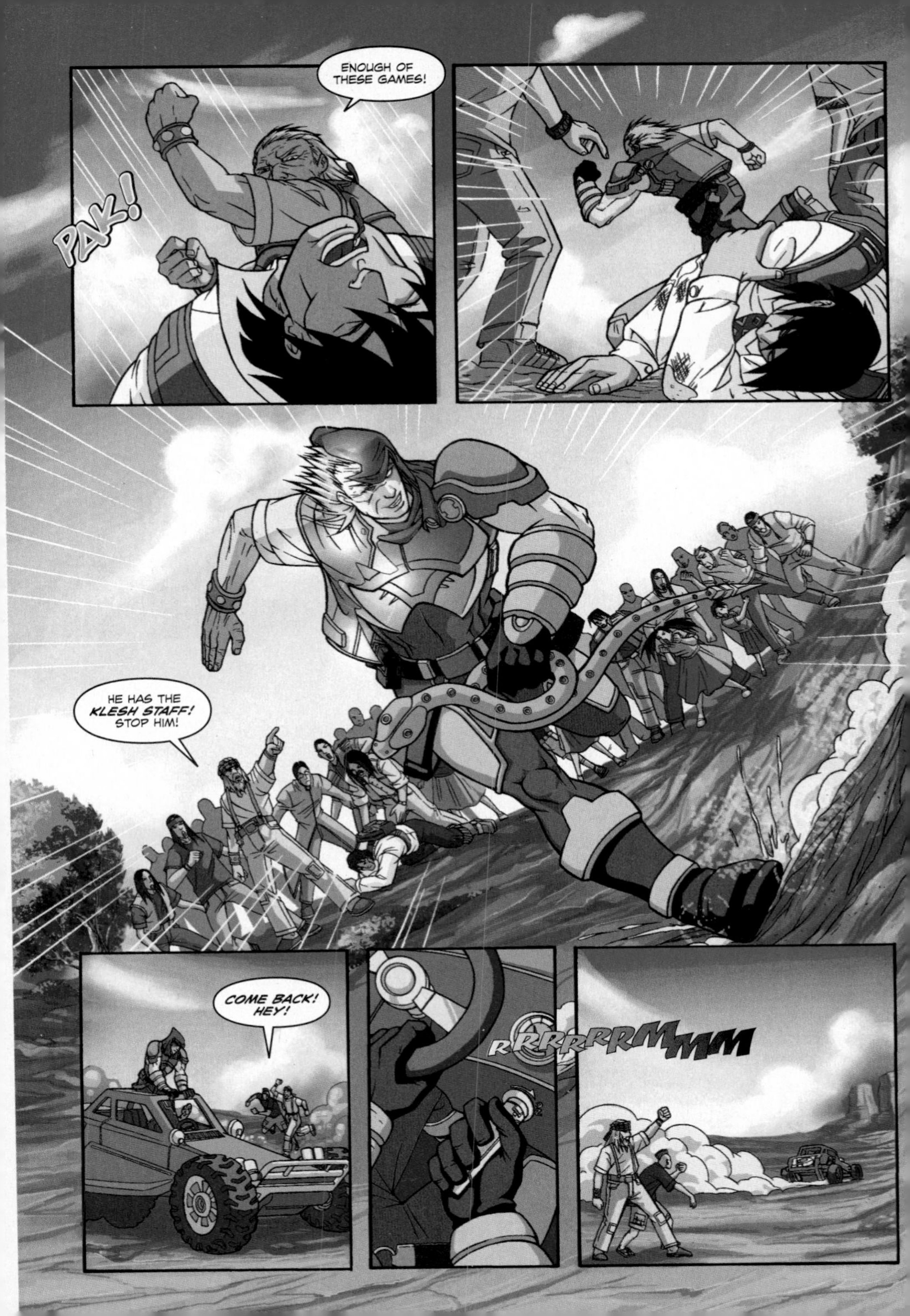
ENOUGH OF THESE GAMES!
PAK!
HE HAS THE KLESH STAFF! STOP HIM!
COME BACK! HEY!
RRRRRRRMMMM

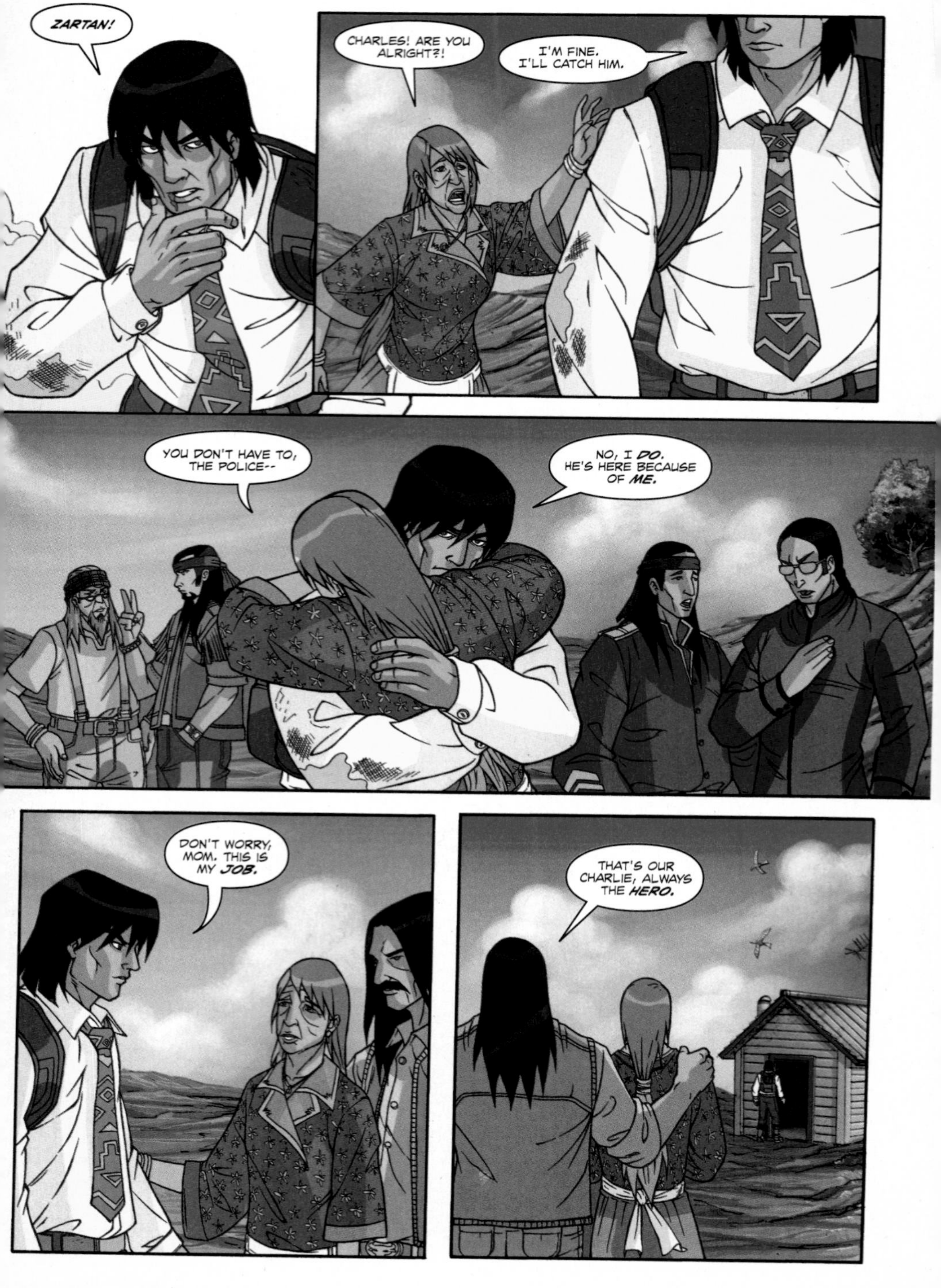
ZARTAN!
CHARLES! ARE YOU ALRIGHT?!
I'M FINE. I'LL CATCH HIM.
YOU DON'T HAVE TO, THE POLICE--
NO, I DO. HE'S HERE BECAUSE OF ME.
DON'T WORRY, MOM. THIS IS MY JOB.
THAT'S OUR CHARLIE, ALWAYS THE HERO.

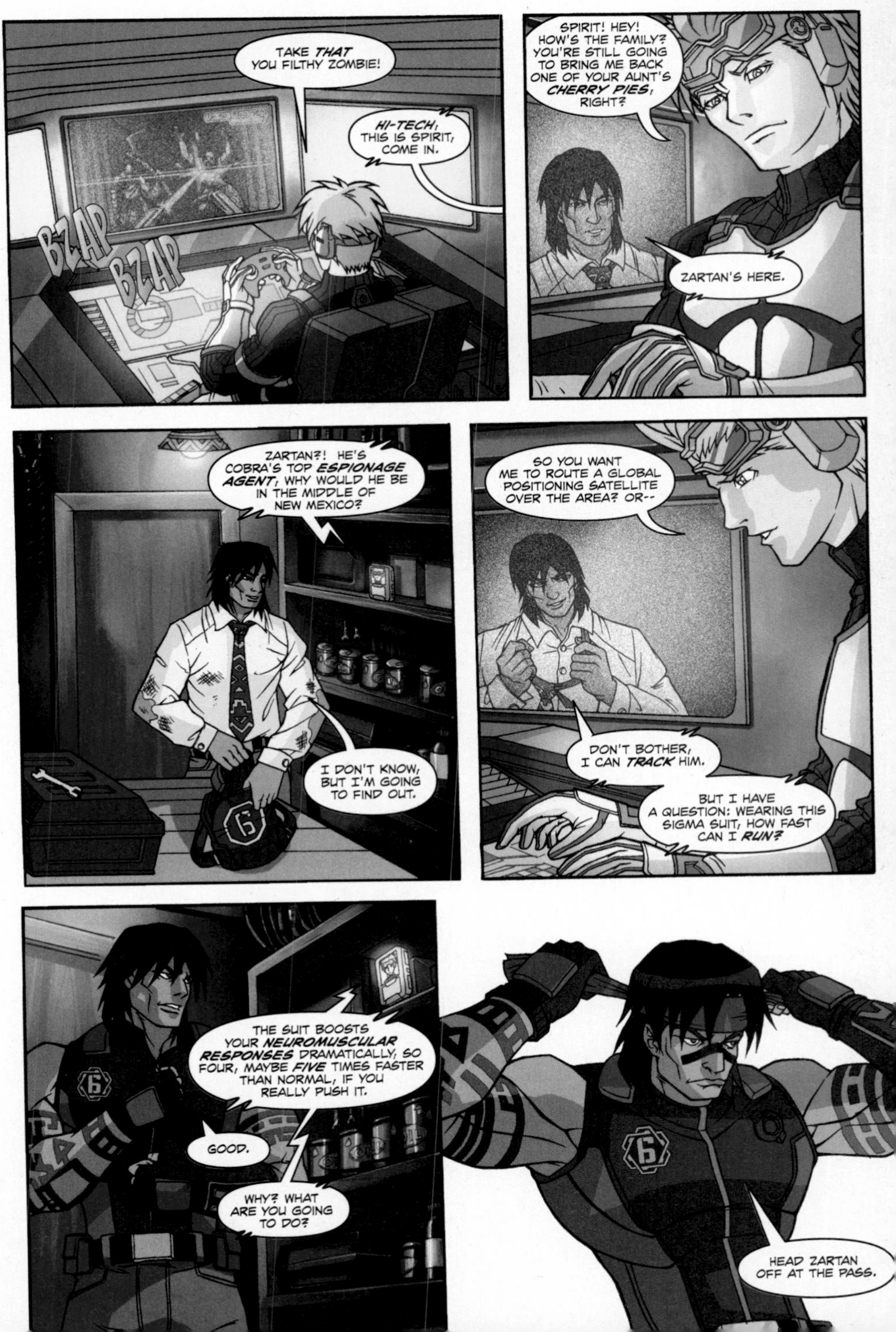
TAKE THAT YOU FILTHY ZOMBIE!
BZAP BZAP
HI-TECH, THIS IS SPIRIT, COME IN.
SPIRIT! HEY! HOW'S THE FAMILY? YOU'RE STILL GOING TO BRING ME BACK ONE OF YOUR AUNT'S CHERRY PIES, RIGHT?
ZARTAN'S HERE.
ZARTAN?! HE'S COBRA'S TOP ESPIONAGE AGENT, WHY WOULD HE BE IN THE MIDDLE OF NEW MEXICO?
I DON'T KNOW, BUT I'M GOING TO FIND OUT.
SO YOU WANT ME TO ROUTE A GLOBAL POSITIONING SATELLITE OVER THE AREA? OR--
DON'T BOTHER, I CAN TRACK HIM.
BUT I HAVE A QUESTION: WEARING THIS SIGMA SUIT, HOW FAST CAN I RUN?
THE SUIT BOOSTS YOUR NEUROMUSCULAR RESPONSES DRAMATICALLY, SO FOUR, MAYBE FIVE TIMES FASTER THAN NORMAL, IF YOU REALLY PUSH IT.
GOOD.
WHY? WHAT ARE YOU GOING TO DO?
HEAD ZARTAN OFF AT THE PASS.

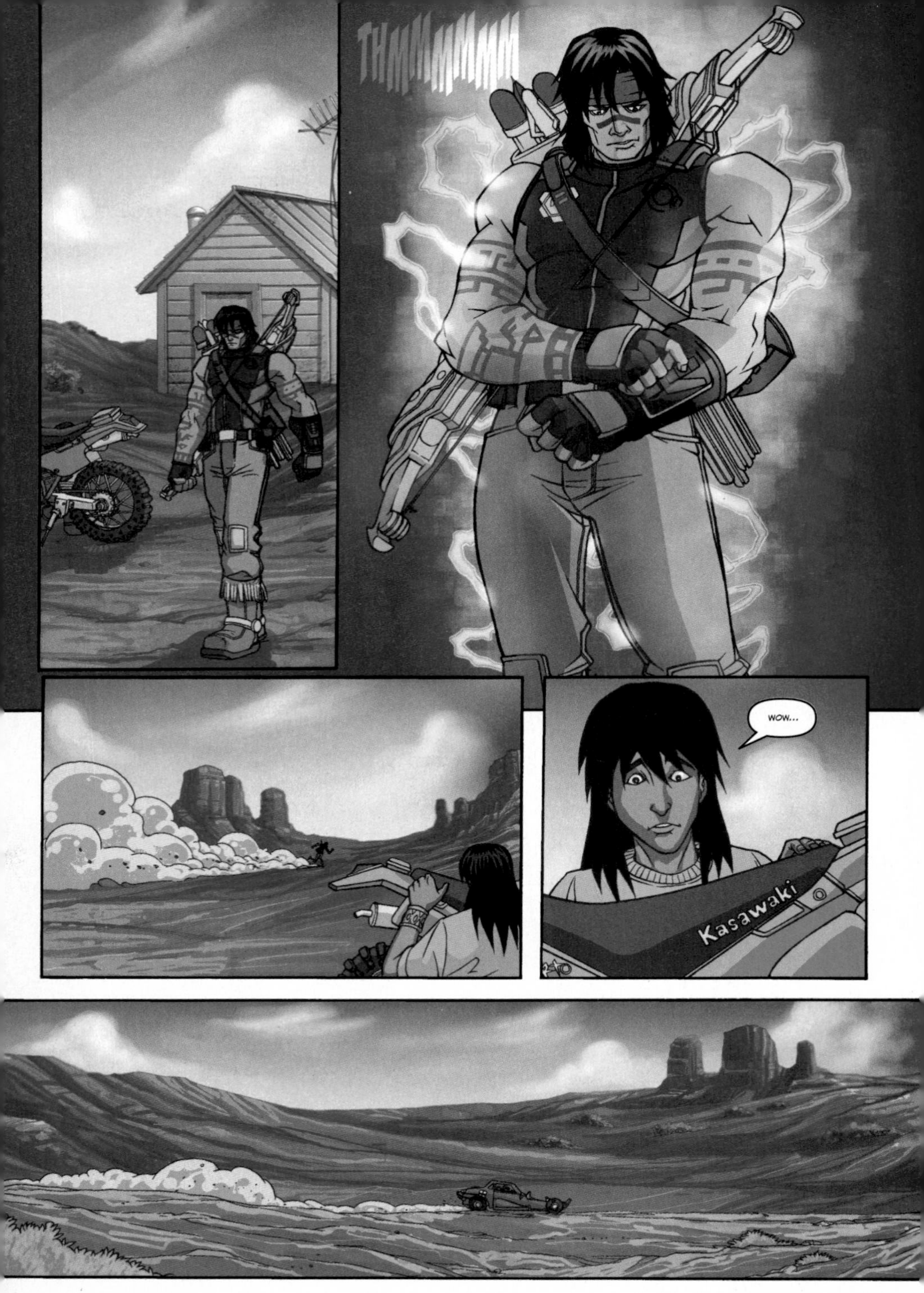
THMMMMMMM
WOW...
Kasawaki

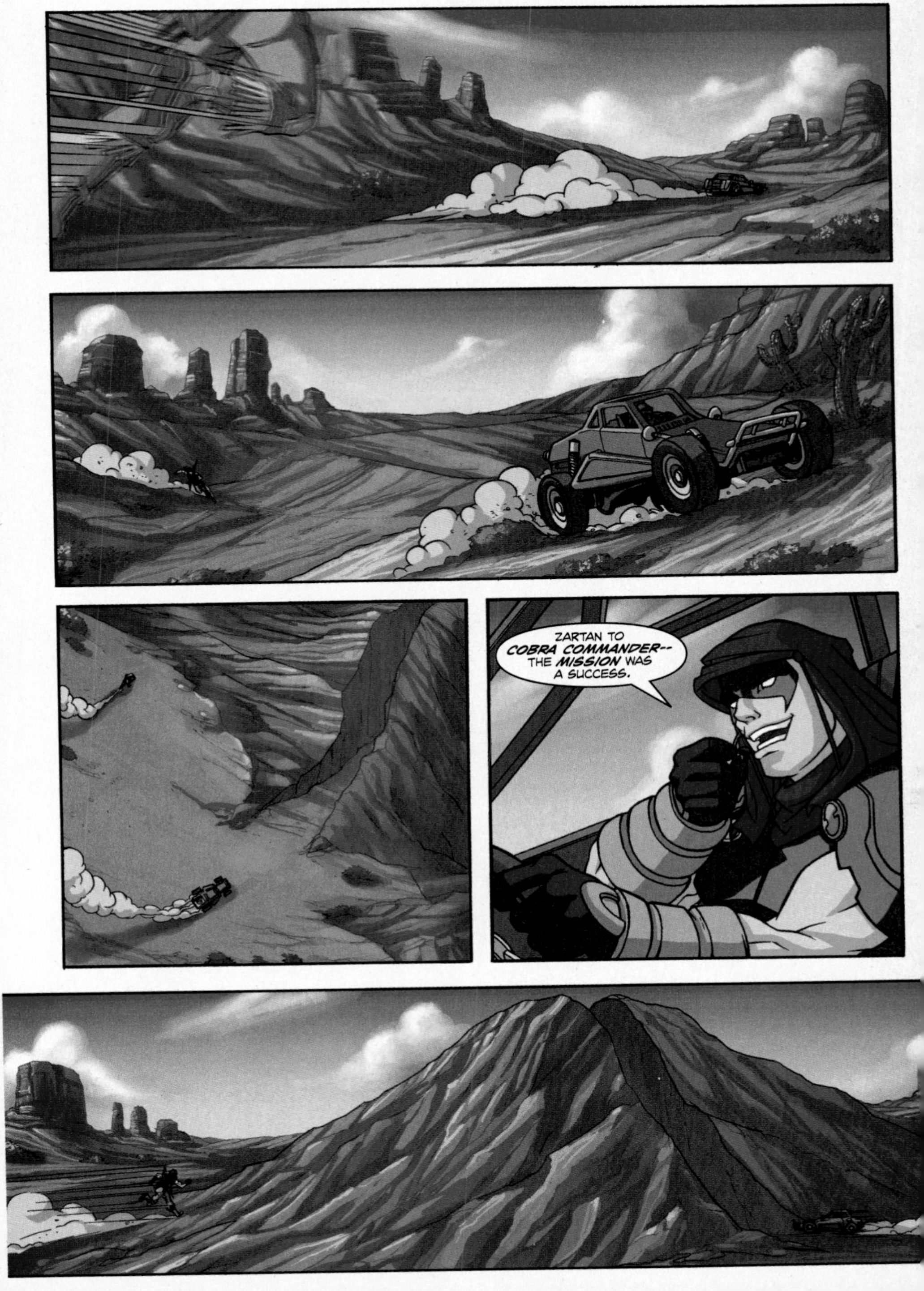
ZARTAN TO COBRA COMMANDER-- THE MISSION WAS A SUCCESS.

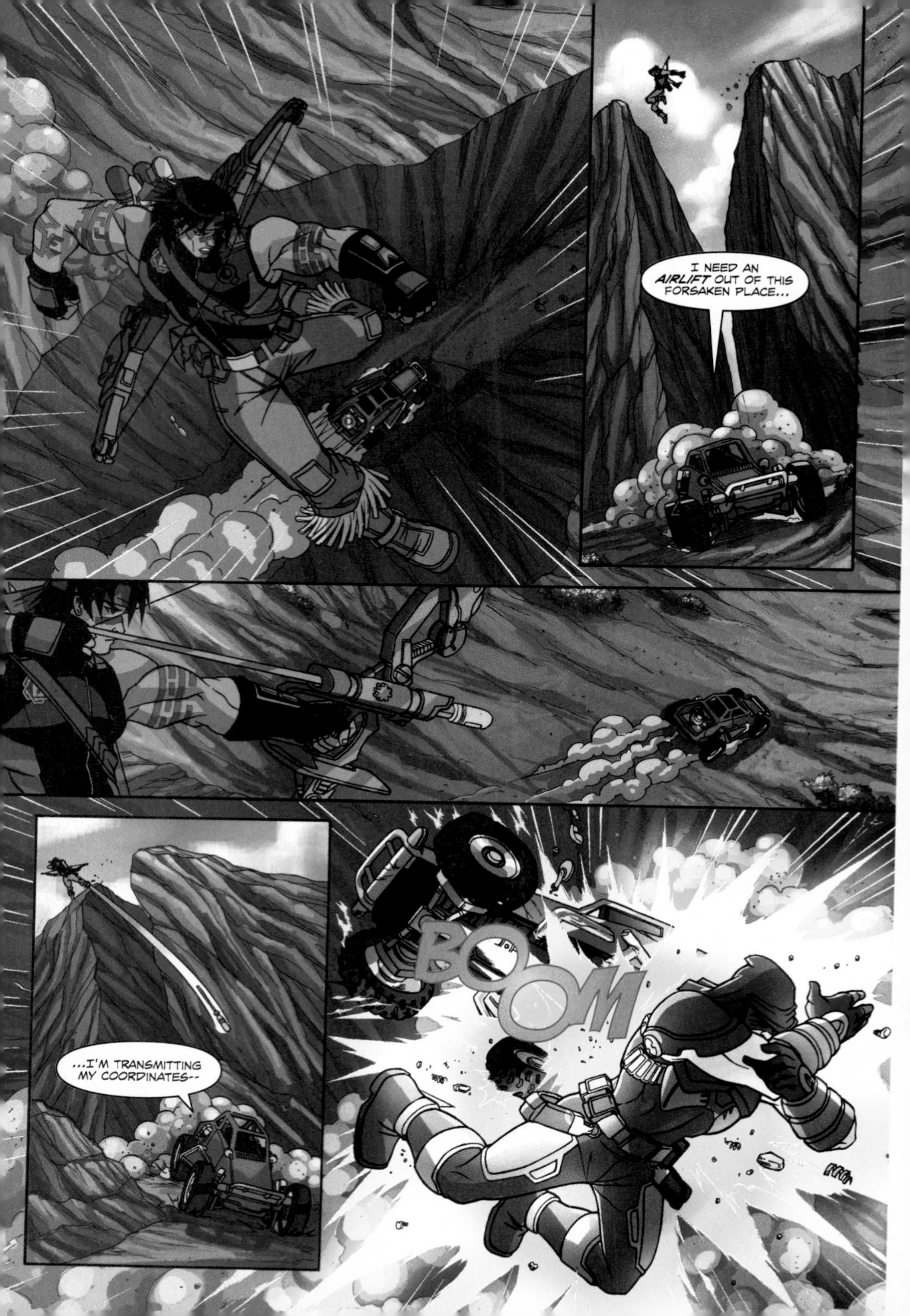
I NEED AN AIRLIFT OUT OF THIS FORSAKEN PLACE...
...I'M TRANSMITTING MY COORDINATES--
BOOOM

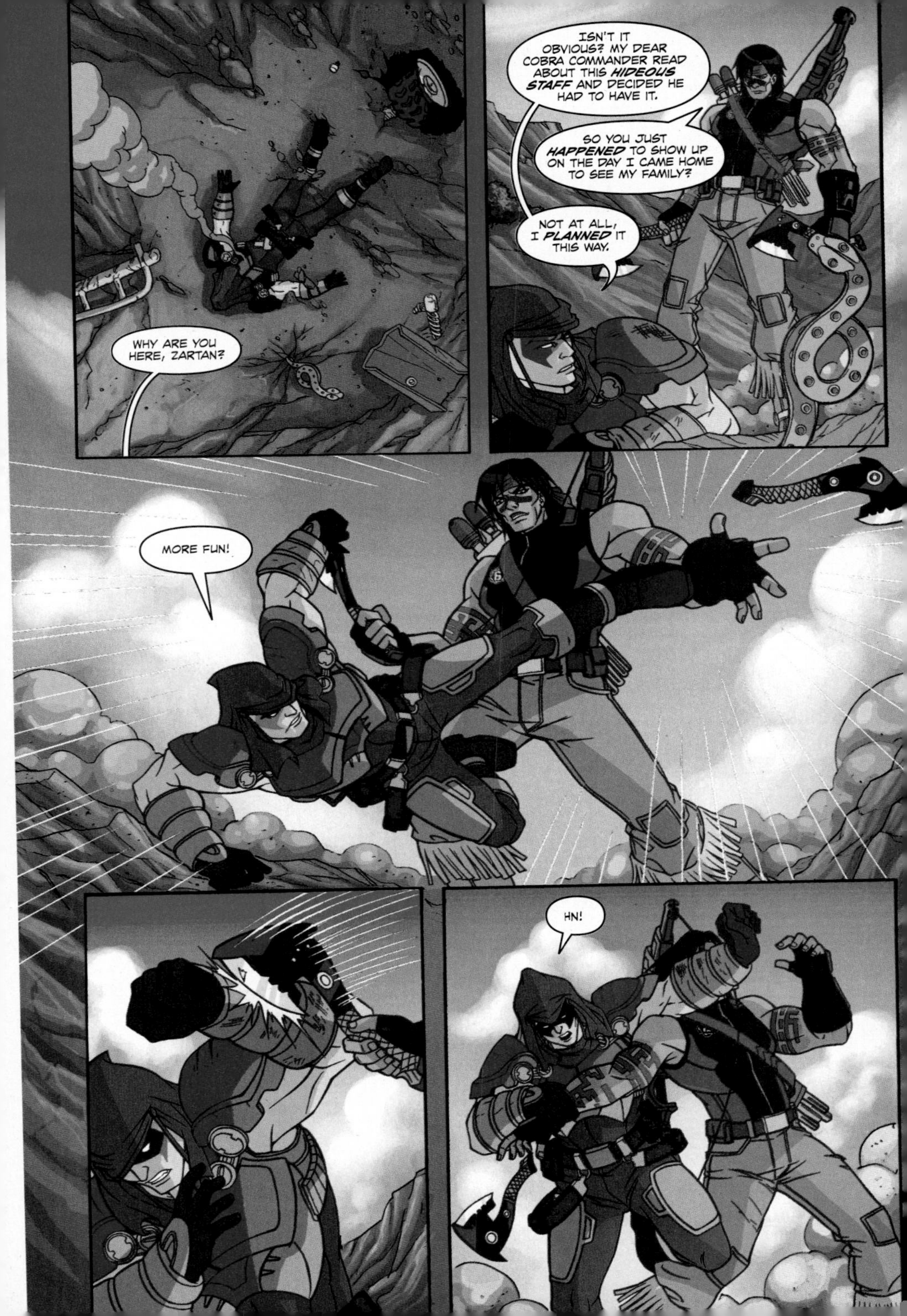
WHY ARE YOU HERE, ZARTAN?
ISN'T IT OBVIOUS? MY DEAR COBRA COMMANDER READ ABOUT THIS HIDEOUS STAFF AND DECIDED HE HAD TO HAVE IT.
SO YOU JUST HAPPENED TO SHOW UP ON THE DAY I CAME HOME TO SEE MY FAMILY?
NOT AT ALL, I PLANNED IT THIS WAY.
MORE FUN!
HN!

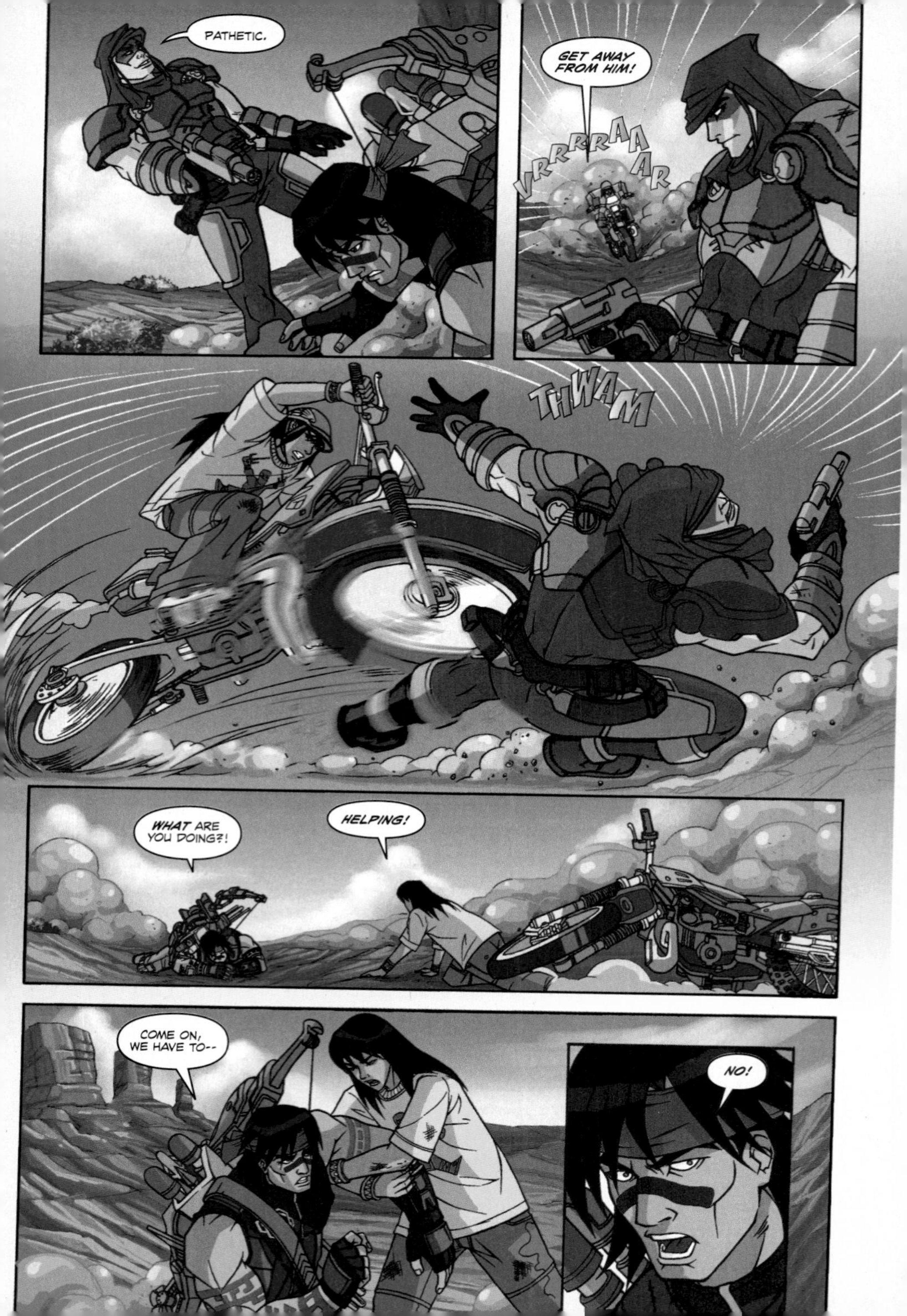
PATHETIC.
GET AWAY FROM HIM!
VRRRRAAAAR
THWAM
WHAT ARE YOU DOING?!
HELPING!
COME ON, WE HAVE TO--
NO!

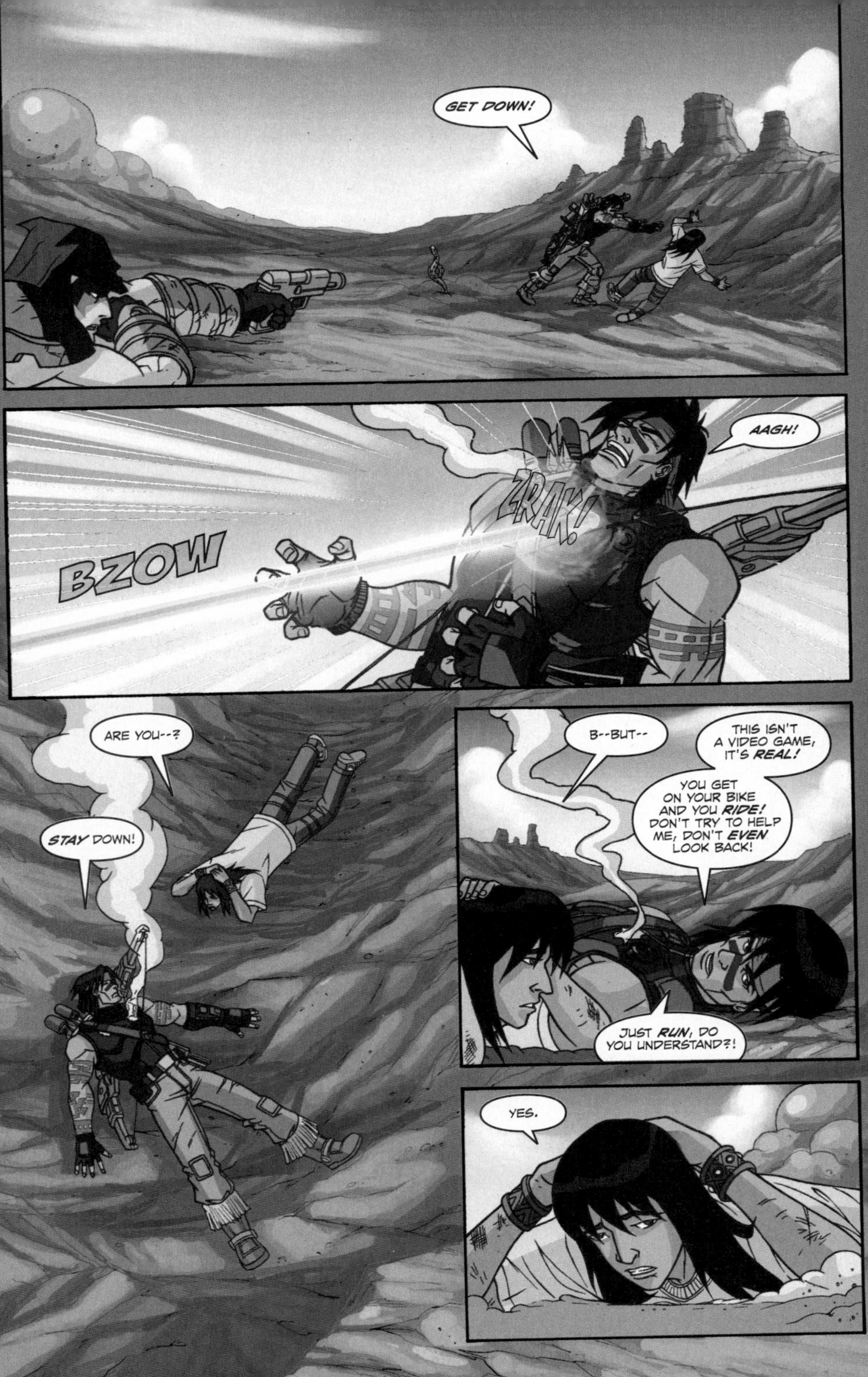
GET DOWN!
AAGH!
BZOW
ZRAK!
ARE YOU--?
STAY DOWN!
B--BUT--
THIS ISN'T A VIDEO GAME, IT'S REAL!
YOU GET ON YOUR BIKE AND YOU RIDE! DON'T TRY TO HELP ME, DON'T EVEN LOOK BACK!
JUST RUN, DO YOU UNDERSTAND?!
YES.

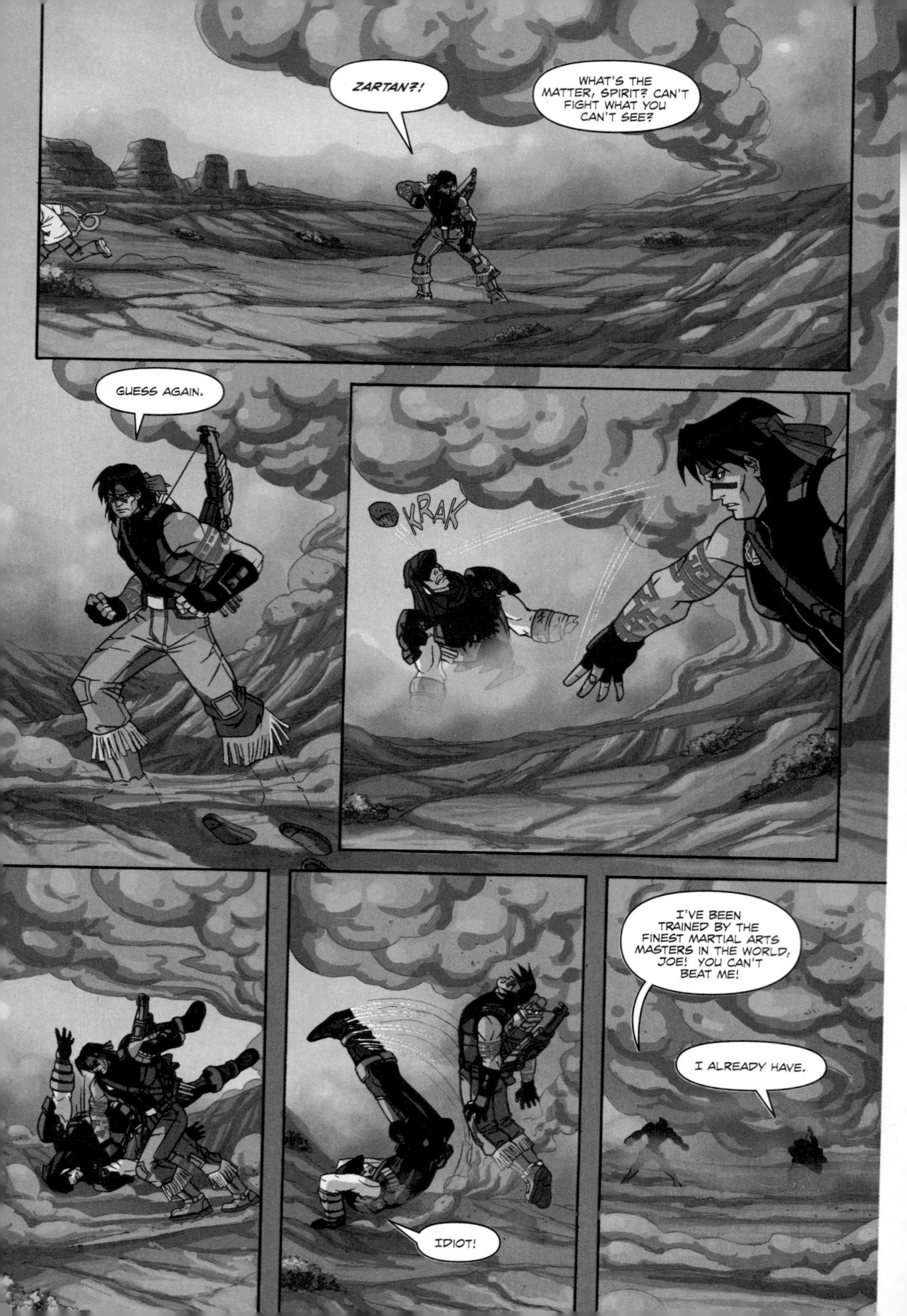
ZARTAN?!
WHAT'S THE MATTER, SPIRIT? CAN'T FIGHT WHAT YOU CAN'T SEE?
GUESS AGAIN.
KRAK
IDIOT!
I'VE BEEN TRAINED BY THE FINEST MARTIAL ARTS MASTERS IN THE WORLD, JOE! YOU CAN'T BEAT ME!
I ALREADY HAVE.

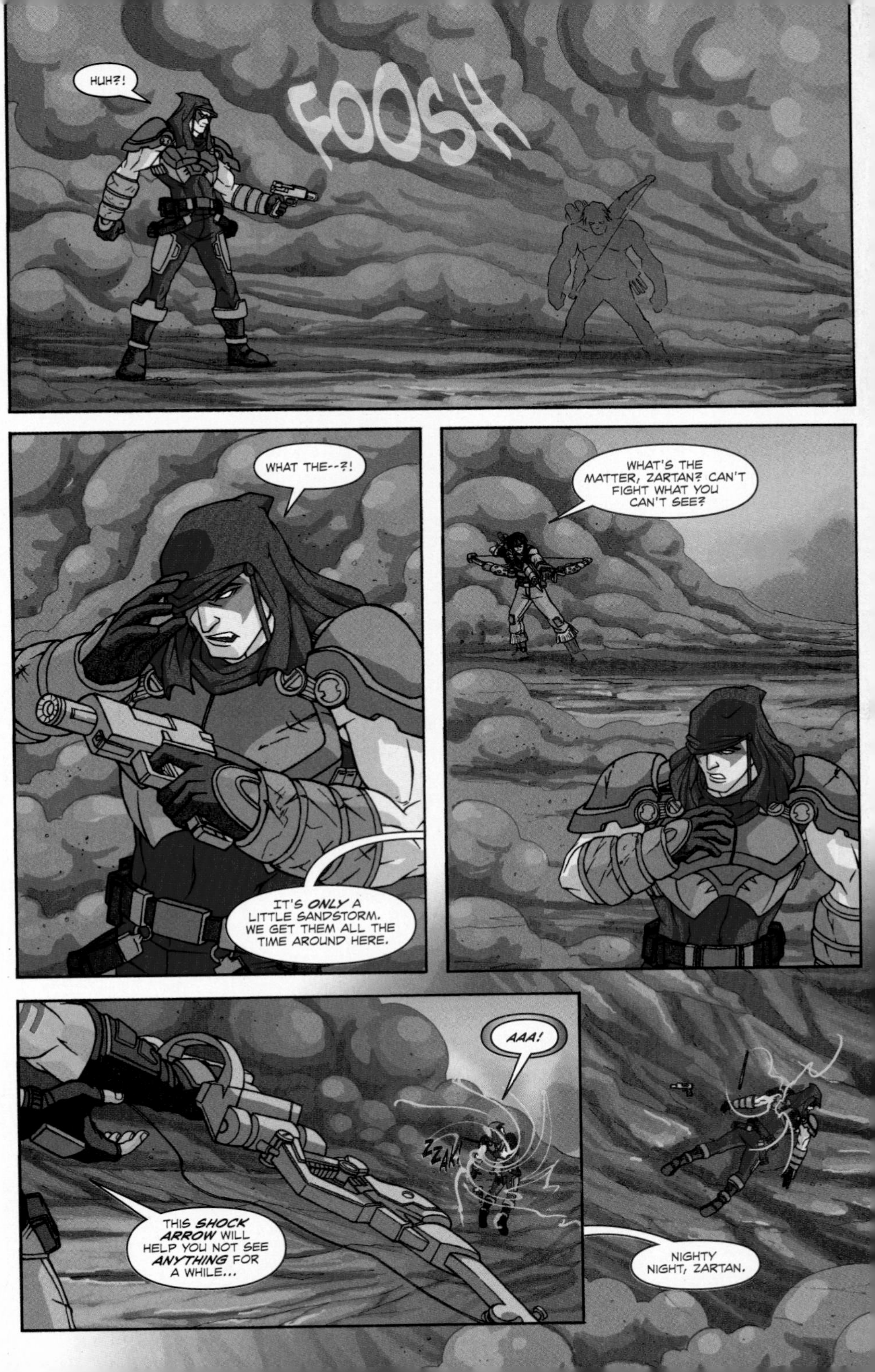
HUH?!
FOOSH
WHAT THE--?!
IT'S ONLY A LITTLE SANDSTORM. WE GET THEM ALL THE TIME AROUND HERE.
WHAT'S THE MATTER, ZARTAN? CAN'T FIGHT WHAT YOU CAN'T SEE?
AAA!
ZZAK!
THIS SHOCK ARROW WILL HELP YOU NOT SEE ANYTHING FOR A WHILE...
NIGHTY NIGHT, ZARTAN.

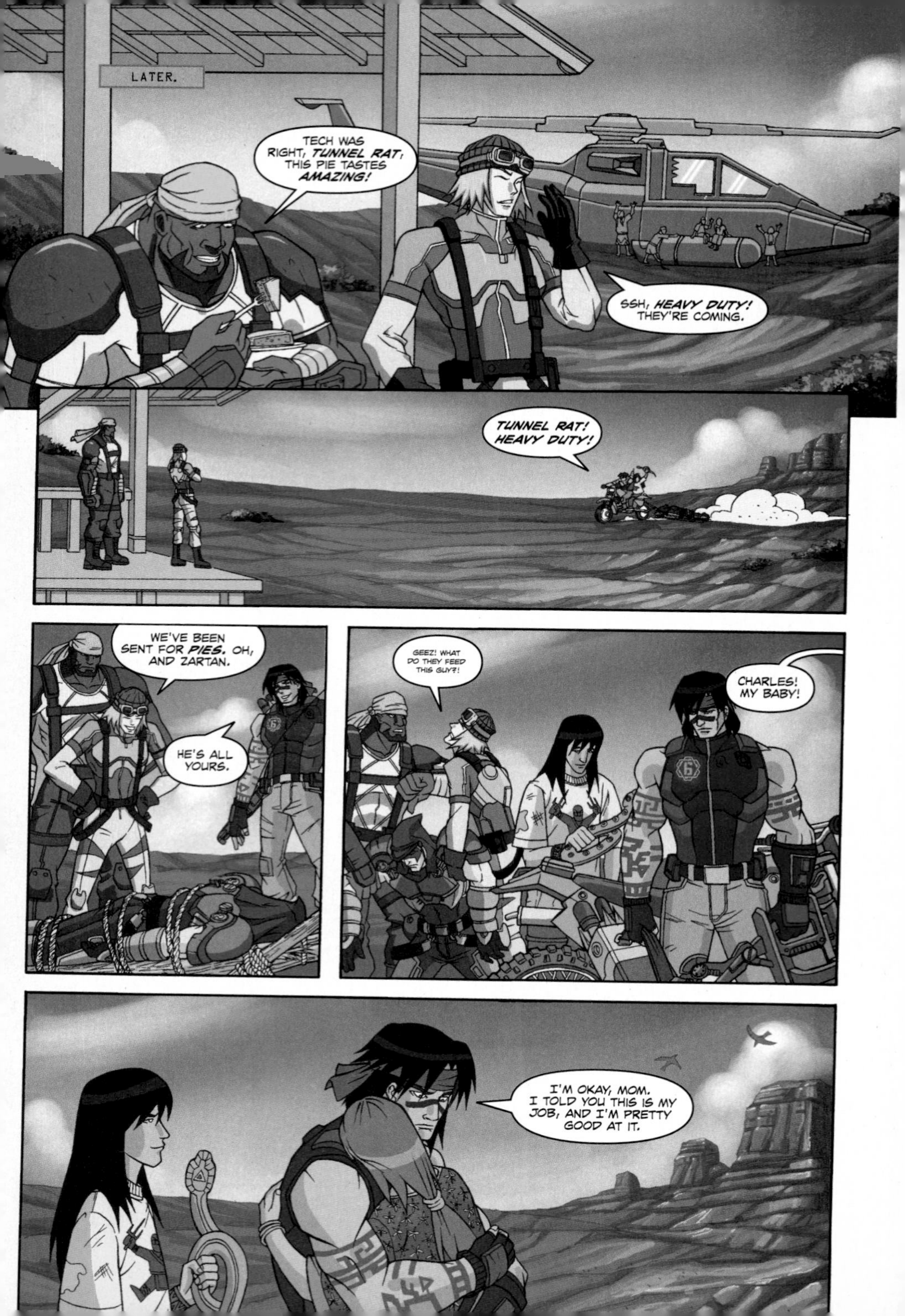
LATER.
TECH WAS RIGHT, TUNNEL RAT; THIS PIE TASTES AMAZING!
SSH, HEAVY DUTY! THEY'RE COMING.
TUNNEL RAT! HEAVY DUTY!
WE'VE BEEN SENT FOR PIES. OH, AND ZARTAN.
HE'S ALL YOURS.
GEEZ! WHAT DO THEY FEED THIS GUY?!
CHARLES! MY BABY!
I'M OKAY, MOM. I TOLD YOU THIS IS MY JOB, AND I'M PRETTY GOOD AT IT.

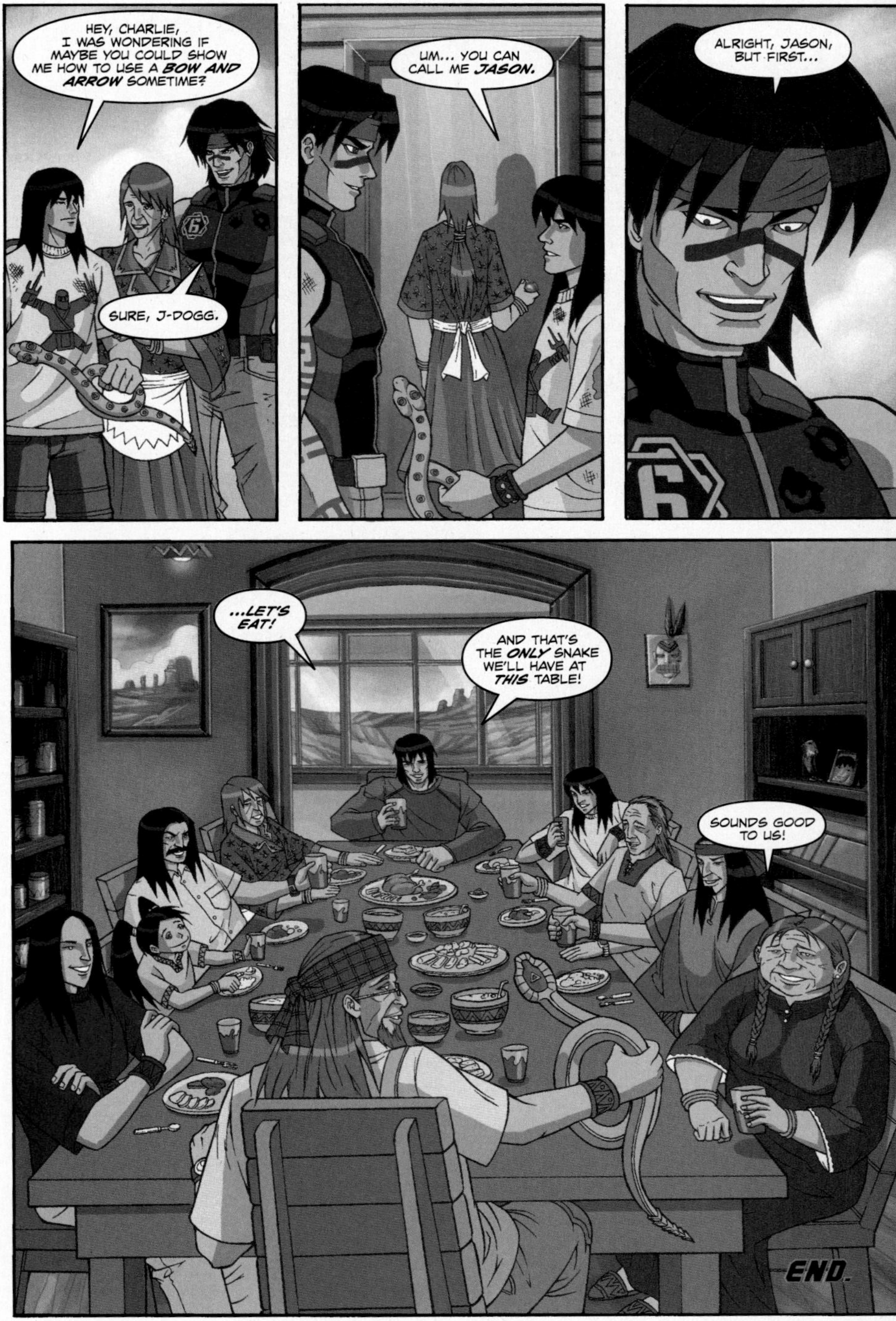
HEY, CHARLIE, I WAS WONDERING IF MAYBE YOU COULD SHOW ME HOW TO USE A BOW AND ARROW SOMETIME?
SURE, J-DOGG.
UM... YOU CAN CALL ME JASON.
ALRIGHT, JASON, BUT FIRST...
...LET'S EAT!
AND THAT'S THE ONLY SNAKE WE'LL HAVE AT THIS TABLE!
SOUNDS GOOD TO US!
END.

SIGMA 6 is the code name for a new group of covert G.I. JOE operatives. Few highly specialize capabilities. They use innovative technology and gear designed exclusively for each their missions. Working against them is the evil COBRA organization, whose goal is t take control of the world by sabotage, espionage and outright destruction. SIGMA 6 figh them at every turn and provides a swift solution to critical situations around the glob

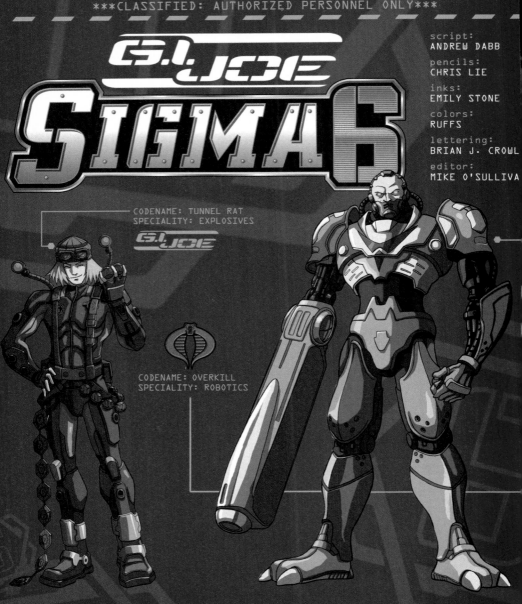

CLASSIFIED: AUTHORIZED PERSONNEL ONLY

G.I. JOE
SIGMA 6

script:
ANDREW DABB

pencils:
CHRIS LIE

inks:
EMILY STONE

colors:
RUFFS

lettering:
BRIAN J. CROWL

editor:
MIKE O'SULLIVA

CODENAME: TUNNEL RAT
SPECIALITY: EXPLOSIVES

CODENAME: OVERKILL
SPECIALITY: ROBOTICS

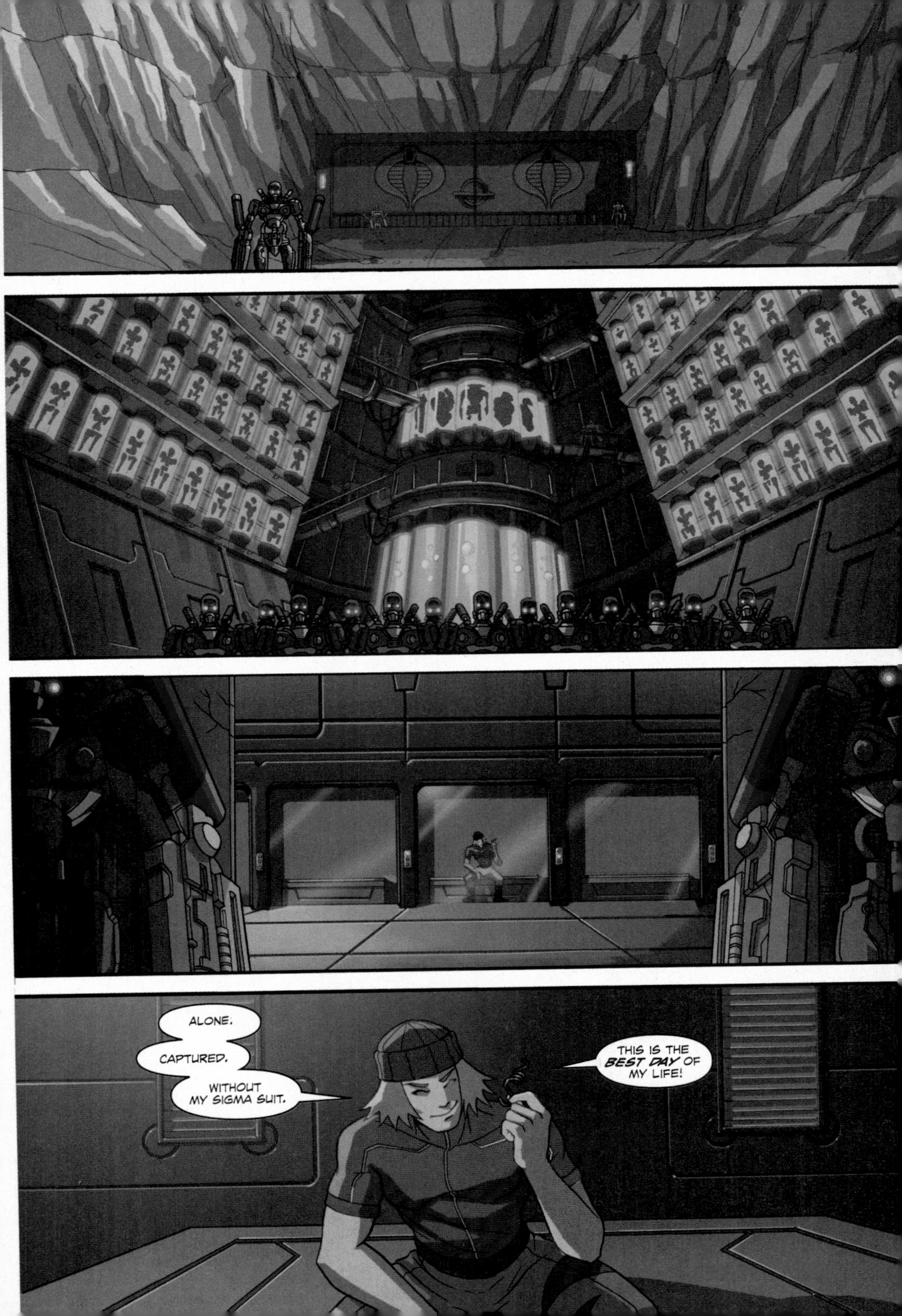
ALONE.
CAPTURED.
WITHOUT MY SIGMA SUIT.
THIS IS THE BEST DAY OF MY LIFE!

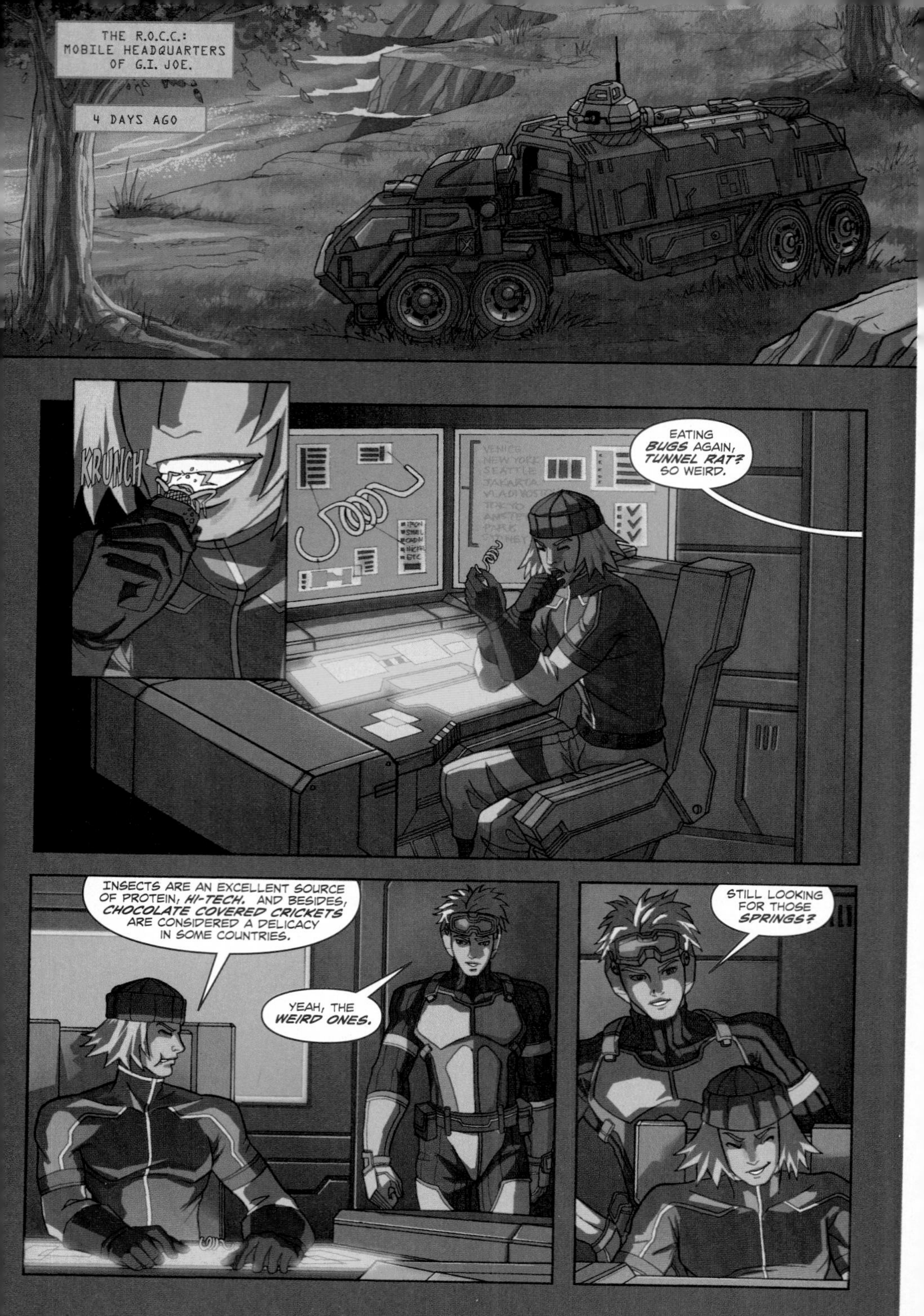

THE R.O.C.C.: MOBILE HEADQUARTERS OF G.I. JOE.
4 DAYS AGO
KRUNCH
EATING BUGS AGAIN, TUNNEL RAT? SO WEIRD.
INSECTS ARE AN EXCELLENT SOURCE OF PROTEIN, HI-TECH. AND BESIDES, CHOCOLATE COVERED CRICKETS ARE CONSIDERED A DELICACY IN SOME COUNTRIES.
YEAH, THE WEIRD ONES.
STILL LOOKING FOR THOSE SPRINGS?

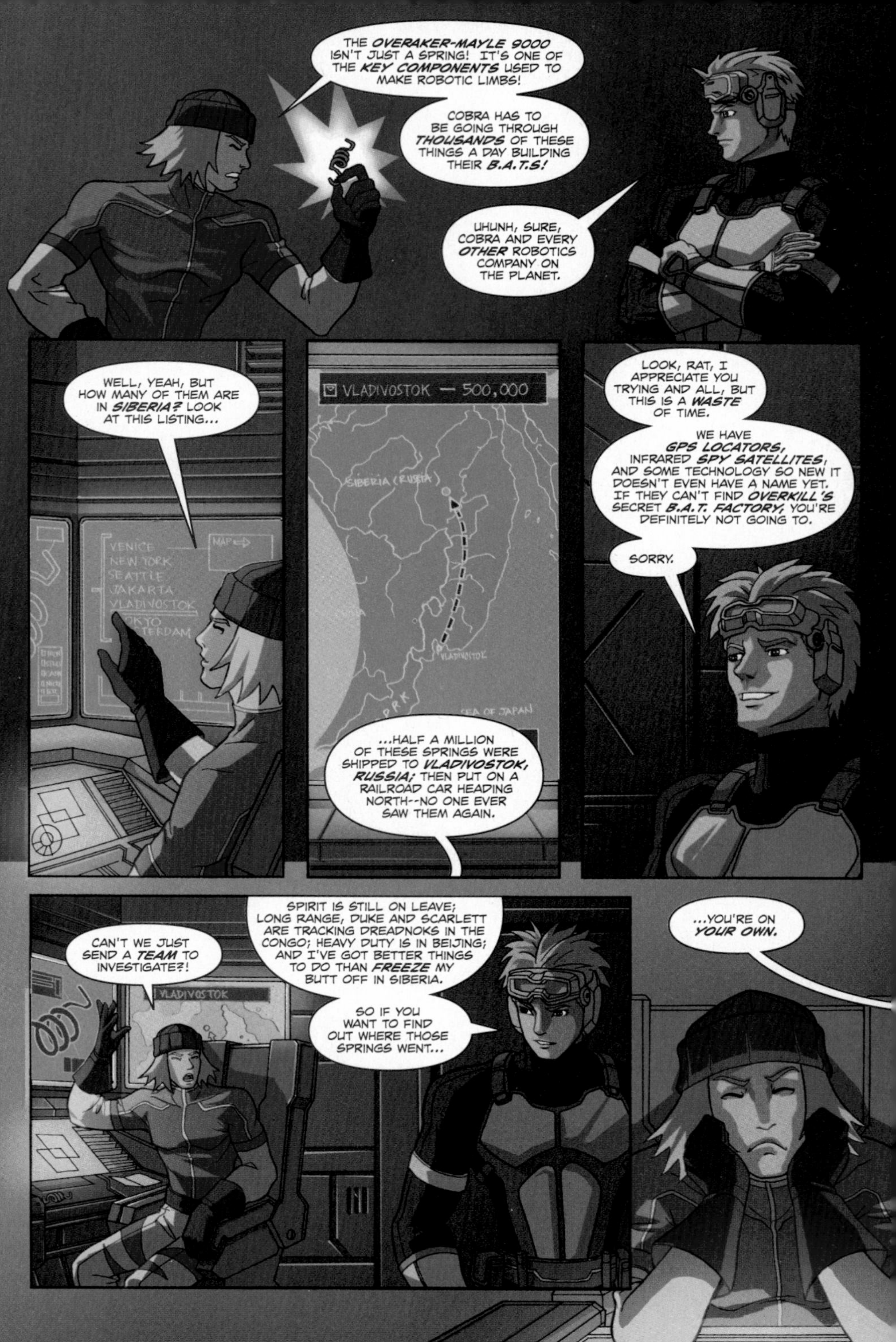
THE OVERAKER-MAYLE 9000 ISN'T JUST A SPRING! IT'S ONE OF THE KEY COMPONENTS USED TO MAKE ROBOTIC LIMBS!
COBRA HAS TO BE GOING THROUGH THOUSANDS OF THESE THINGS A DAY BUILDING THEIR B.A.T.S!
UHUNH, SURE, COBRA AND EVERY OTHER ROBOTICS COMPANY ON THE PLANET.
WELL, YEAH, BUT HOW MANY OF THEM ARE IN SIBERIA? LOOK AT THIS LISTING...
VENICE
NEW YORK
SEATTLE
JAKARTA
VLADIVOSTOK
MAP
VLADIVOSTOK — 500,000
SIBERIA (RUSSIA)
VLADIVOSTOK
PRK
SEA OF JAPAN
...HALF A MILLION OF THESE SPRINGS WERE SHIPPED TO VLADIVOSTOK, RUSSIA; THEN PUT ON A RAILROAD CAR HEADING NORTH--NO ONE EVER SAW THEM AGAIN.
LOOK, RAT, I APPRECIATE YOU TRYING AND ALL, BUT THIS IS A WASTE OF TIME.
WE HAVE GPS LOCATORS, INFRARED SPY SATELLITES, AND SOME TECHNOLOGY SO NEW IT DOESN'T EVEN HAVE A NAME YET. IF THEY CAN'T FIND OVERKILL'S SECRET B.A.T. FACTORY, YOU'RE DEFINITELY NOT GOING TO.
SORRY.
CAN'T WE JUST SEND A TEAM TO INVESTIGATE?!
VLADIVOSTOK
SPIRIT IS STILL ON LEAVE; LONG RANGE, DUKE AND SCARLETT ARE TRACKING DREADNOKS IN THE CONGO; HEAVY DUTY IS IN BEIJING; AND I'VE GOT BETTER THINGS TO DO THAN FREEZE MY BUTT OFF IN SIBERIA.
SO IF YOU WANT TO FIND OUT WHERE THOSE SPRINGS WENT...
...YOU'RE ON YOUR OWN.

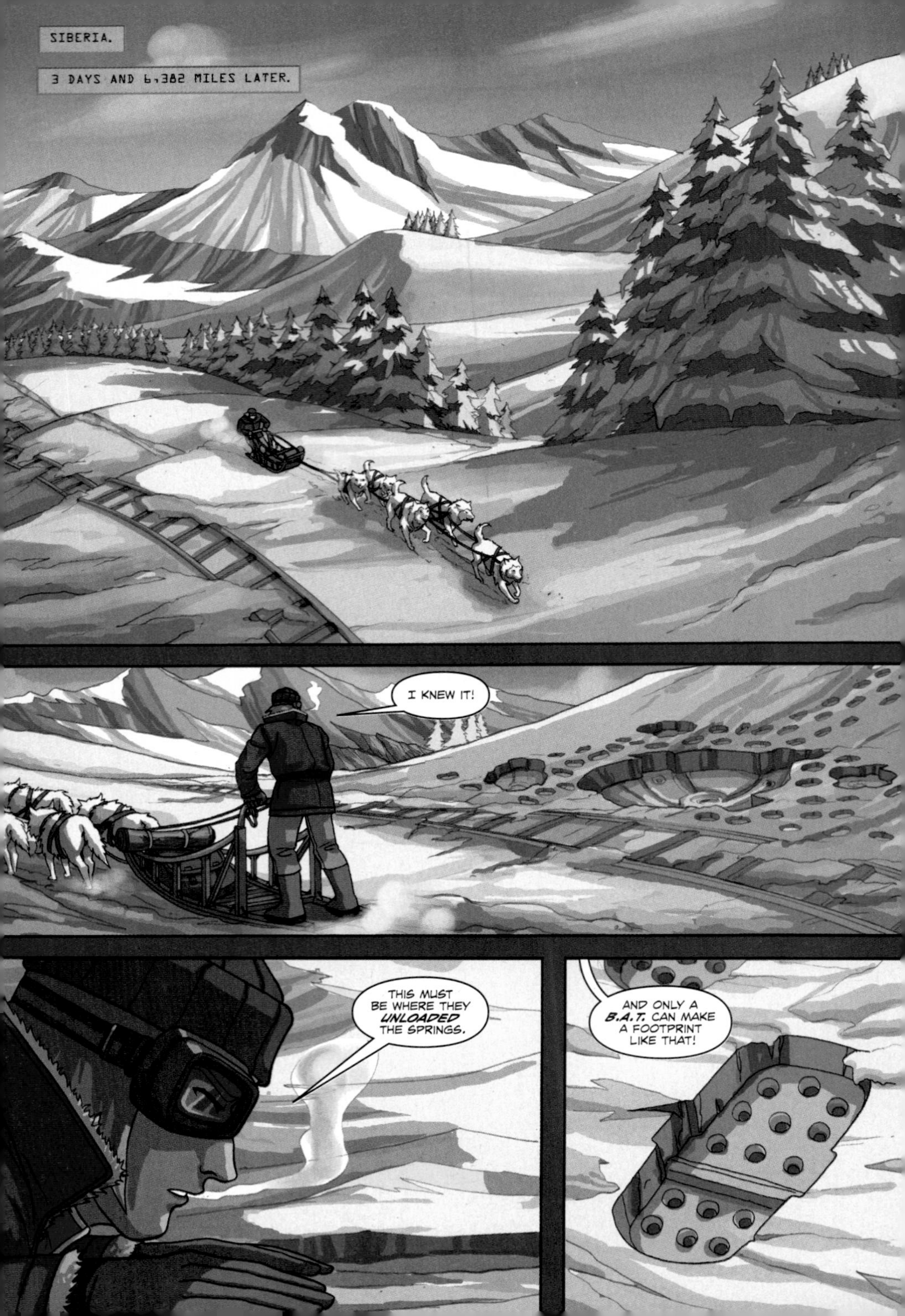
SIBERIA.
3 DAYS AND 6,382 MILES LATER.
I KNEW IT!
THIS MUST BE WHERE THEY UNLOADED THE SPRINGS.
AND ONLY A B.A.T. CAN MAKE A FOOTPRINT LIKE THAT!

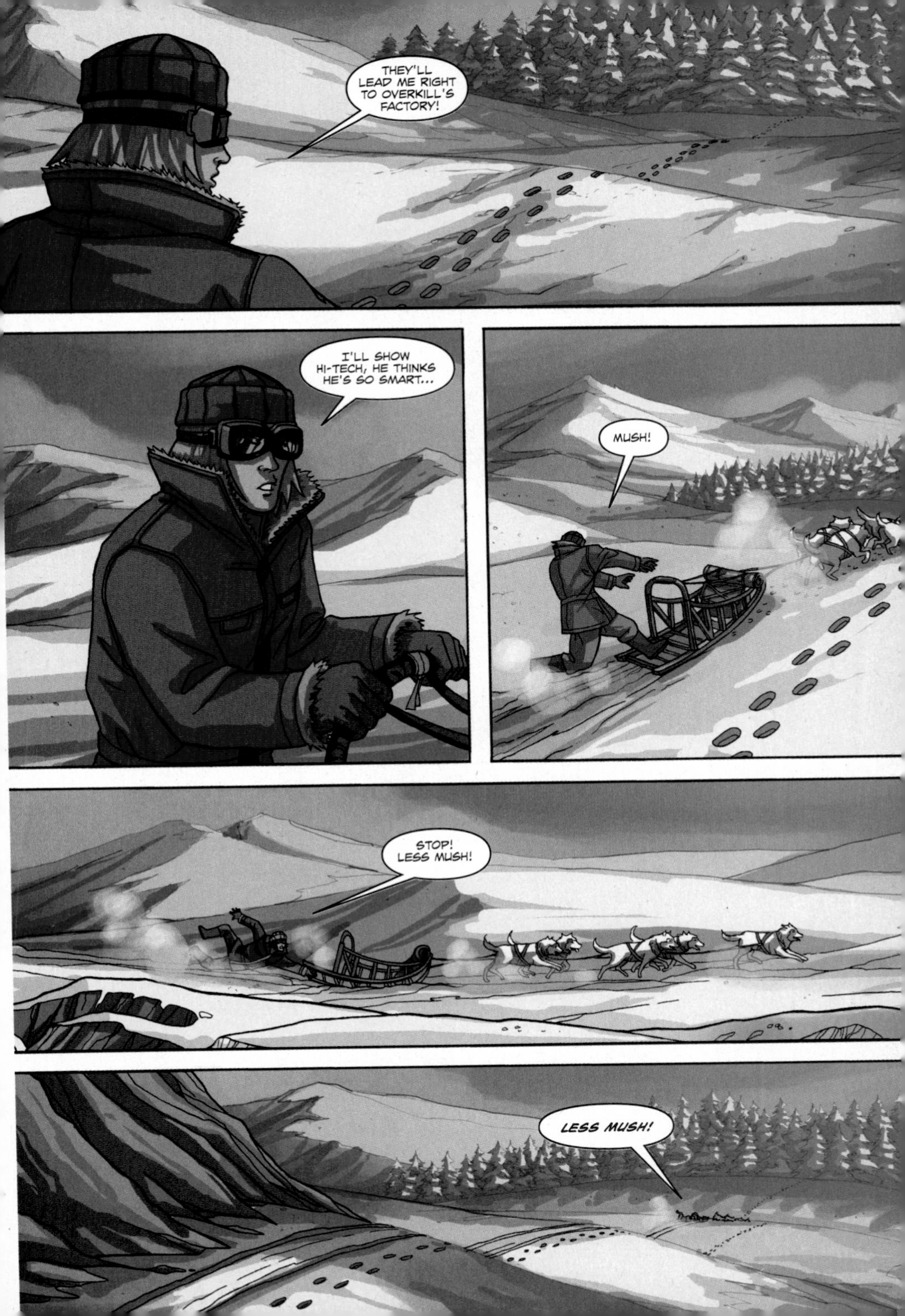
THEY'LL LEAD ME RIGHT TO OVERKILL'S FACTORY!
I'LL SHOW HI-TECH, HE THINKS HE'S SO SMART...
MUSH!
STOP! LESS MUSH!
LESS MUSH!

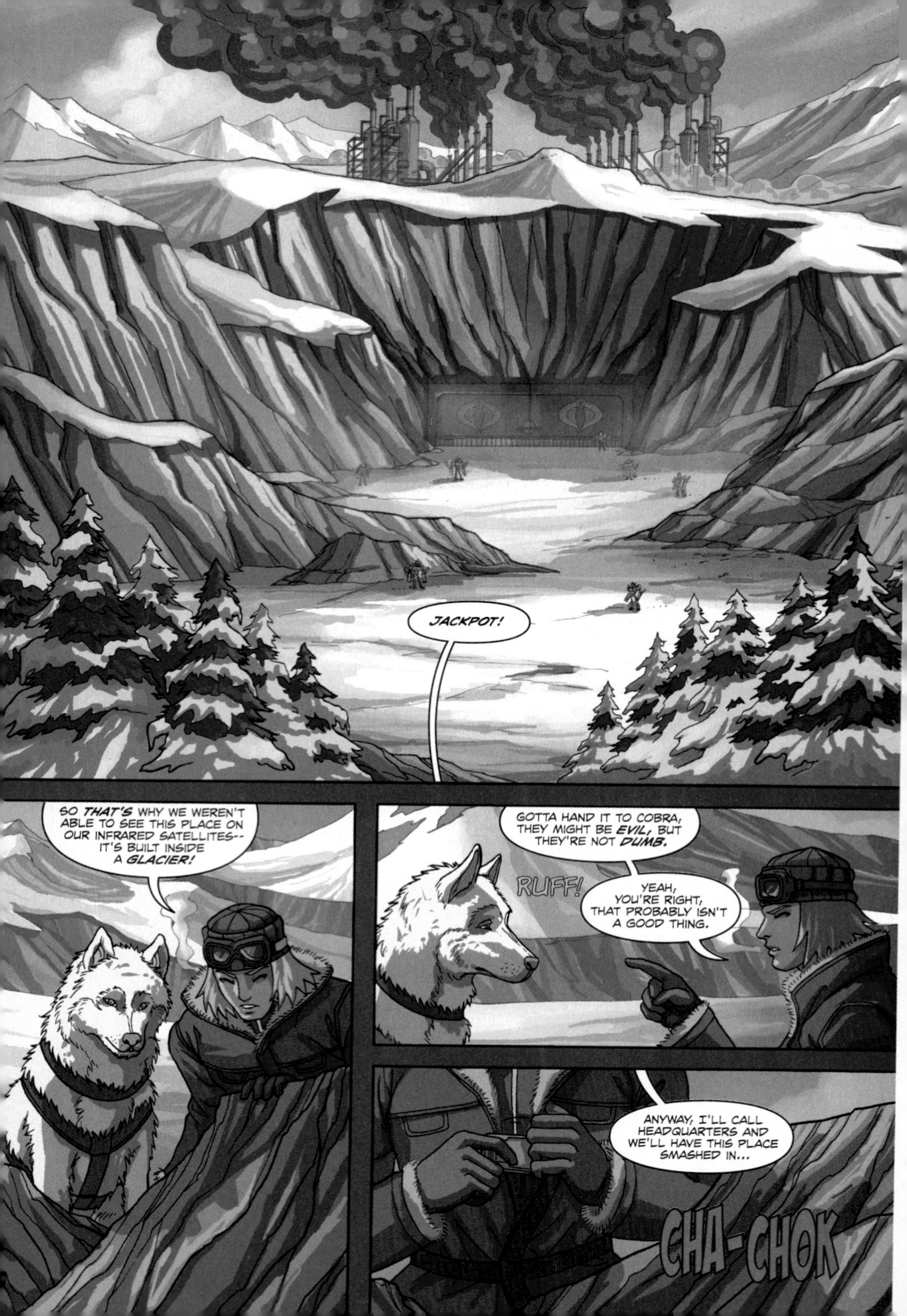
JACKPOT!
SO THAT'S WHY WE WEREN'T ABLE TO SEE THIS PLACE ON OUR INFRARED SATELLITES-- IT'S BUILT INSIDE A GLACIER!
GOTTA HAND IT TO COBRA, THEY MIGHT BE EVIL, BUT THEY'RE NOT DUMB.
RUFF!
YEAH, YOU'RE RIGHT, THAT PROBABLY ISN'T A GOOD THING.
ANYWAY, I'LL CALL HEADQUARTERS AND WE'LL HAVE THIS PLACE SMASHED IN...
CHA-CHOK

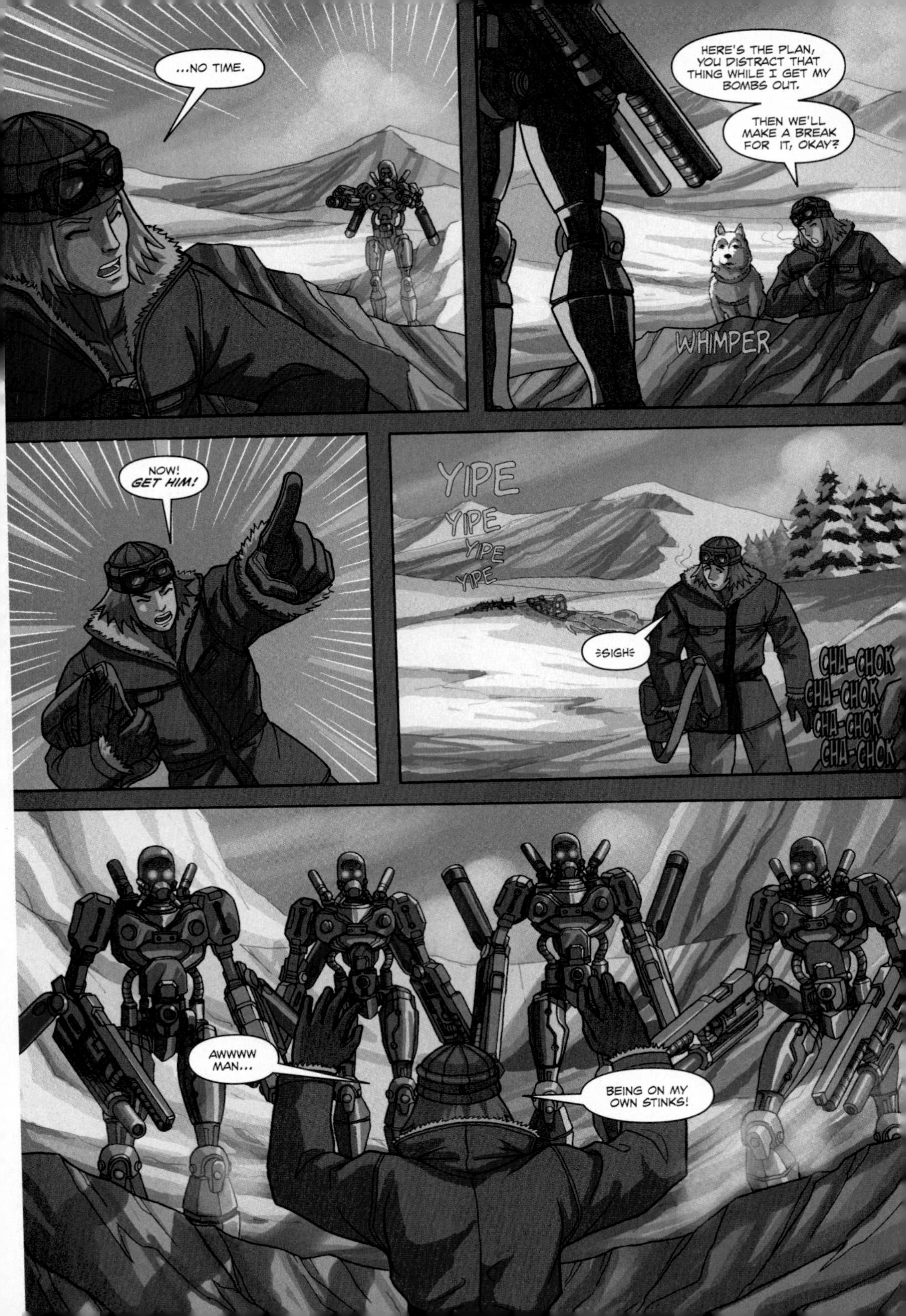
...NO TIME.
HERE'S THE PLAN, YOU DISTRACT THAT THING WHILE I GET MY BOMBS OUT.
THEN WE'LL MAKE A BREAK FOR IT, OKAY?
WHIMPER
NOW! *GET HIM!*
YIPE
YIPE
YIPE
YIPE
=SIGH=
CHA-CHOK
CHA-CHOK
CHA-CHOK
CHA-CHOK
AWWWW MAN...
BEING ON MY OWN STINKS!

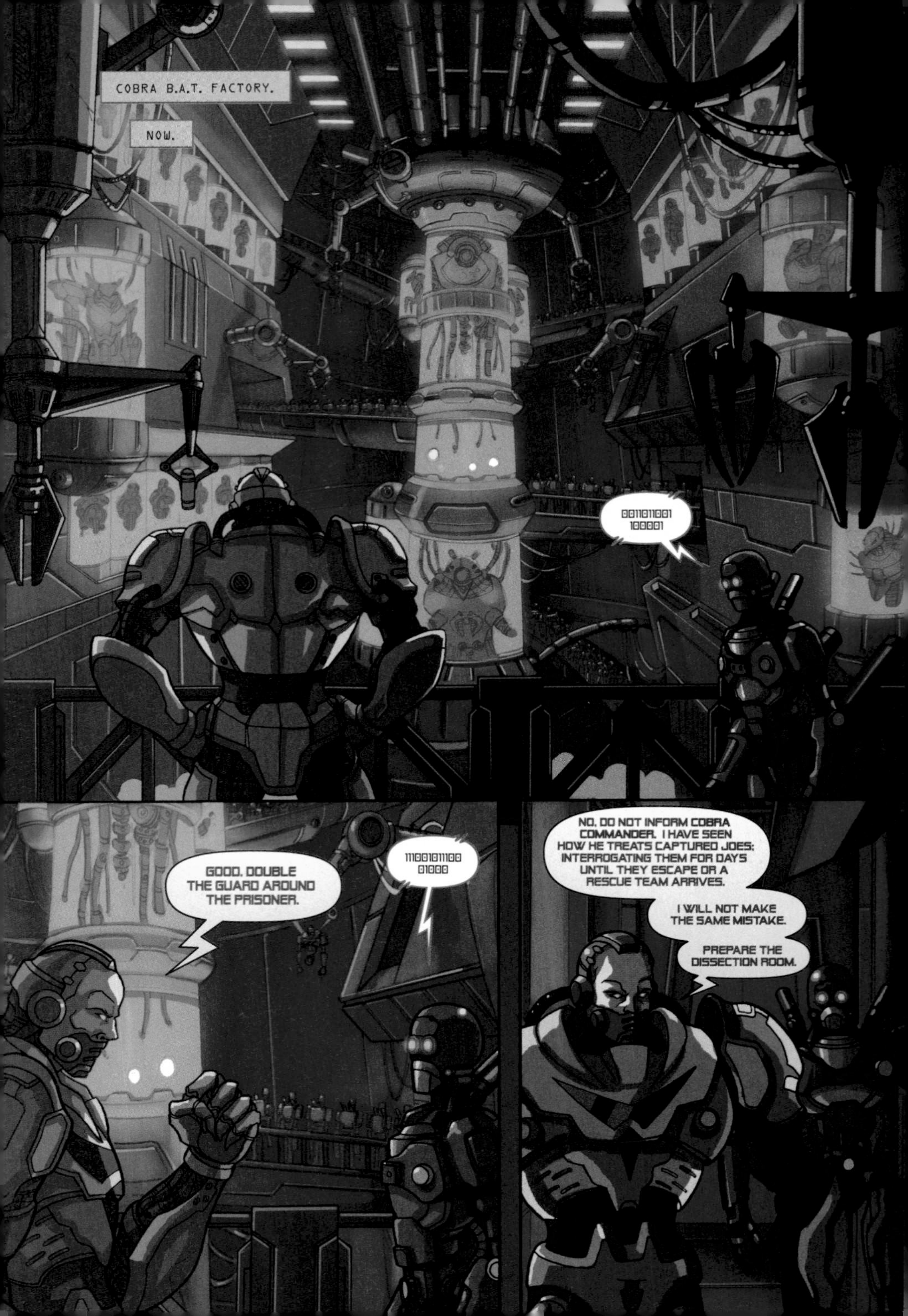
COBRA B.A.T. FACTORY.
NOW.
0011011001 100001
GOOD. DOUBLE THE GUARD AROUND THE PRISONER.
11100101100 01000
NO, DO NOT INFORM COBRA COMMANDER. I HAVE SEEN HOW HE TREATS CAPTURED JOES: INTERROGATING THEM FOR DAYS UNTIL THEY ESCAPE OR A RESCUE TEAM ARRIVES.
I WILL NOT MAKE THE SAME MISTAKE.
PREPARE THE DISSECTION ROOM.

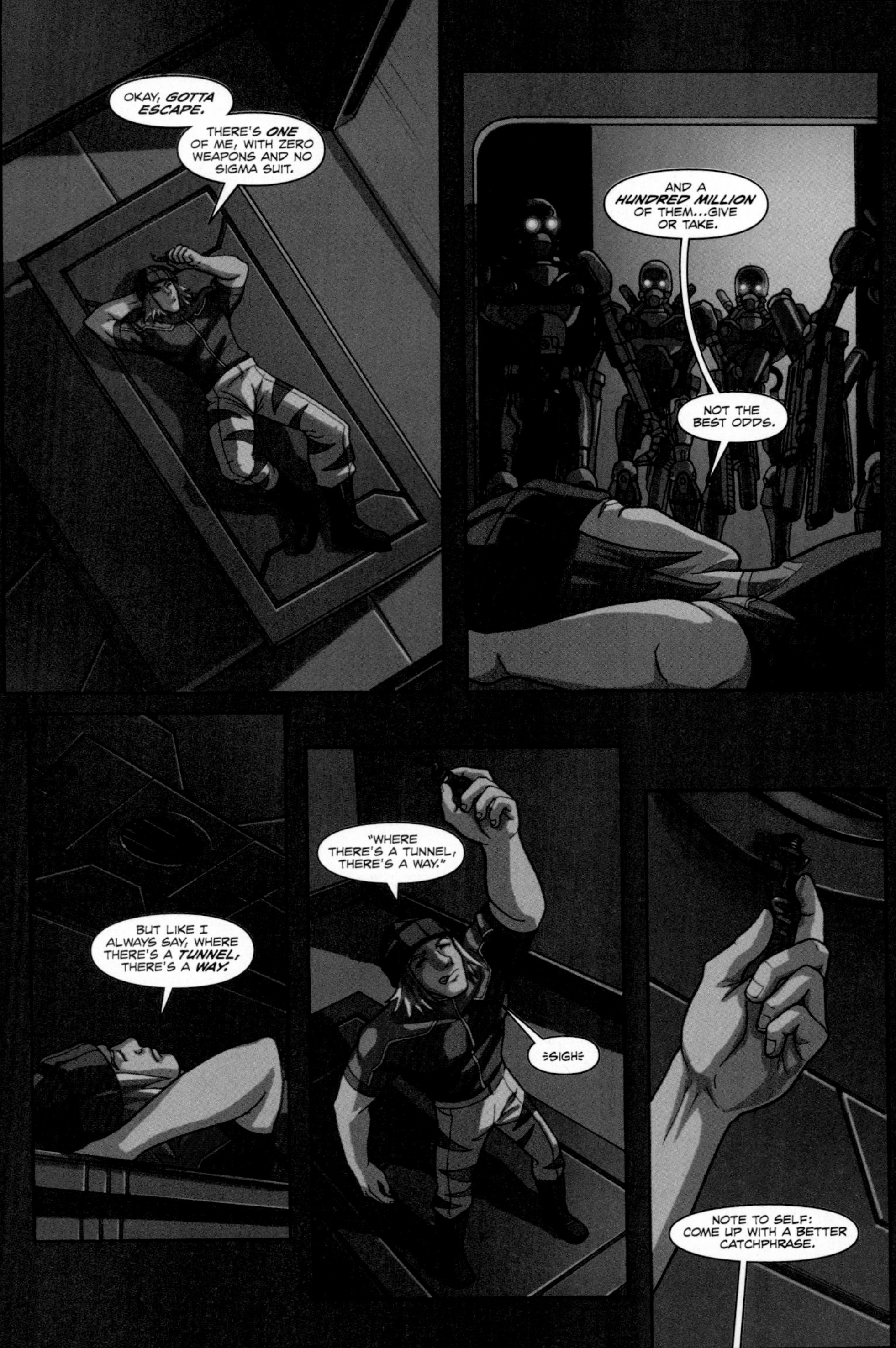
OKAY, GOTTA ESCAPE.
THERE'S ONE OF ME, WITH ZERO WEAPONS AND NO SIGMA SUIT.
AND A HUNDRED MILLION OF THEM...GIVE OR TAKE.
NOT THE BEST ODDS.
BUT LIKE I ALWAYS SAY, WHERE THERE'S A TUNNEL, THERE'S A WAY.
"WHERE THERE'S A TUNNEL, THERE'S A WAY."
SIGH
NOTE TO SELF: COME UP WITH A BETTER CATCHPHRASE.

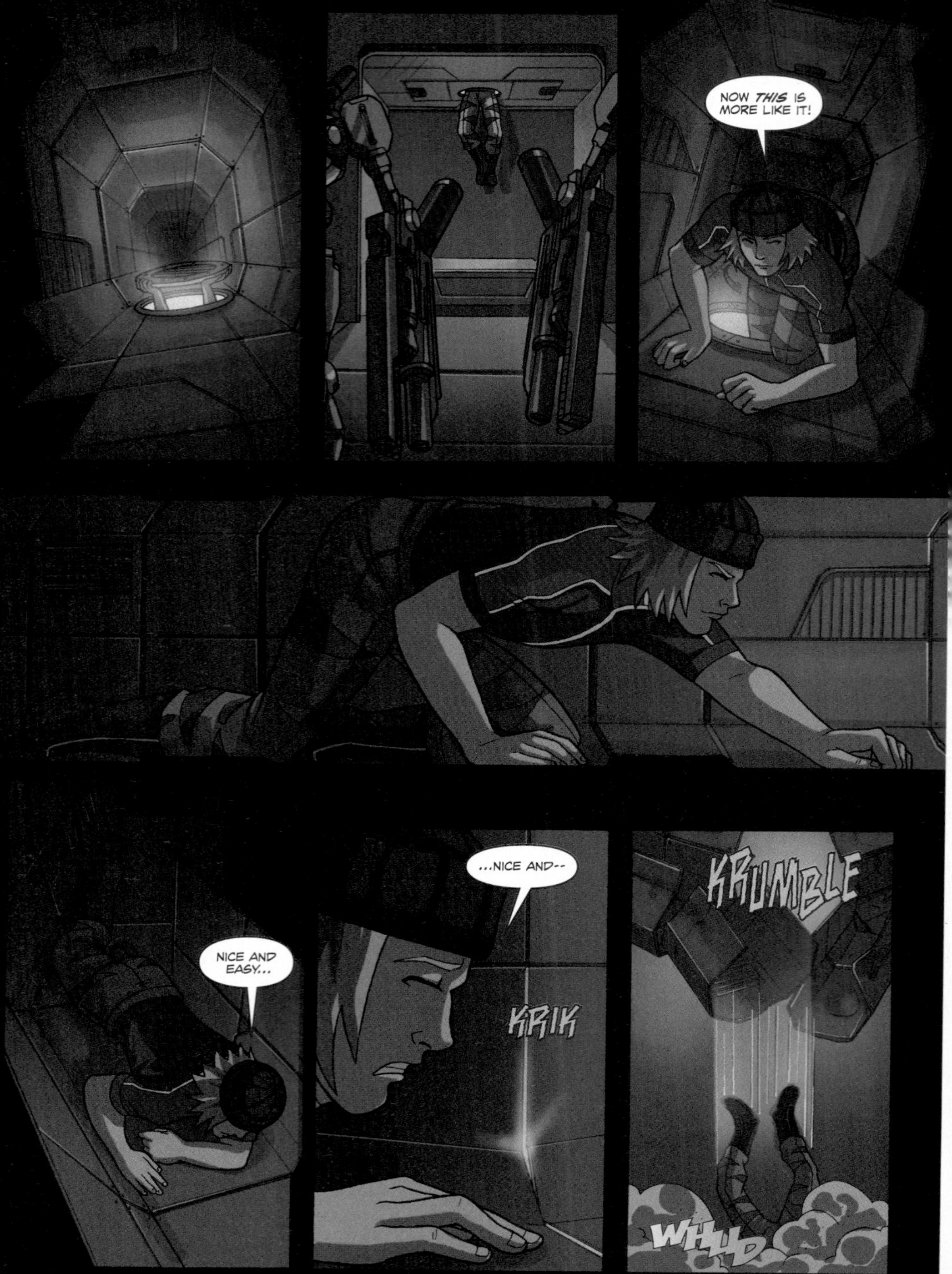
NOW *THIS* IS MORE LIKE IT!
NICE AND EASY...
...NICE AND--
KRIK
KRUMBLE
WHUD

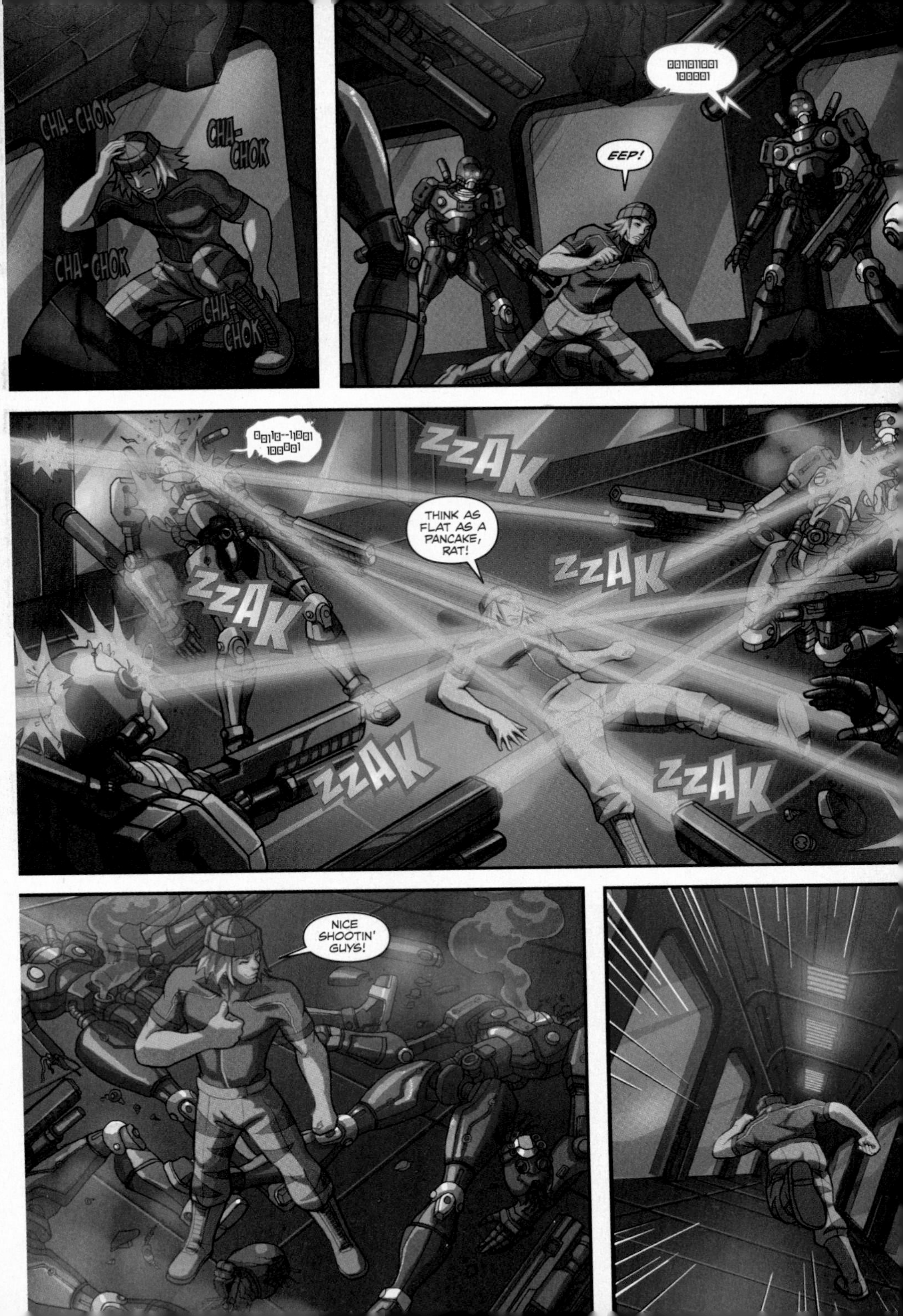
CHA-CHOK
CHA-CHOK
CHA-CHOK
CHA-CHOK
0011011001 100001
EEP!
0010--1001 100001
ZZAK
THINK AS FLAT AS A PANCAKE, RAT!
ZZAK
ZZAK
ZZAK
ZZAK
NICE SHOOTIN' GUYS!

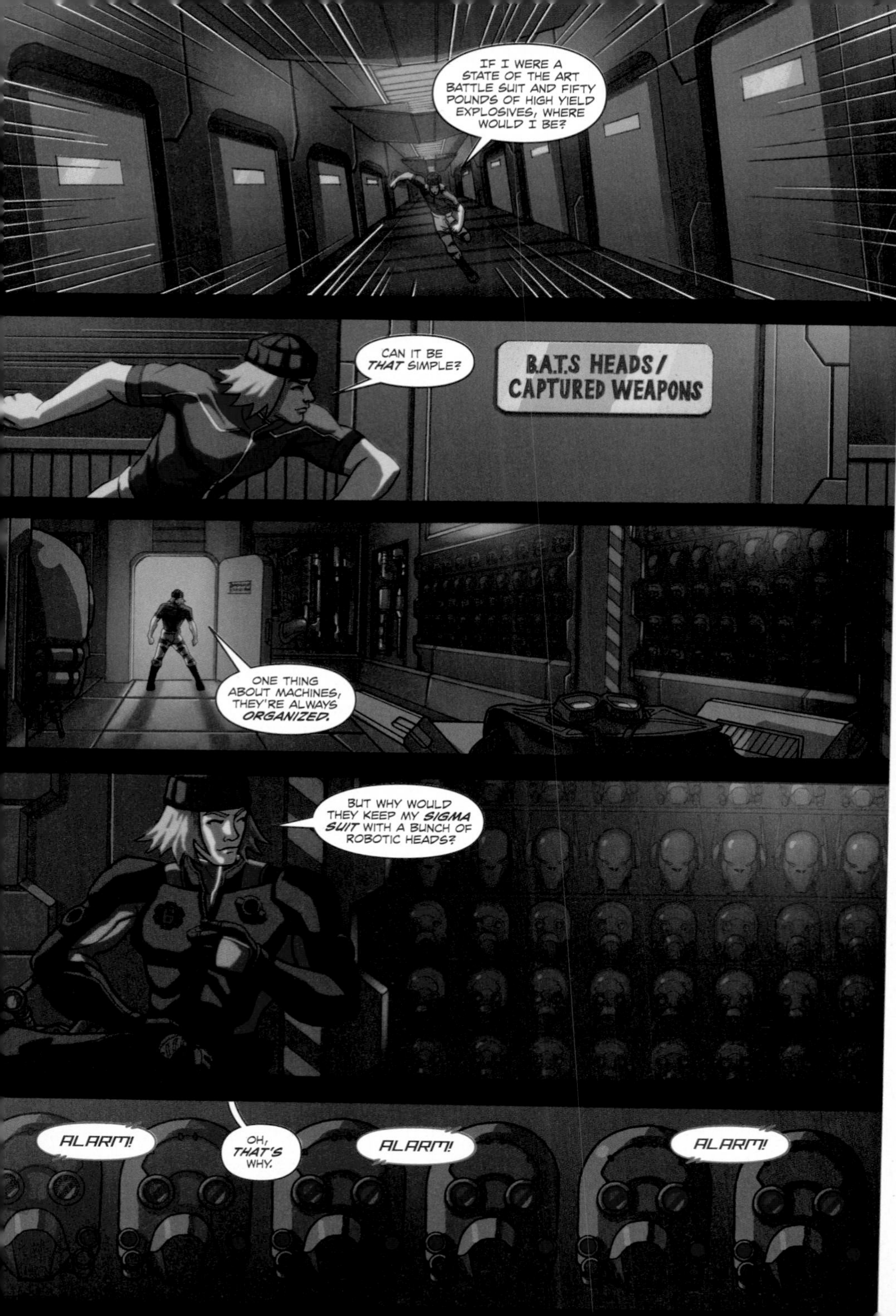

IF I WERE A STATE OF THE ART BATTLE SUIT AND FIFTY POUNDS OF HIGH YIELD EXPLOSIVES, WHERE WOULD I BE?
CAN IT BE THAT SIMPLE?
B.A.T.S HEADS/ CAPTURED WEAPONS
ONE THING ABOUT MACHINES, THEY'RE ALWAYS ORGANIZED.
BUT WHY WOULD THEY KEEP MY SIGMA SUIT WITH A BUNCH OF ROBOTIC HEADS?
ALARM!
OH, THAT'S WHY.
ALARM!
ALARM!

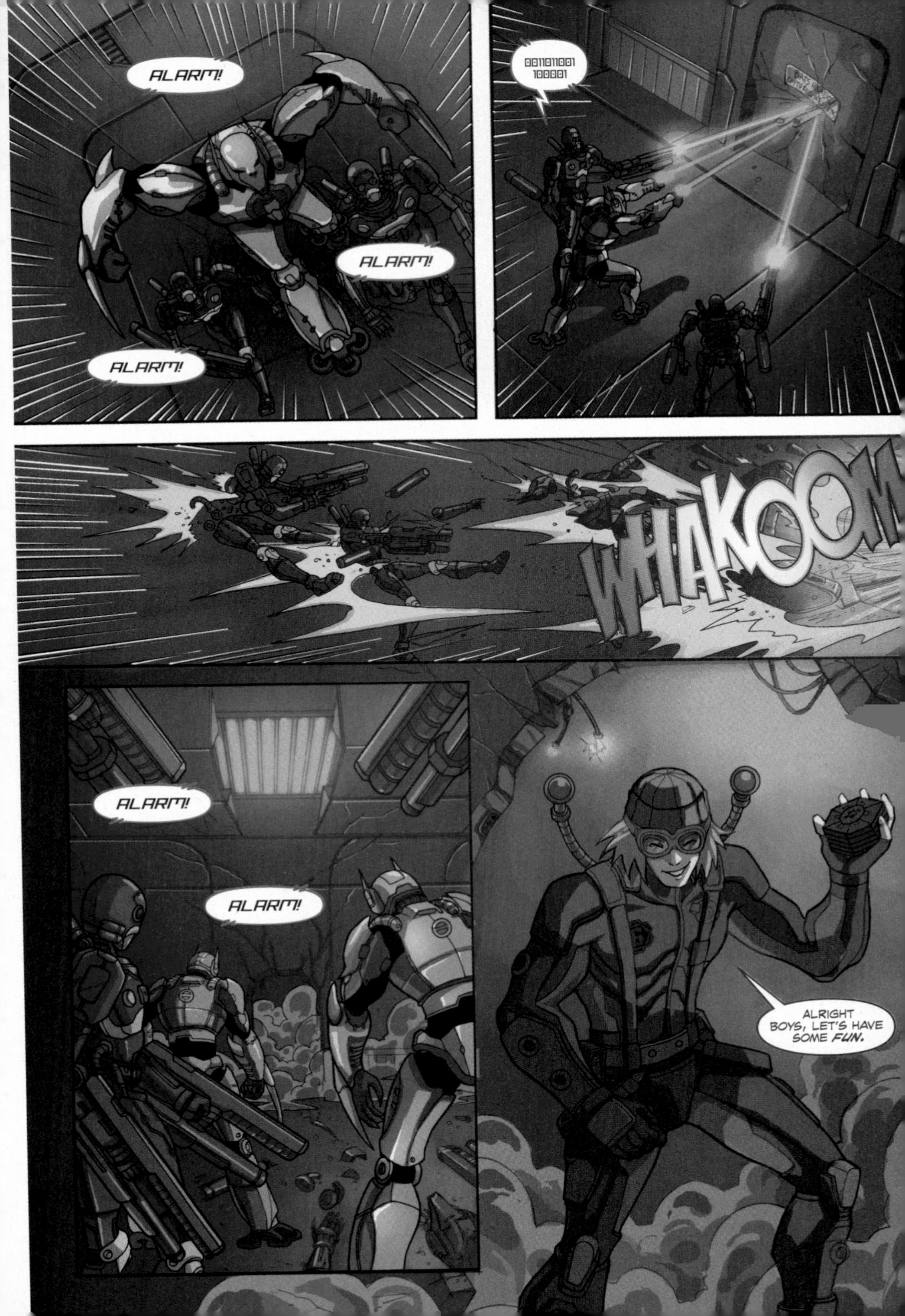
ALARM!
ALARM!
ALARM!
0011011001
100001
WHAKOOM
ALARM!
ALARM!
ALRIGHT BOYS, LET'S HAVE SOME *FUN*.

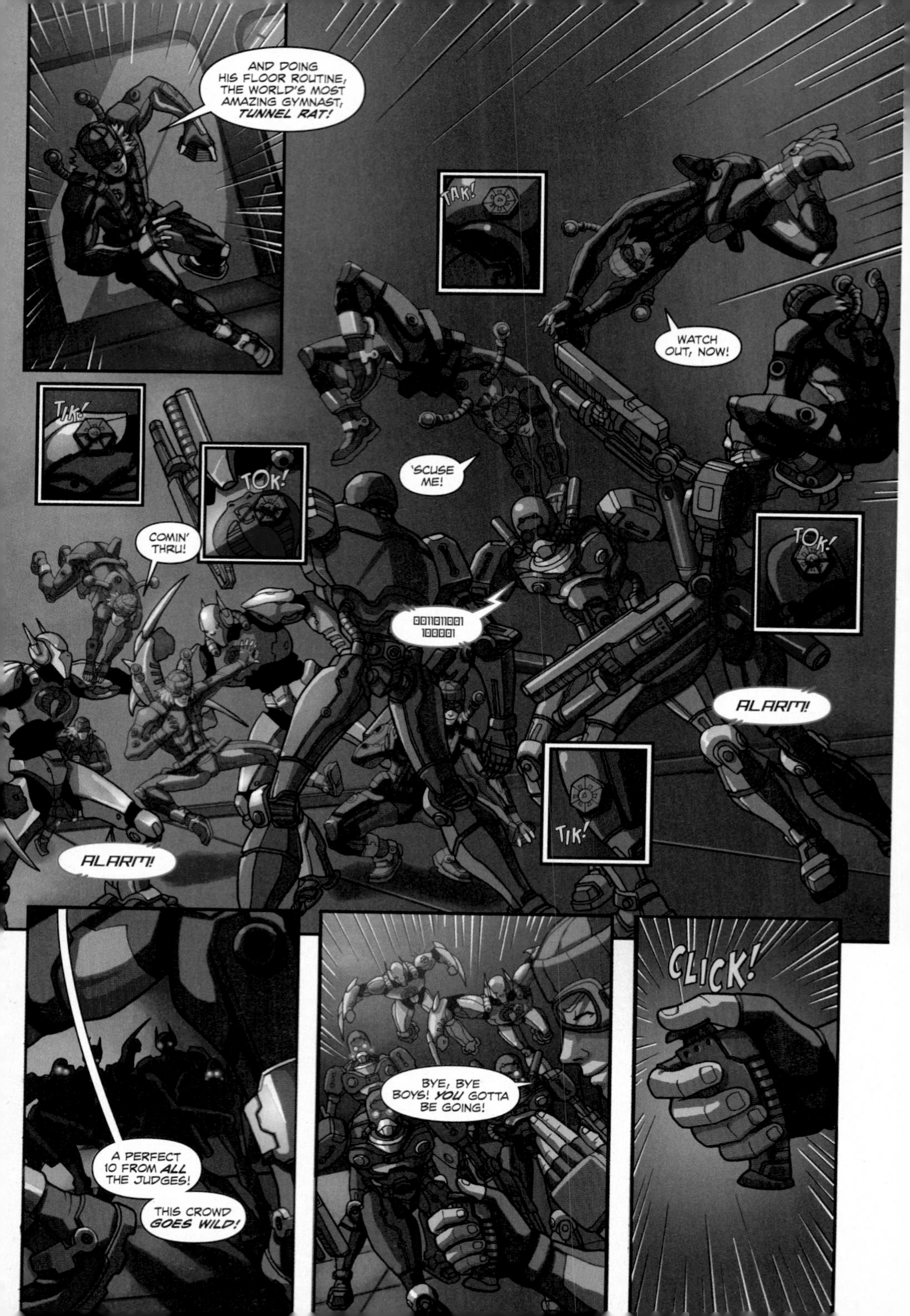
AND DOING HIS FLOOR ROUTINE, THE WORLD'S MOST AMAZING GYMNAST, *TUNNEL RAT!*
TAK!
WATCH OUT, NOW!
TIK!
'SCUSE ME!
TOK!
COMIN' THRU!
TOK!
0011011001 100001
ALARM!
TIK!
ALARM!
A PERFECT 10 FROM *ALL* THE JUDGES!
THIS CROWD *GOES WILD!*
BYE, BYE BOYS! *YOU* GOTTA BE GOING!
CLICK!

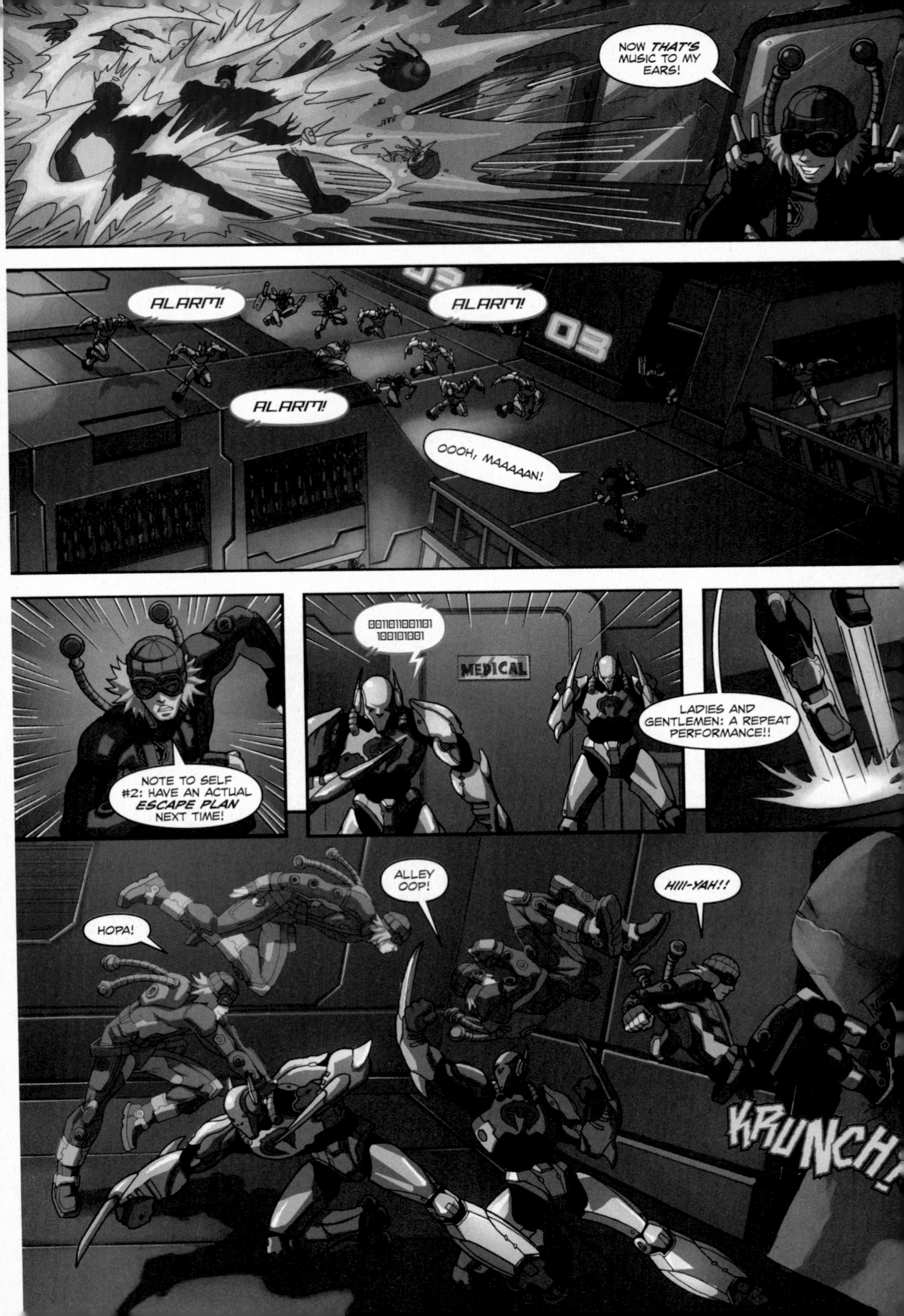

NOW *THAT'S* MUSIC TO MY EARS!
ALARM!
ALARM!
ALARM!
OOOH, MAAAAAN!
NOTE TO SELF #2: HAVE AN ACTUAL *ESCAPE PLAN* NEXT TIME!
001101100110 1100101001
MEDICAL
LADIES AND GENTLEMEN: A REPEAT PERFORMANCE!!
HOPA!
ALLEY OOP!
HIII-YAH!!
KRUNCH!

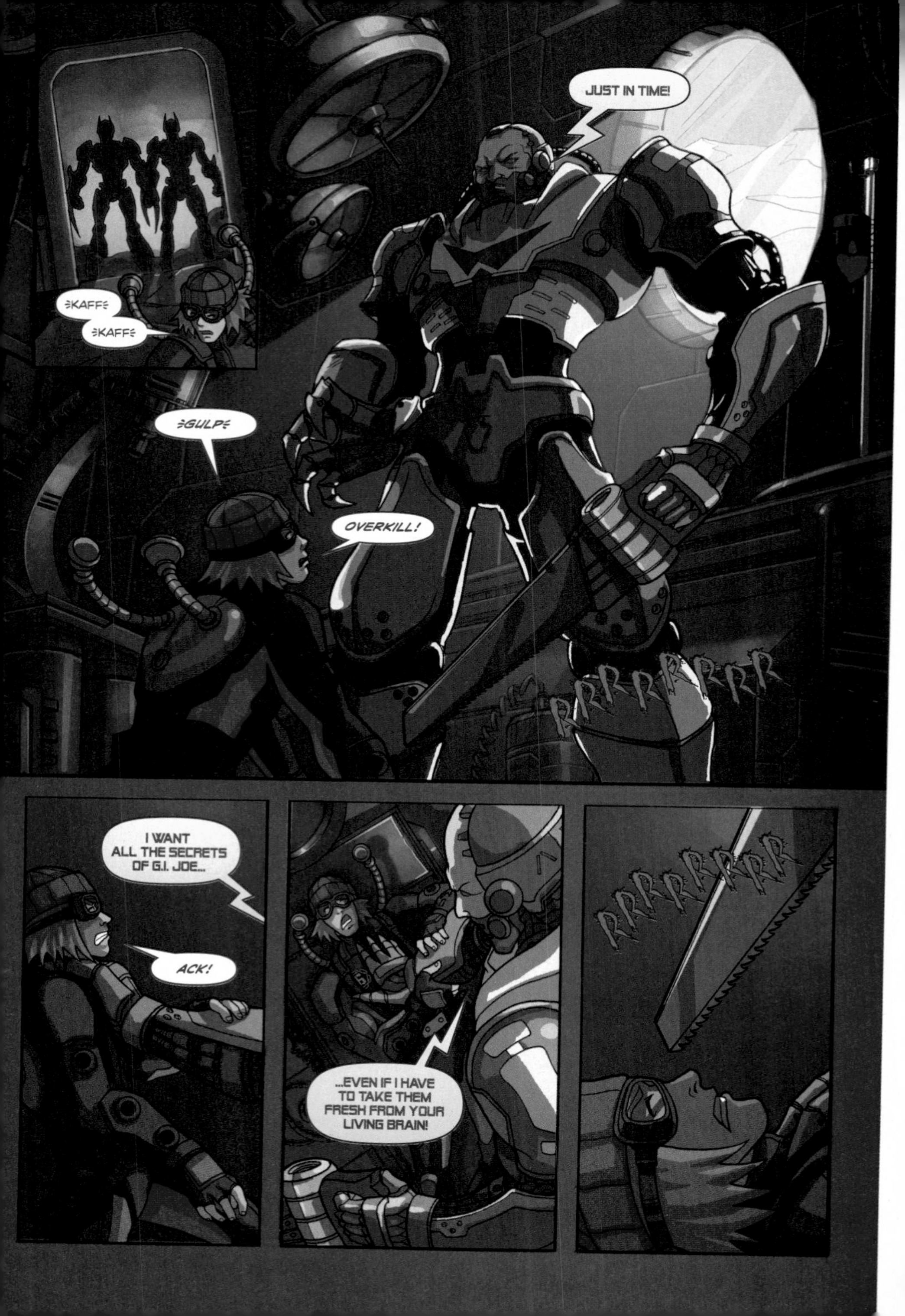
KAFF
KAFF
JUST IN TIME!
GULP
OVERKILL!
RRRRRRRRR
I WANT ALL THE SECRETS OF G.I. JOE...
ACK!
...EVEN IF I HAVE TO TAKE THEM FRESH FROM YOUR LIVING BRAIN!
RRRRRRRRR

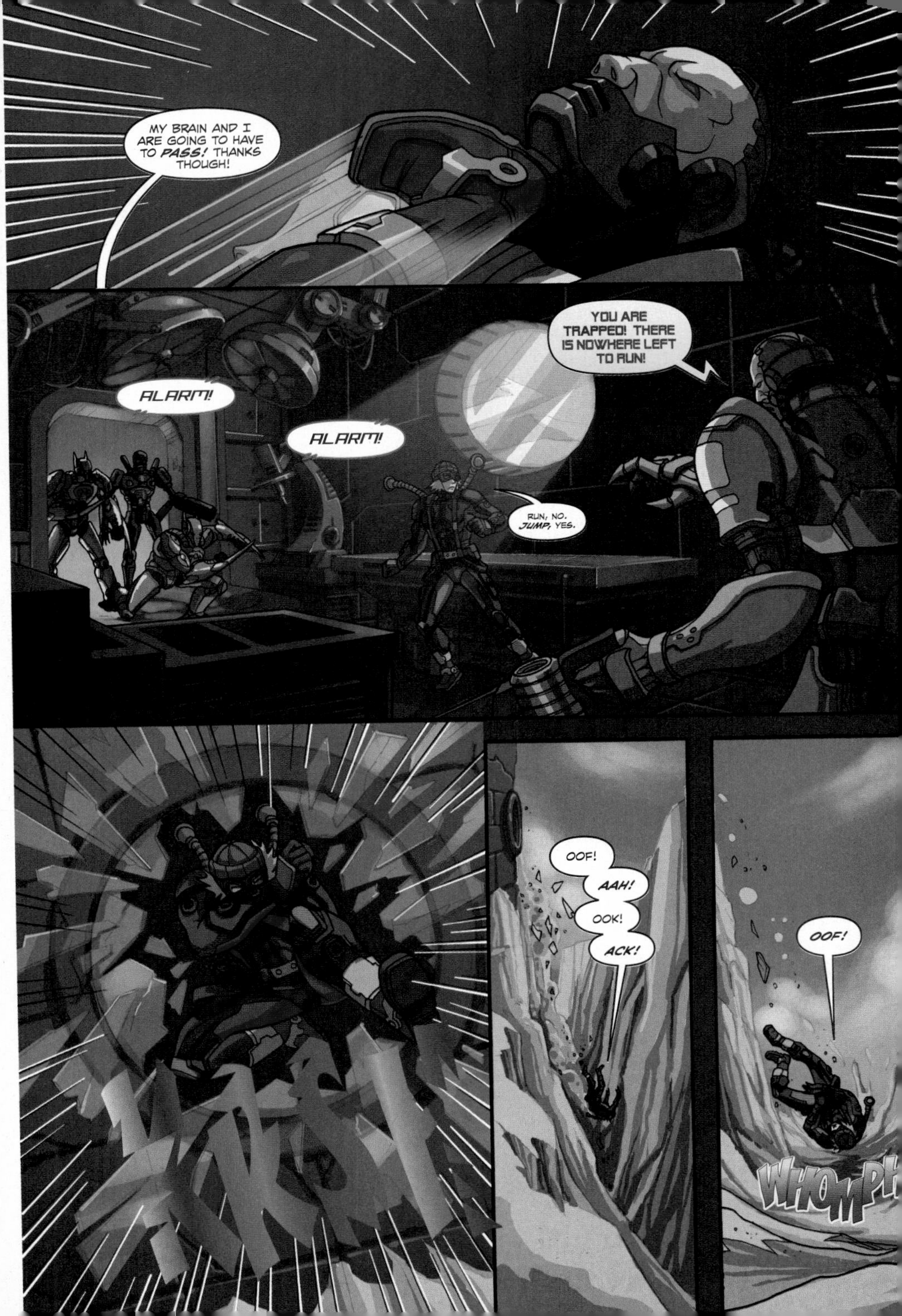
MY BRAIN AND I ARE GOING TO HAVE TO PASS! THANKS THOUGH!
YOU ARE TRAPPED! THERE IS NOWHERE LEFT TO RUN!
ALARM!
ALARM!
RUN, NO. JUMP, YES.
OOF!
AAH!
OOK!
ACK!
OOF!
WHOMP!

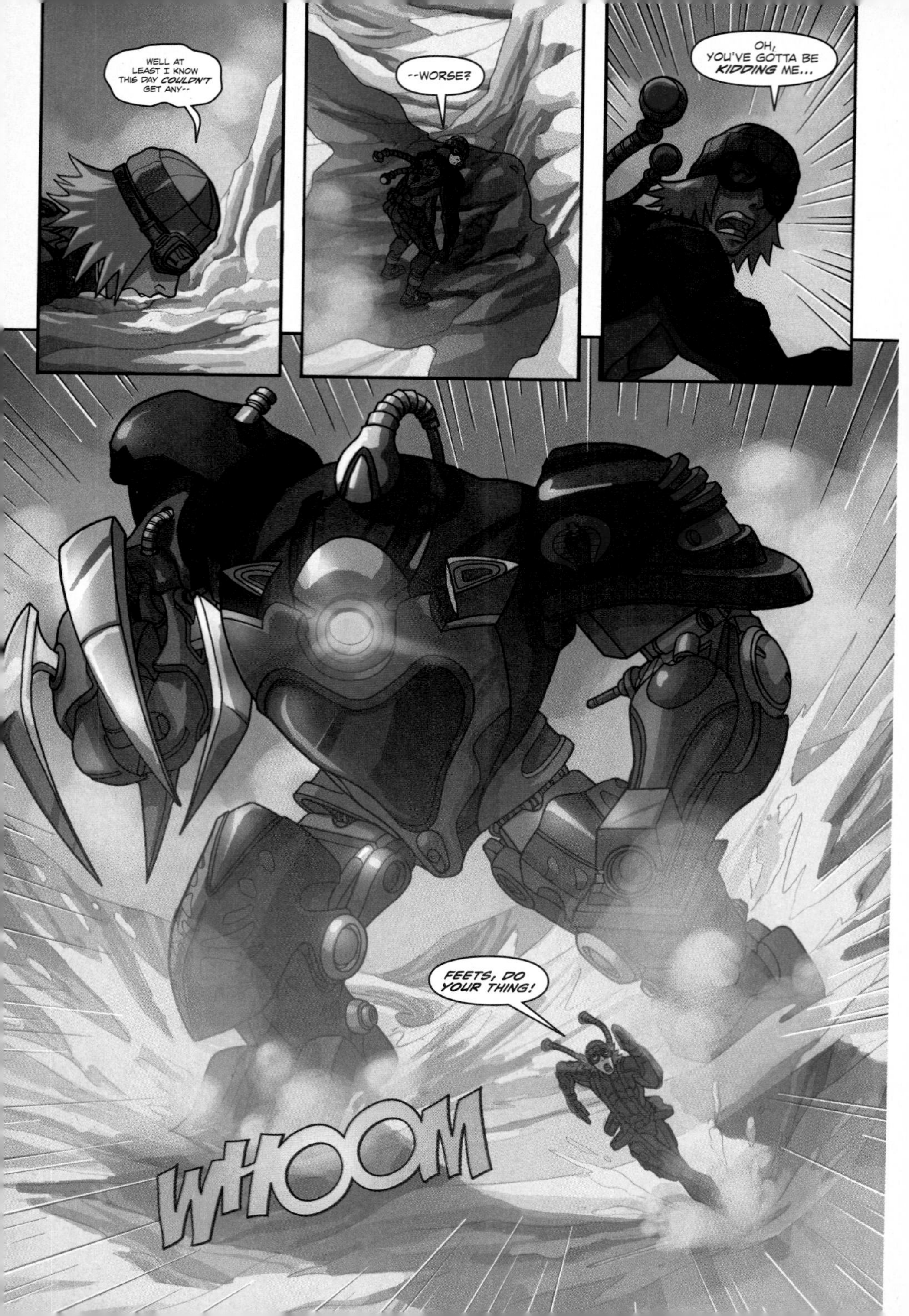

WELL AT LEAST I KNOW THIS DAY COULDN'T GET ANY--
--WORSE?
OH, YOU'VE GOTTA BE KIDDING ME...
FEETS, DO YOUR THING!
WHOOM

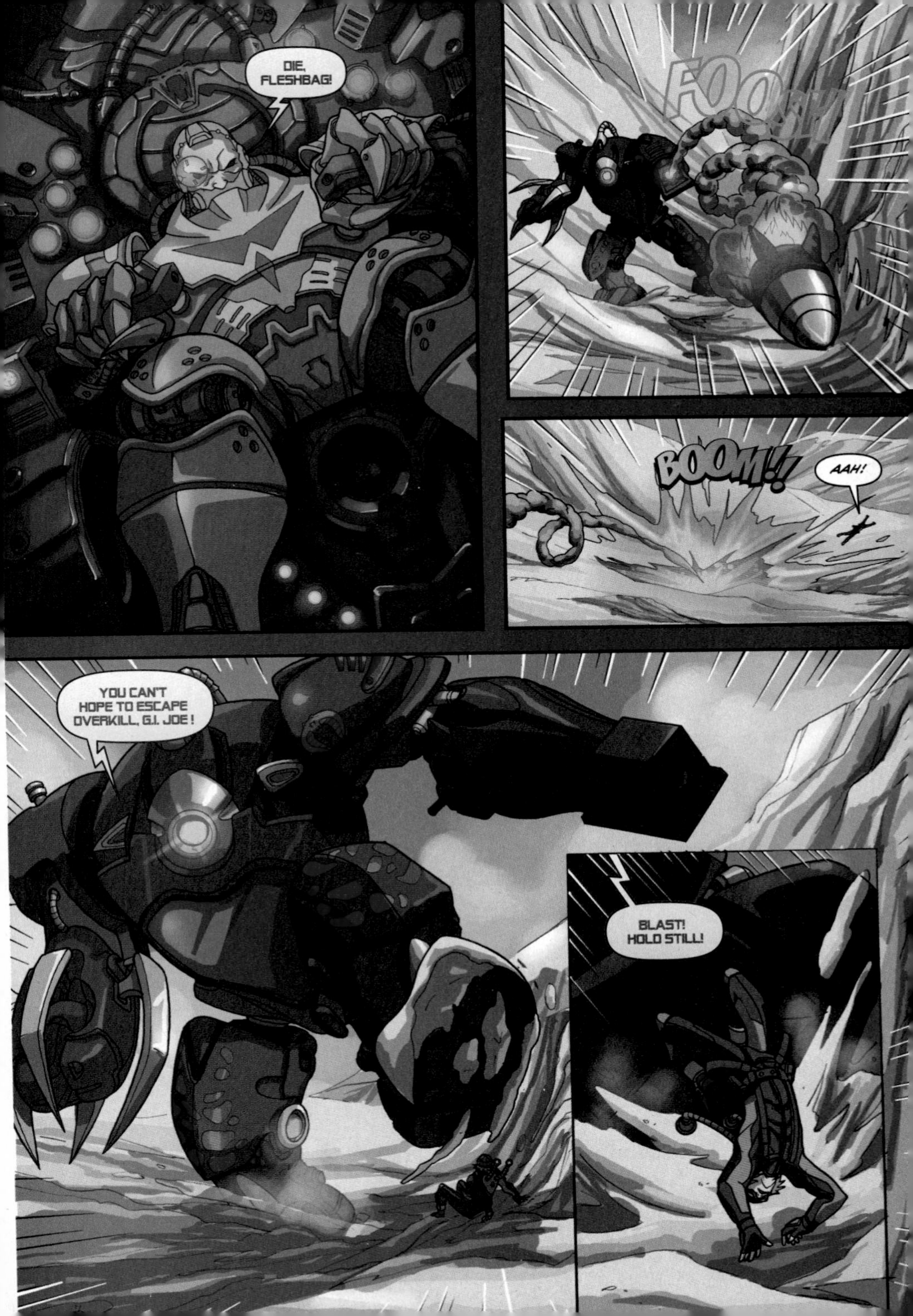
DIE, FLESHBAG!
BOOM!!
AAH!
YOU CAN'T HOPE TO ESCAPE OVERKILL, G.I. JOE!
BLAST! HOLD STILL!

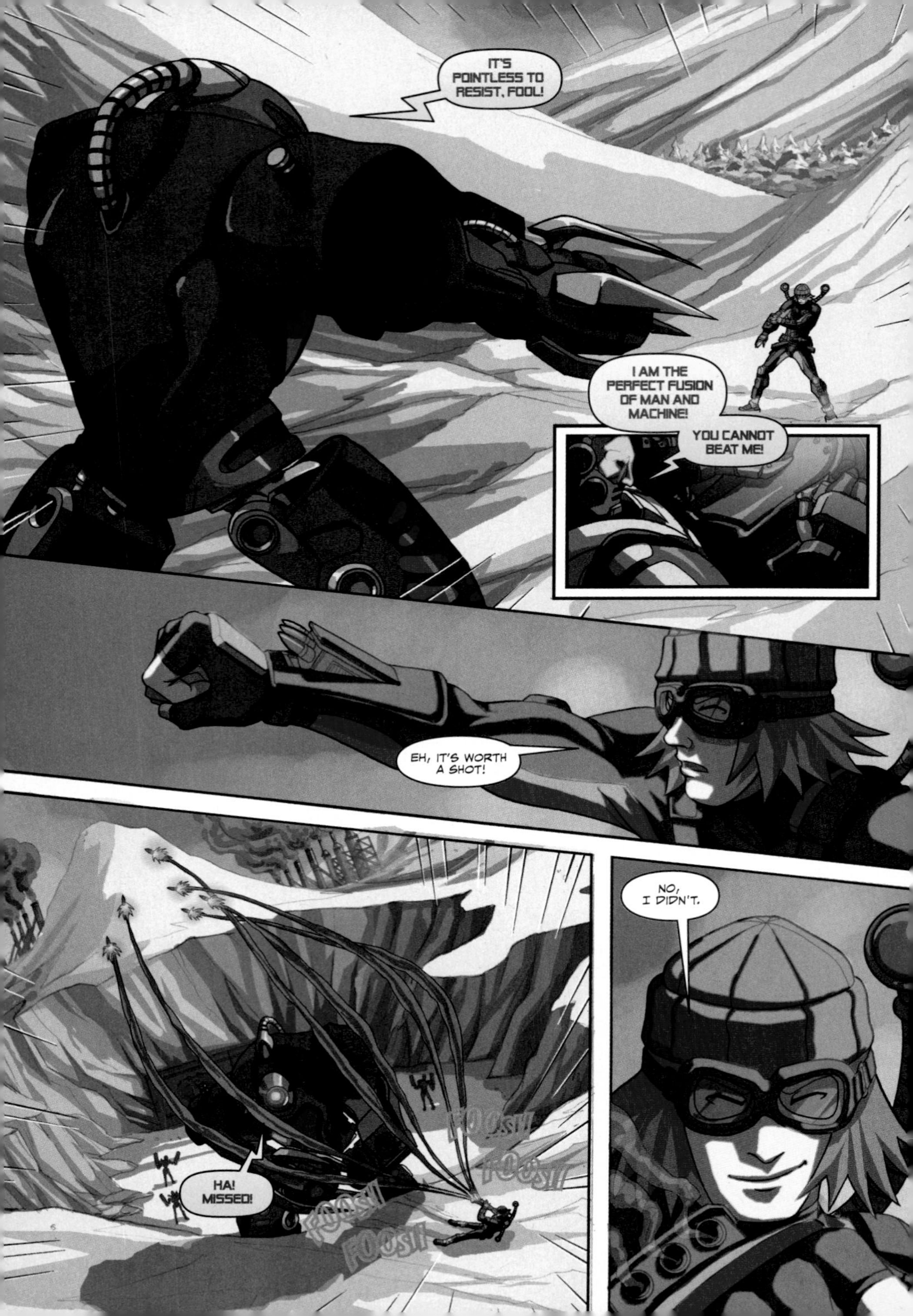
IT'S POINTLESS TO RESIST, FOOL!
I AM THE PERFECT FUSION OF MAN AND MACHINE!
YOU CANNOT BEAT ME!
EH, IT'S WORTH A SHOT!
HA! MISSED!
FOOSH
FOOSH
FOOSH
FOOSH
NO, I DIDN'T.

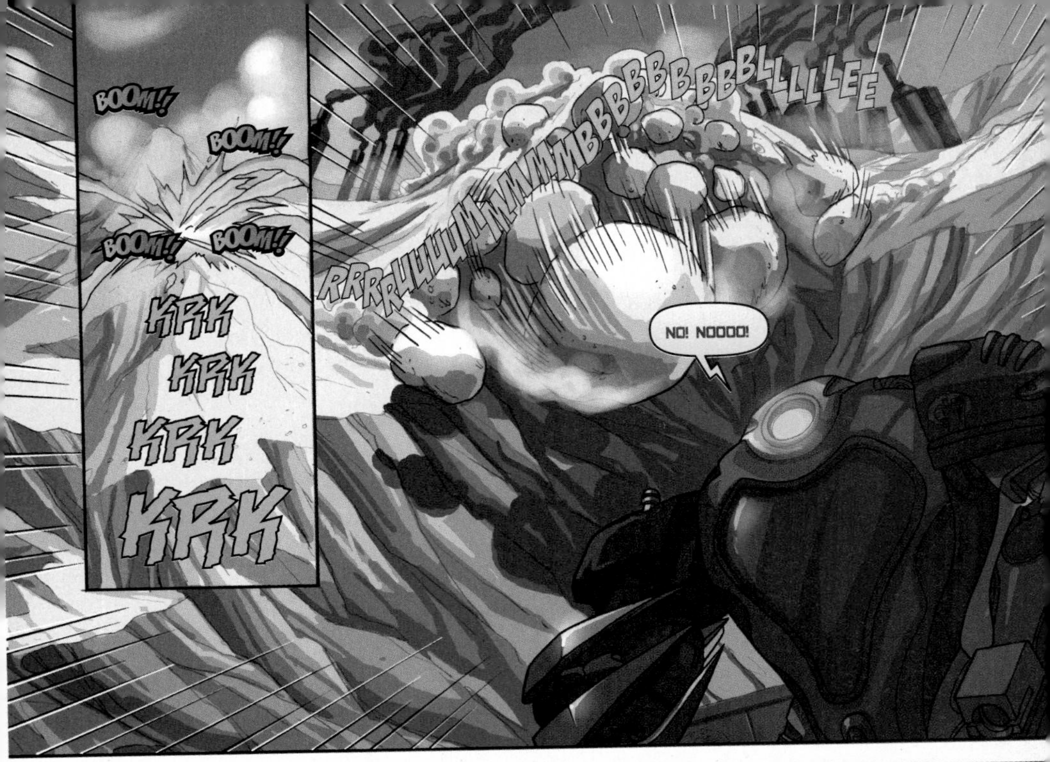
BOOM!!
BOOM!!
BOOM!!
BOOM!!
KRK
KRK
KRK
KRK
RRRRUUUUMMMMMMBBBBBBBBLLLLLLEE
NO! NOOOO!

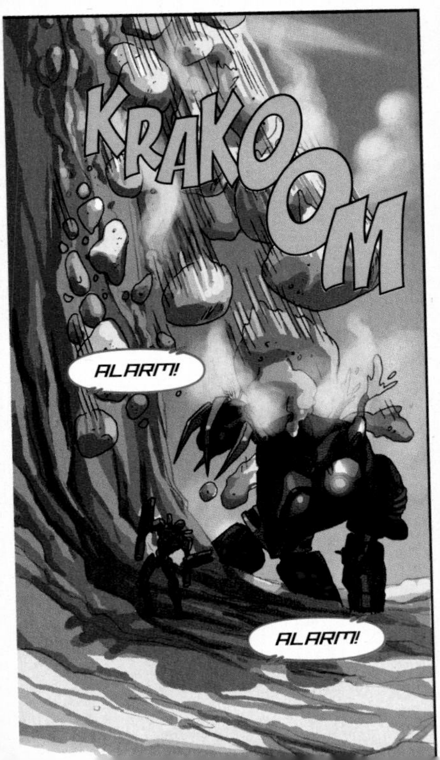
KRAKOOOM
ALARM!
ALARM!

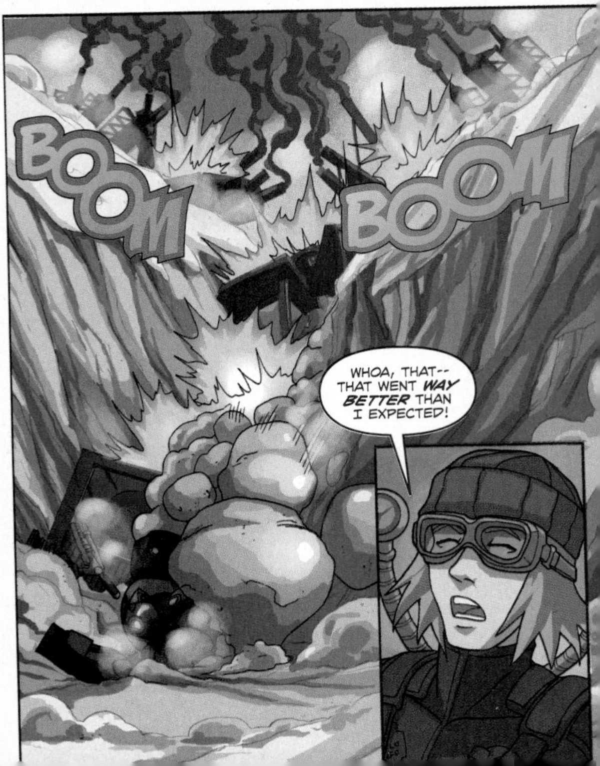
BOOOM
BOOOM
WHOA, THAT-- THAT WENT *WAY BETTER* THAN I EXPECTED!

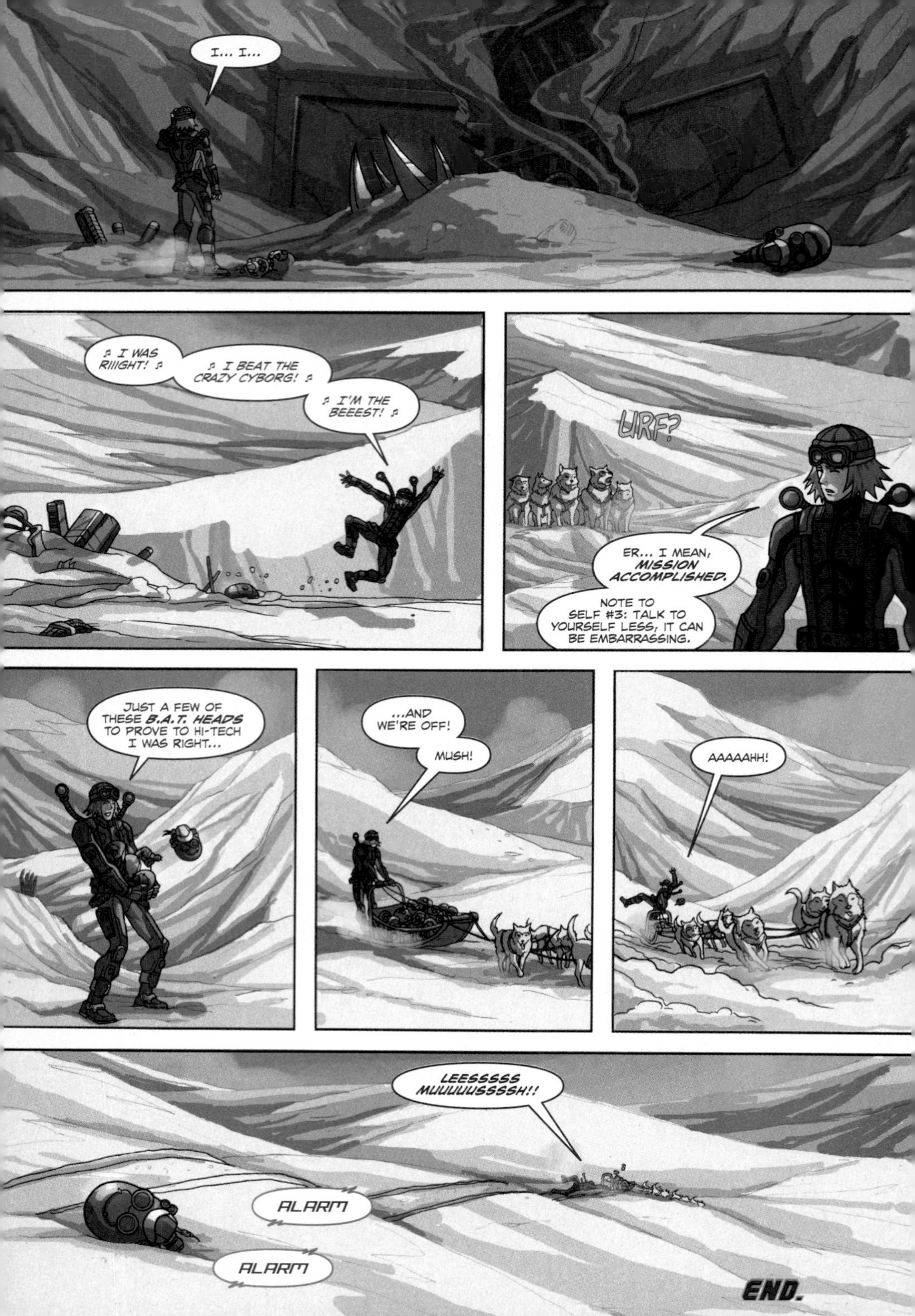
I... I...
♫ I WAS RIIIGHT! ♫
♫ I BEAT THE CRAZY CYBORG! ♫
♫ I'M THE BEEEST! ♫
URF?
ER... I MEAN, MISSION ACCOMPLISHED.
NOTE TO SELF #3: TALK TO YOURSELF LESS, IT CAN BE EMBARRASSING.
JUST A FEW OF THESE B.A.T. HEADS TO PROVE TO HI-TECH I WAS RIGHT...
...AND WE'RE OFF!
MUSH!
AAAAAHH!
LEESSSSS MUUUUUUSSSSH!!
ALARM
ALARM
END.

SIGMA 6 is the code name for a new group of covert G.I. Joe operatives with highly specialized capabilities. They use innovative technology and gear designed exclusively for each of their missions. Working against them is the evil COBRA organization, whose goal is to take control of the world by sabotage, espionage and outright destruction. SIGMA 6 fights them at every turn and provides a swift solution to critical situations around the globe.

CLASSIFIED: AUTHORIZED PERSONNEL ONLY

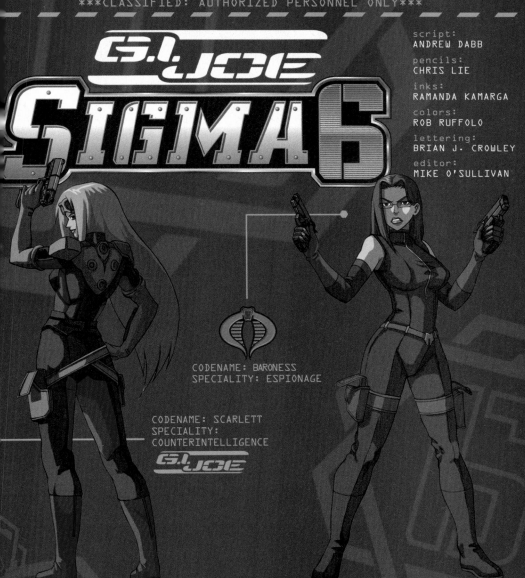

G.I.JOE SIGMA 6

script:
ANDREW DABB

pencils:
CHRIS LIE

inks:
RAMANDA KAMARGA

colors:
ROB RUFFOLO

lettering:
BRIAN J. CROWLEY

editor:
MIKE O'SULLIVAN

CODENAME: BARONESS
SPECIALITY: ESPIONAGE

CODENAME: SCARLETT
SPECIALITY:
COUNTERINTELLIGENCE

G.I.JOE

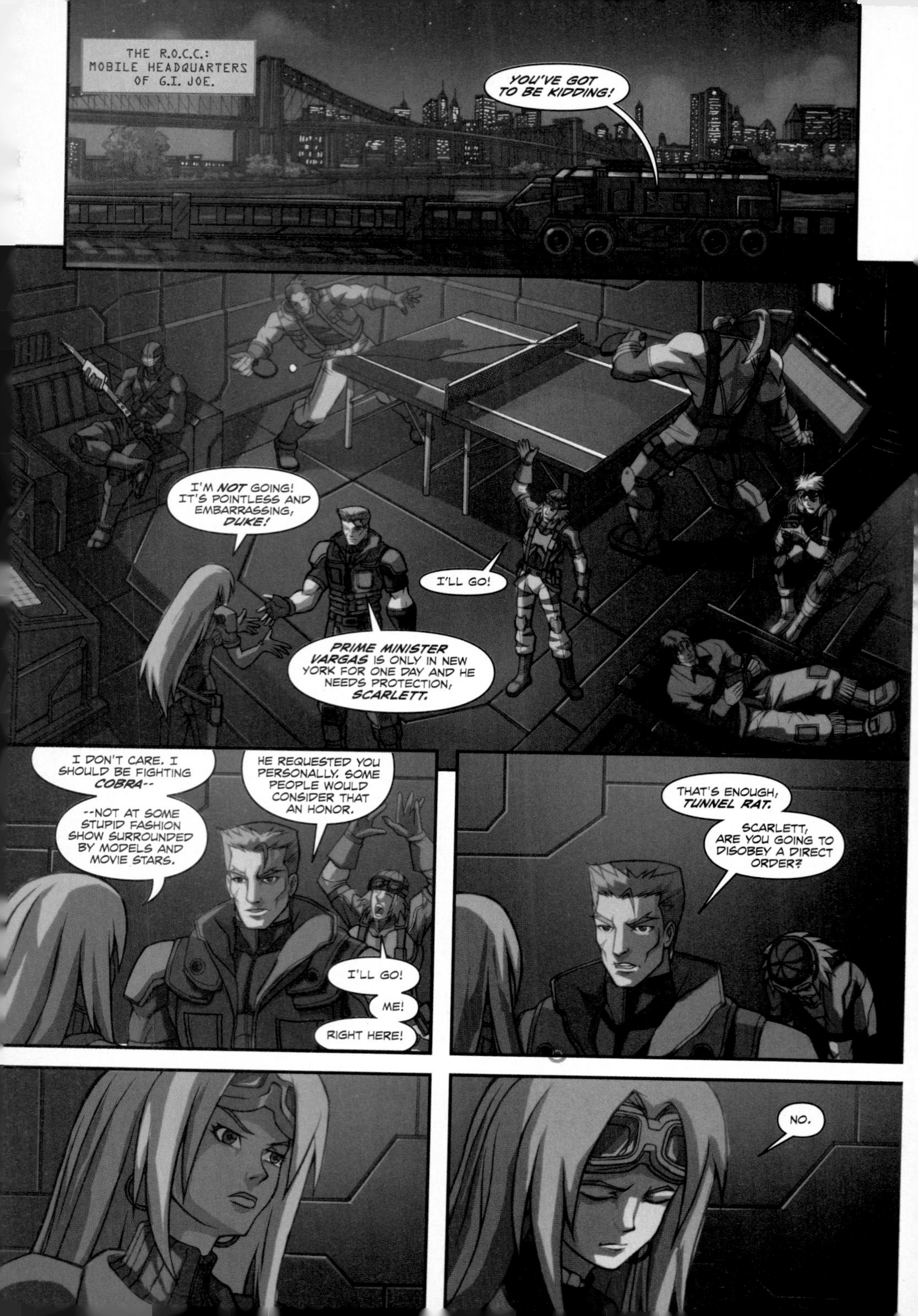
THE R.O.C.C.: MOBILE HEADQUARTERS OF G.I. JOE.
YOU'VE GOT TO BE KIDDING!
I'M NOT GOING! IT'S POINTLESS AND EMBARRASSING, DUKE!
I'LL GO!
PRIME MINISTER VARGAS IS ONLY IN NEW YORK FOR ONE DAY AND HE NEEDS PROTECTION, SCARLETT.
I DON'T CARE. I SHOULD BE FIGHTING COBRA--
--NOT AT SOME STUPID FASHION SHOW SURROUNDED BY MODELS AND MOVIE STARS.
HE REQUESTED YOU PERSONALLY. SOME PEOPLE WOULD CONSIDER THAT AN HONOR.
I'LL GO!
ME!
RIGHT HERE!
THAT'S ENOUGH, TUNNEL RAT.
SCARLETT, ARE YOU GOING TO DISOBEY A DIRECT ORDER?
NO.

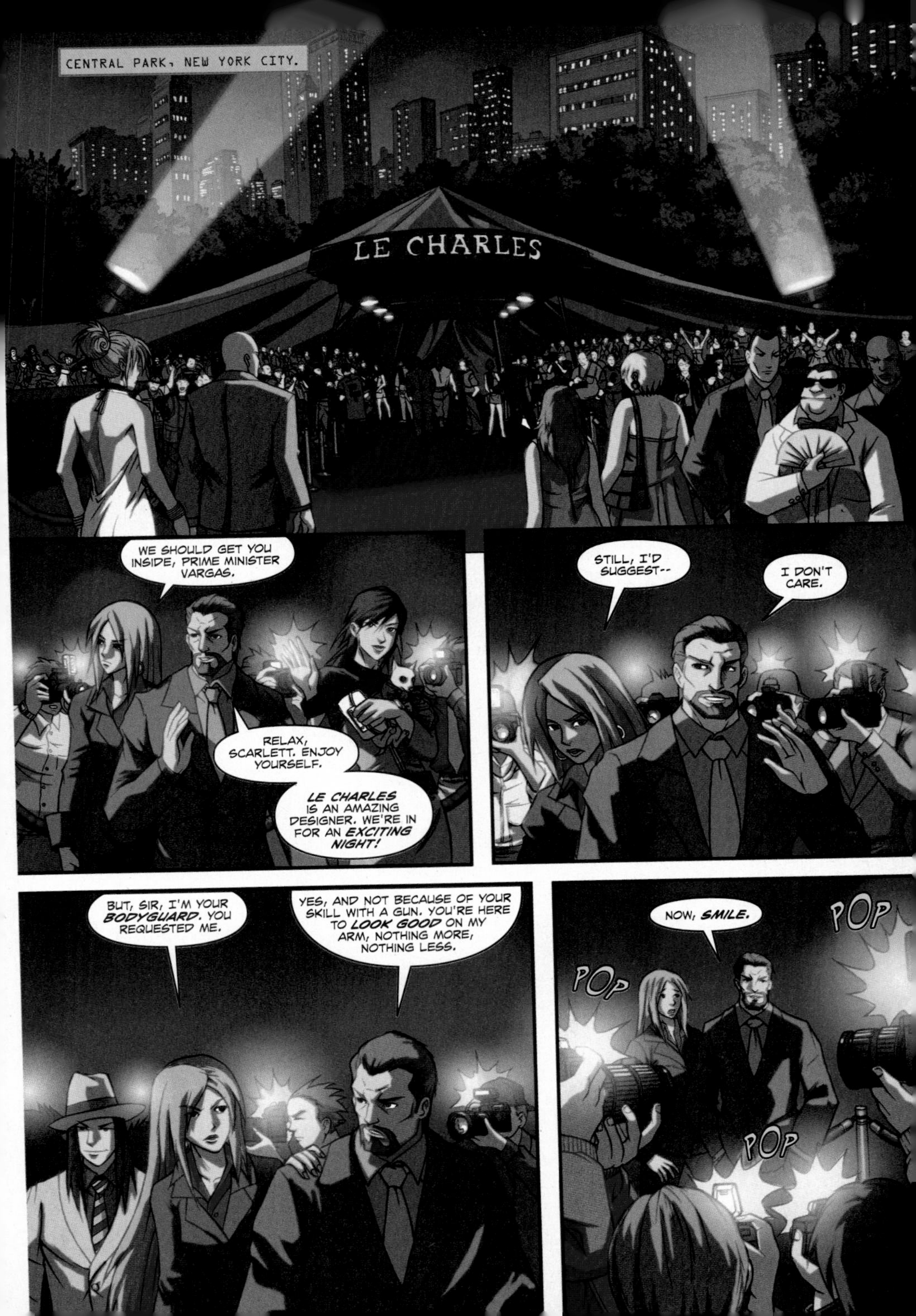
CENTRAL PARK, NEW YORK CITY.
LE CHARLES
WE SHOULD GET YOU INSIDE, PRIME MINISTER VARGAS.
RELAX, SCARLETT. ENJOY YOURSELF.
LE CHARLES IS AN AMAZING DESIGNER. WE'RE IN FOR AN EXCITING NIGHT!
STILL, I'D SUGGEST--
I DON'T CARE.
BUT, SIR, I'M YOUR BODYGUARD. YOU REQUESTED ME.
YES, AND NOT BECAUSE OF YOUR SKILL WITH A GUN. YOU'RE HERE TO LOOK GOOD ON MY ARM, NOTHING MORE, NOTHING LESS.
NOW, SMILE.
POP
POP
POP

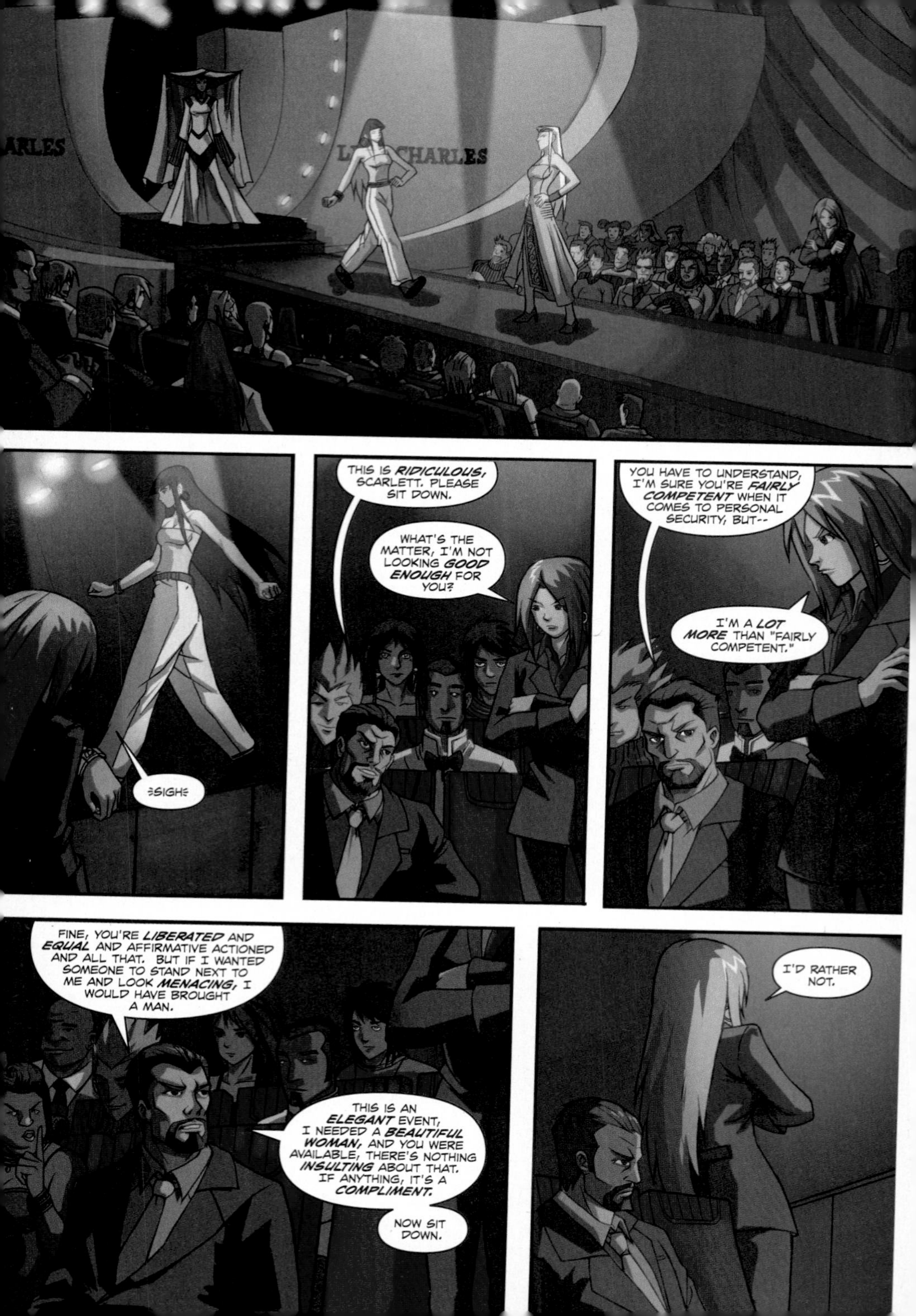
CHARLES
≈SIGH≈
THIS IS *RIDICULOUS,* SCARLETT. PLEASE SIT DOWN.
WHAT'S THE MATTER, I'M NOT LOOKING *GOOD ENOUGH* FOR YOU?
YOU HAVE TO UNDERSTAND, I'M SURE YOU'RE *FAIRLY COMPETENT* WHEN IT COMES TO PERSONAL SECURITY, BUT--
I'M A *LOT MORE* THAN "FAIRLY COMPETENT."
FINE, YOU'RE *LIBERATED* AND *EQUAL* AND AFFIRMATIVE ACTIONED AND ALL THAT. BUT IF I WANTED SOMEONE TO STAND NEXT TO ME AND LOOK *MENACING,* I WOULD HAVE BROUGHT A MAN.
THIS IS AN *ELEGANT* EVENT, I NEEDED A *BEAUTIFUL WOMAN,* AND YOU WERE AVAILABLE, THERE'S NOTHING *INSULTING* ABOUT THAT. IF ANYTHING, IT'S A *COMPLIMENT.*
NOW SIT DOWN.
I'D RATHER NOT.

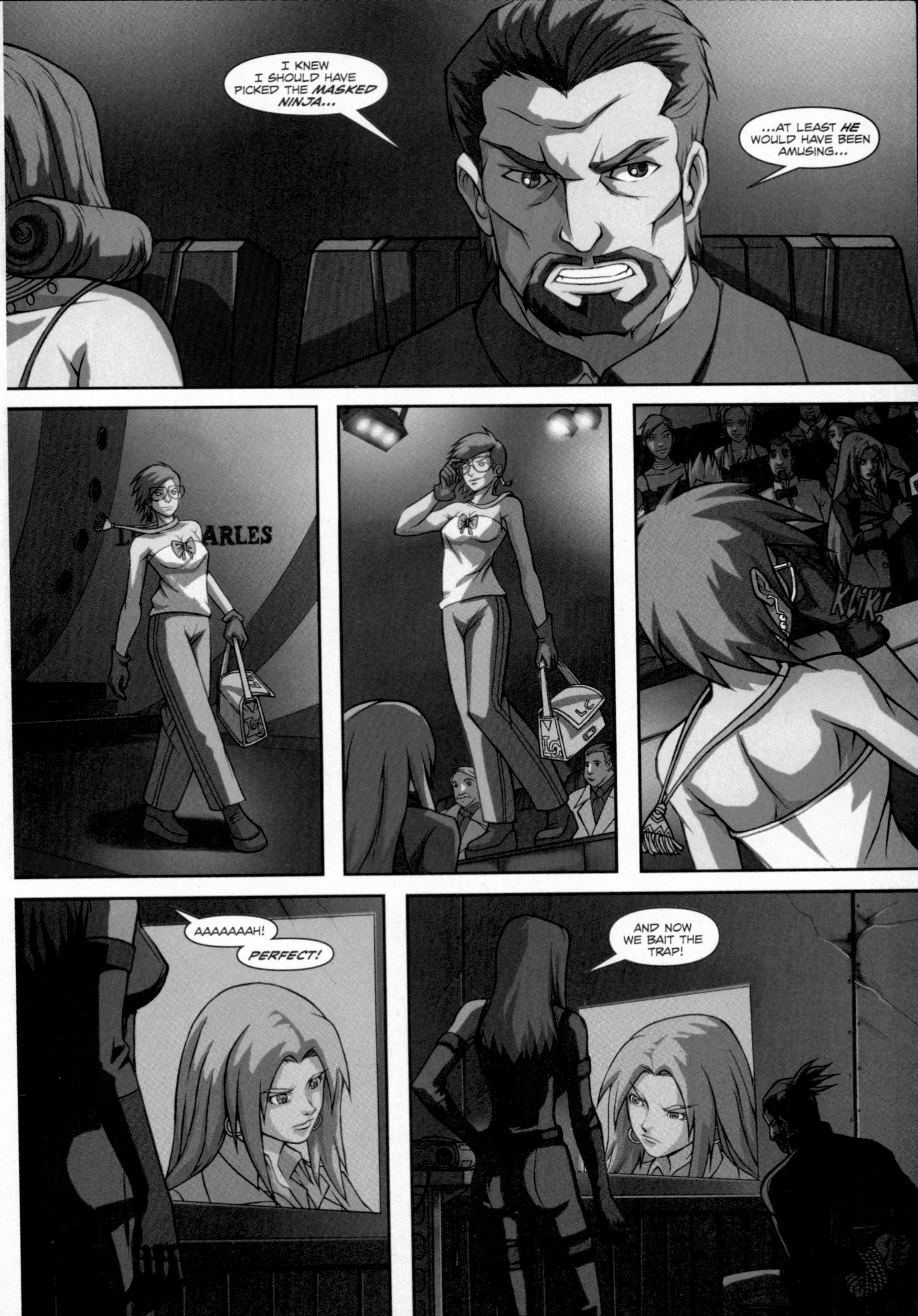
I KNEW I SHOULD HAVE PICKED THE *MASKED NINJA*...
...AT LEAST *HE* WOULD HAVE BEEN AMUSING...
ARLES
LC
KLIK!
AAAAAAAH!
PERFECT!
AND NOW WE BAIT THE TRAP!

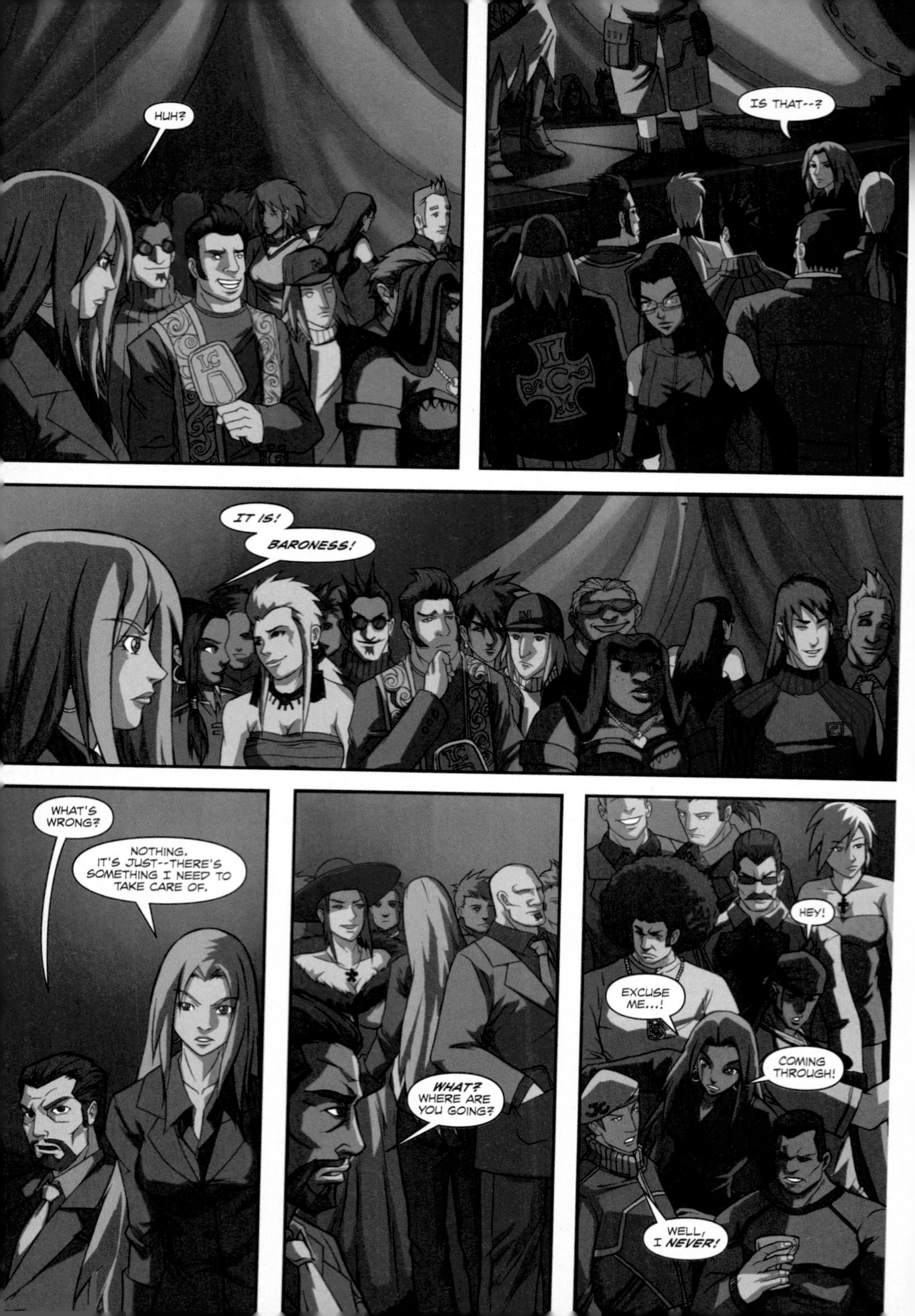
HUH?
IS THAT--?
IT IS!
BARONESS!
WHAT'S WRONG?
NOTHING. IT'S JUST--THERE'S SOMETHING I NEED TO TAKE CARE OF.
WHAT? WHERE ARE YOU GOING?
HEY!
EXCUSE ME...!
COMING THROUGH!
WELL, I NEVER!

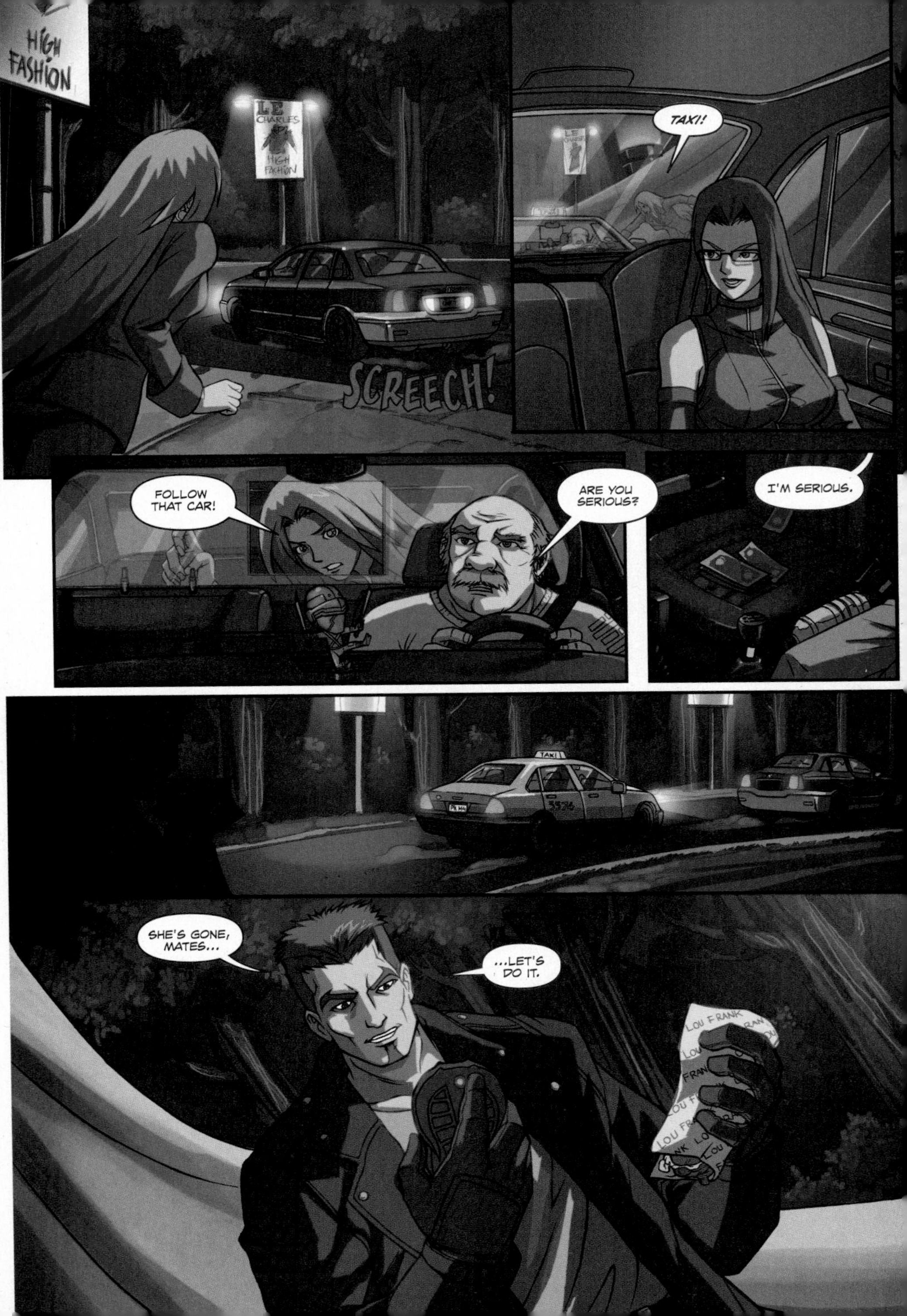
HIGH FASHION
LE CHARLES HIGH FASHION
SCREECH!
TAXI!
FOLLOW THAT CAR!
ARE YOU SERIOUS?
I'M SERIOUS.
TAXI
SHE'S GONE, MATES...
...LET'S DO IT.
LOU FRANK

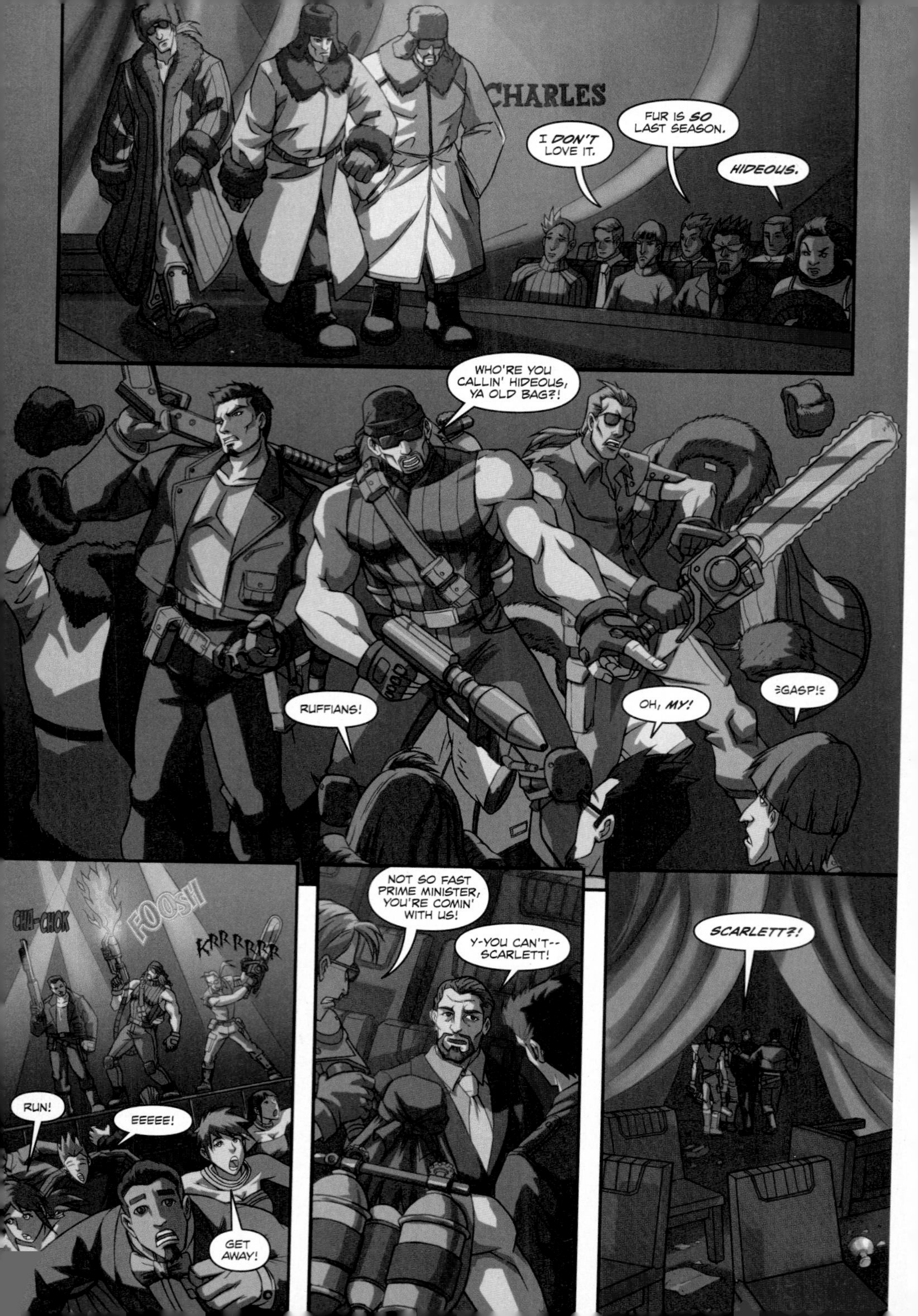
CHARLES
I DON'T LOVE IT.
FUR IS SO LAST SEASON.
HIDEOUS.
WHO'RE YOU CALLIN' HIDEOUS, YA OLD BAG?!
RUFFIANS!
OH, MY!
GASP!
CHA-CHOK
FOOSH
KRRRRRR
RUN!
EEEEE!
GET AWAY!
NOT SO FAST PRIME MINISTER, YOU'RE COMIN' WITH US!
Y-YOU CAN'T-- SCARLETT!
SCARLETT?!

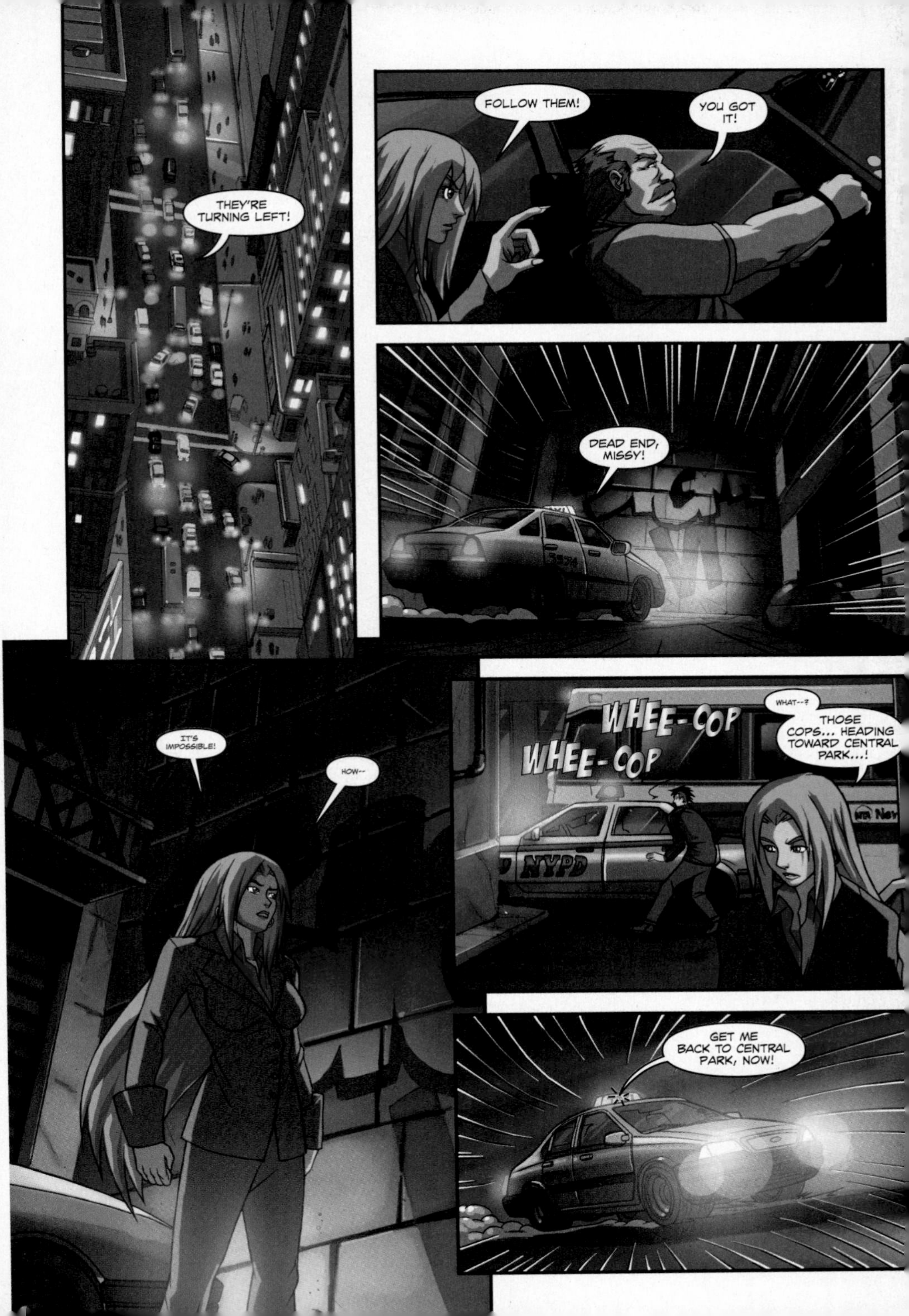
THEY'RE TURNING LEFT!
FOLLOW THEM!
YOU GOT IT!
DEAD END, MISSY!
WHAT--?
THOSE COPS... HEADING TOWARD CENTRAL PARK...!
WHEE-COP
WHEE-COP
NYPD
IT'S IMPOSSIBLE!
HOW--
GET ME BACK TO CENTRAL PARK, NOW!

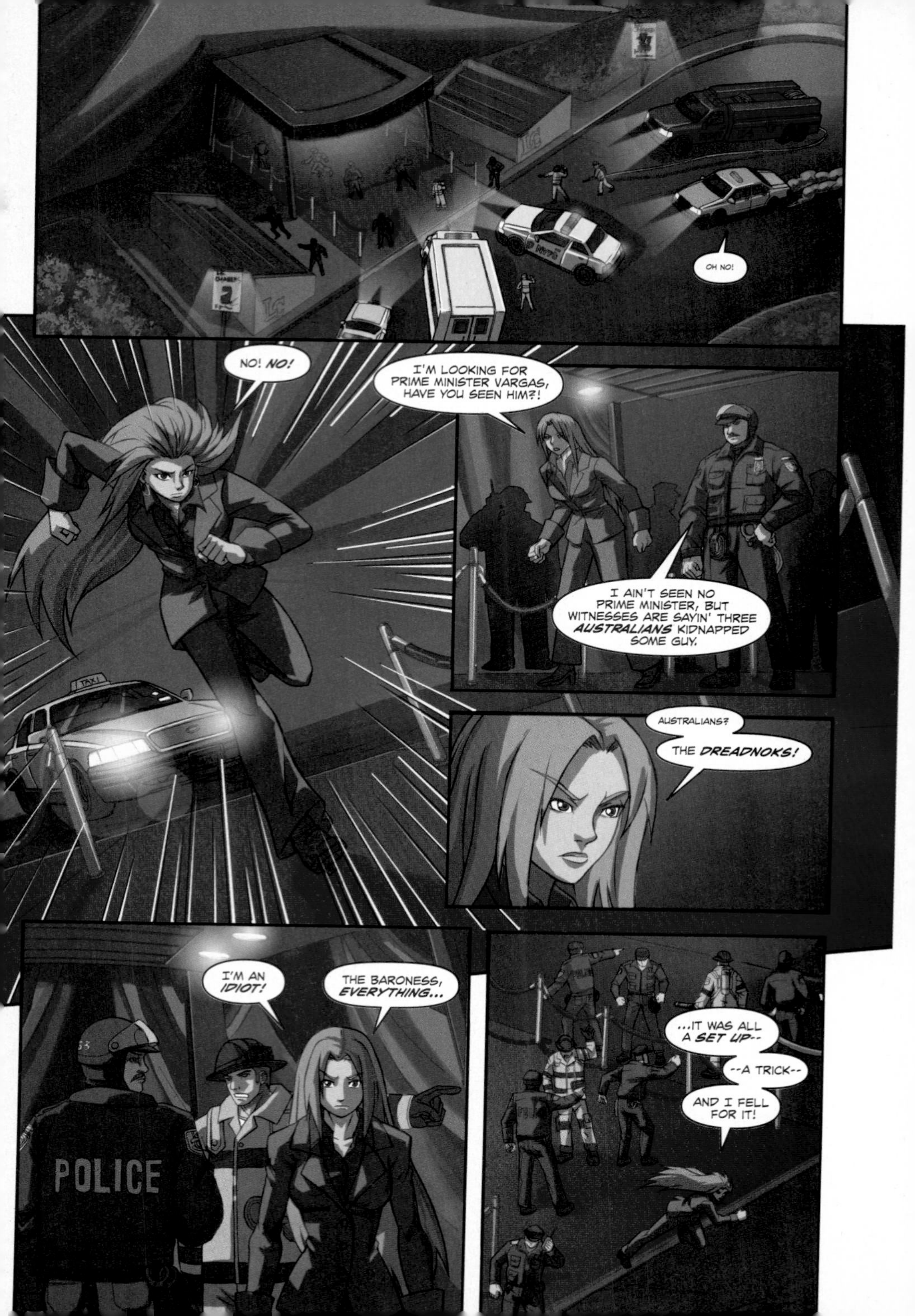

OH NO!
NO! NO!
I'M LOOKING FOR PRIME MINISTER VARGAS, HAVE YOU SEEN HIM?!
I AIN'T SEEN NO PRIME MINISTER, BUT WITNESSES ARE SAYIN' THREE AUSTRALIANS KIDNAPPED SOME GUY.
AUSTRALIANS?
THE DREADNOKS!
I'M AN IDIOT!
THE BARONESS, EVERYTHING...
...IT WAS ALL A SET UP--
--A TRICK--
AND I FELL FOR IT!
POLICE

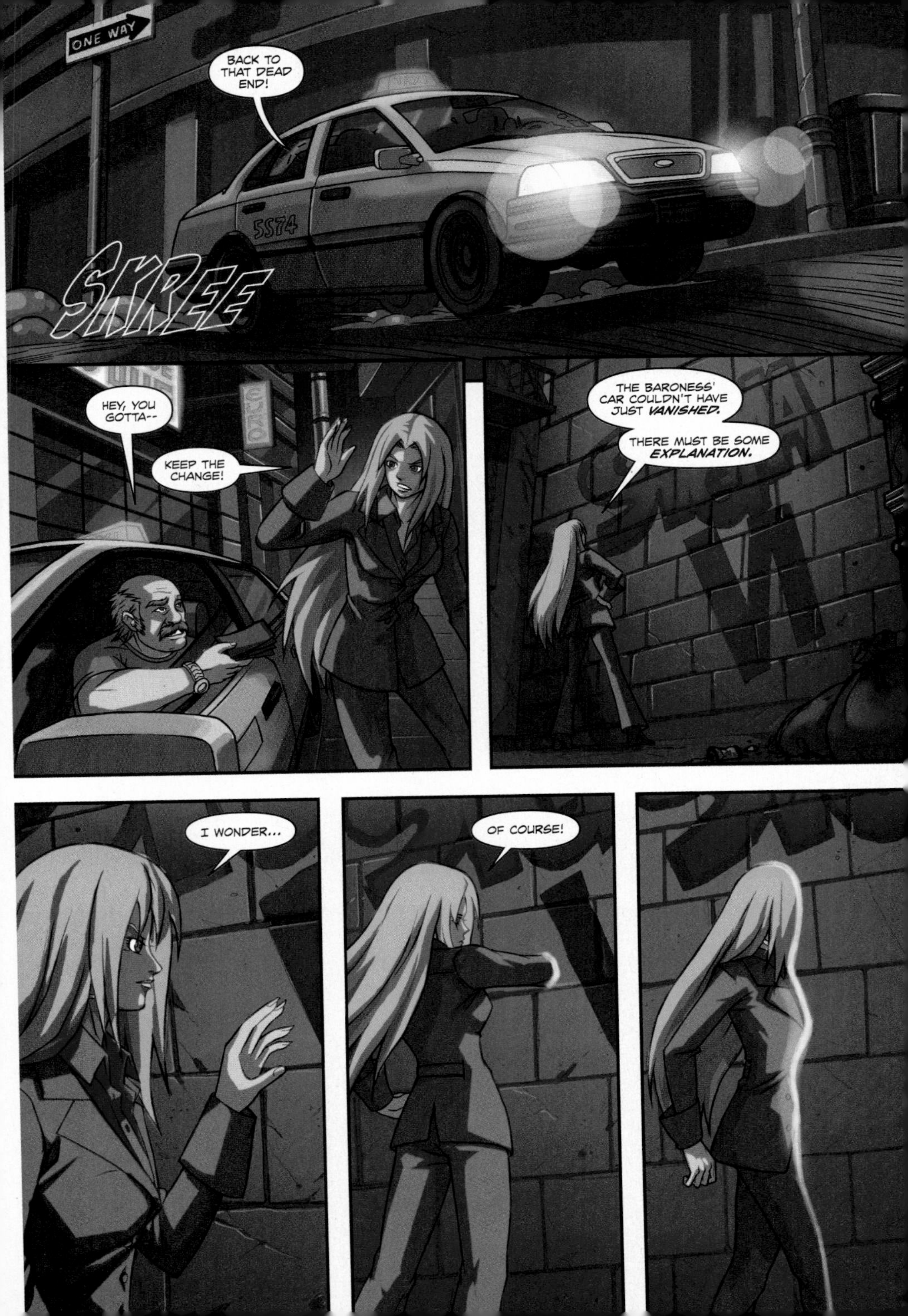
ONE WAY
BACK TO THAT DEAD END!
TAXI
5S74
SKREE
HEY, YOU GOTTA--
KEEP THE CHANGE!
EURO
THE BARONESS' CAR COULDN'T HAVE JUST VANISHED.
THERE MUST BE SOME EXPLANATION.
I WONDER...
OF COURSE!

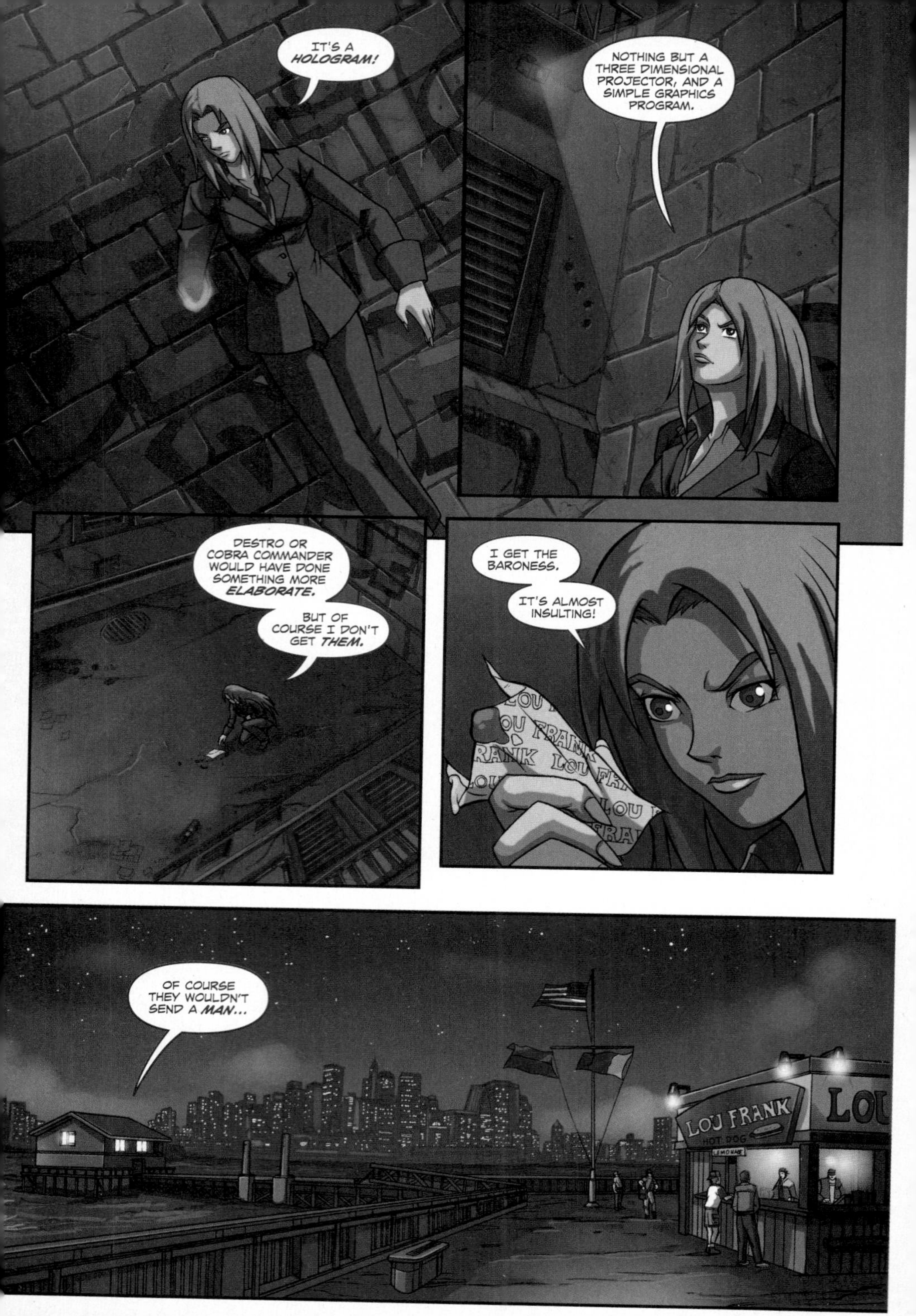
IT'S A *HOLOGRAM!*
NOTHING BUT A THREE DIMENSIONAL PROJECTOR, AND A SIMPLE GRAPHICS PROGRAM.
DESTRO OR COBRA COMMANDER WOULD HAVE DONE SOMETHING MORE *ELABORATE.*
BUT OF COURSE I DON'T GET *THEM.*
I GET THE BARONESS.
IT'S ALMOST INSULTING!
OF COURSE THEY WOULDN'T SEND A *MAN...*
LOU FRANK
HOT DOG
LEMONADE
LOU

NOT SNAKE-EYES, OR SPIRIT, OR EVEN THAT IDIOT WHO EATS BUGS!

NO, IT HAD TO BE *THE GIRL!*

BUT YOU'LL EXCUSE ME, PRIME MINISTER; WE'RE NOT TALKING ABOUT ME.

WE'RE TALKING ABOUT *YOU*, AND SPECIFICALLY HOW MUCH YOUR COUNTRY WILL *PAY* TO GET YOU BACK.

YOU'VE SAID YOU DON'T NEGOTIATE WITH TERRORISTS.

OH, BUT YOU WILL. *EVERYONE* DOES.

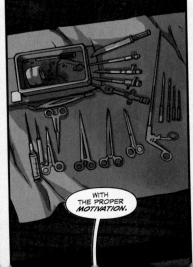

WITH THE PROPER *MOTIVATION.*

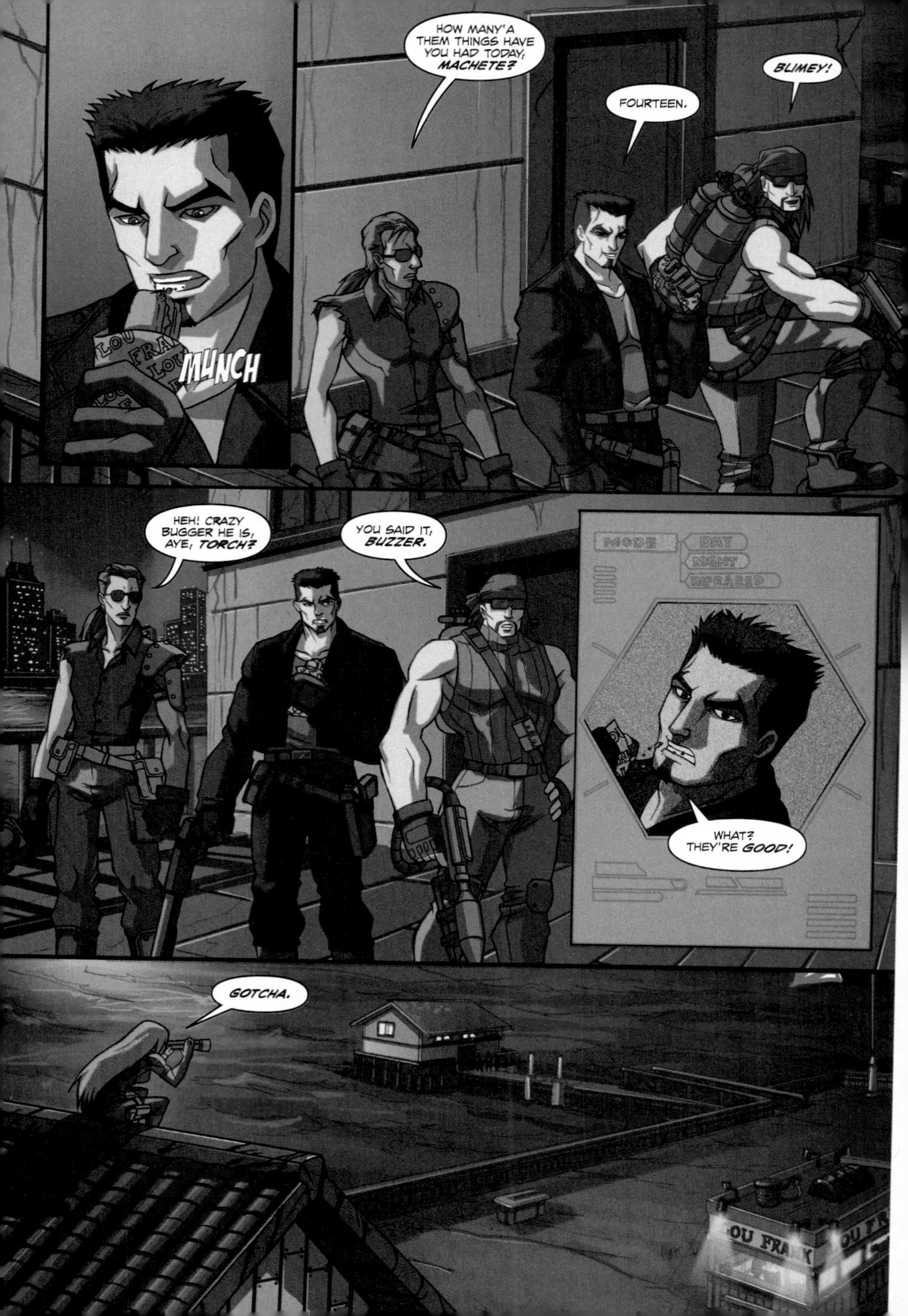
MUNCH
HOW MANY'A THEM THINGS HAVE YOU HAD TODAY, MACHETE?
FOURTEEN.
BLIMEY!
HEH! CRAZY BUGGER HE IS, AYE, TORCH?
YOU SAID IT, BUZZER.
MODE
DAY
NIGHT
INFRARED
WHAT? THEY'RE GOOD!
GOTCHA.
LOU FRANK

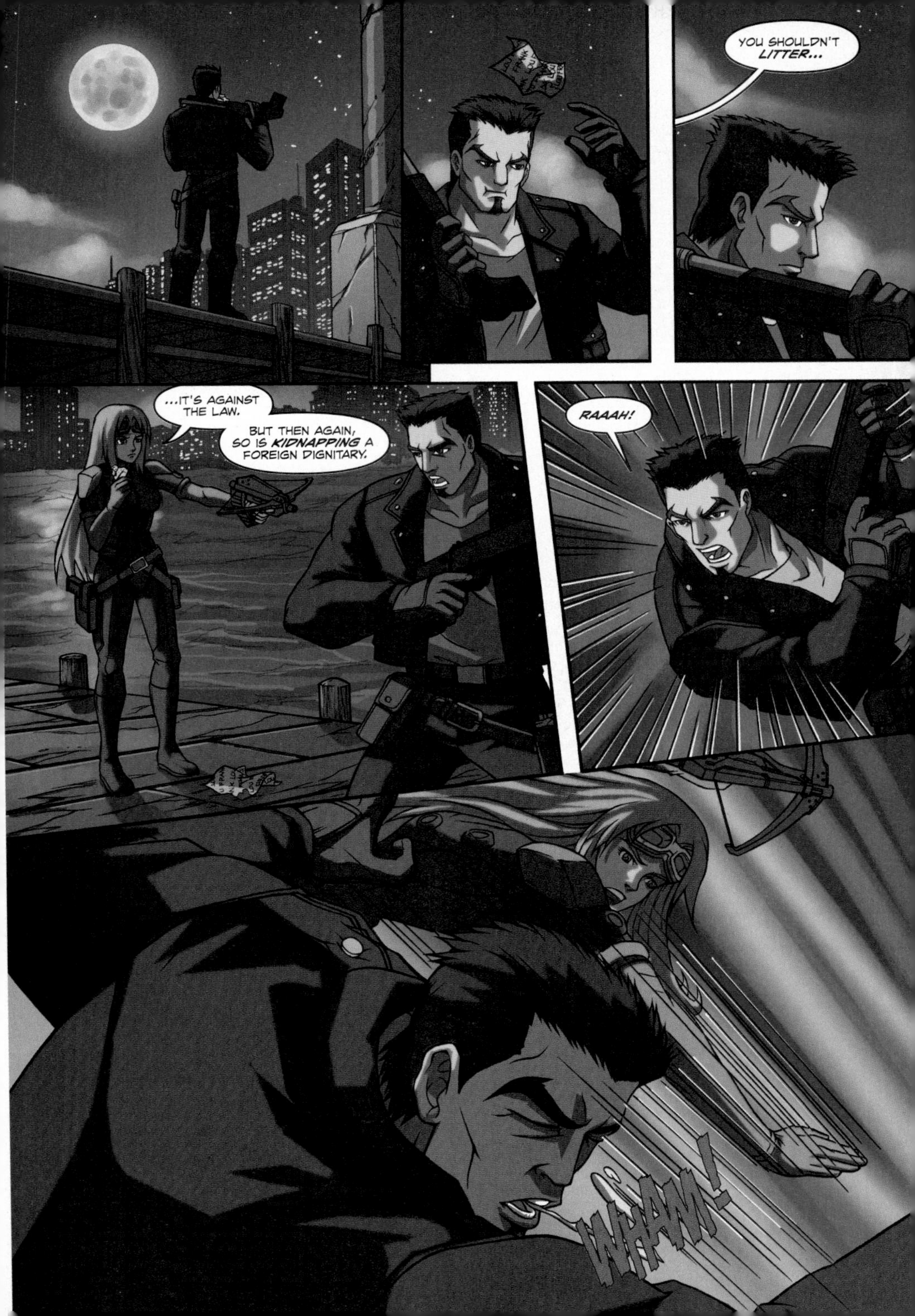

YOU SHOULDN'T *LITTER*...
...IT'S AGAINST THE LAW.
BUT THEN AGAIN, SO IS *KIDNAPPING* A FOREIGN DIGNITARY.
RAAAH!
WHAM!

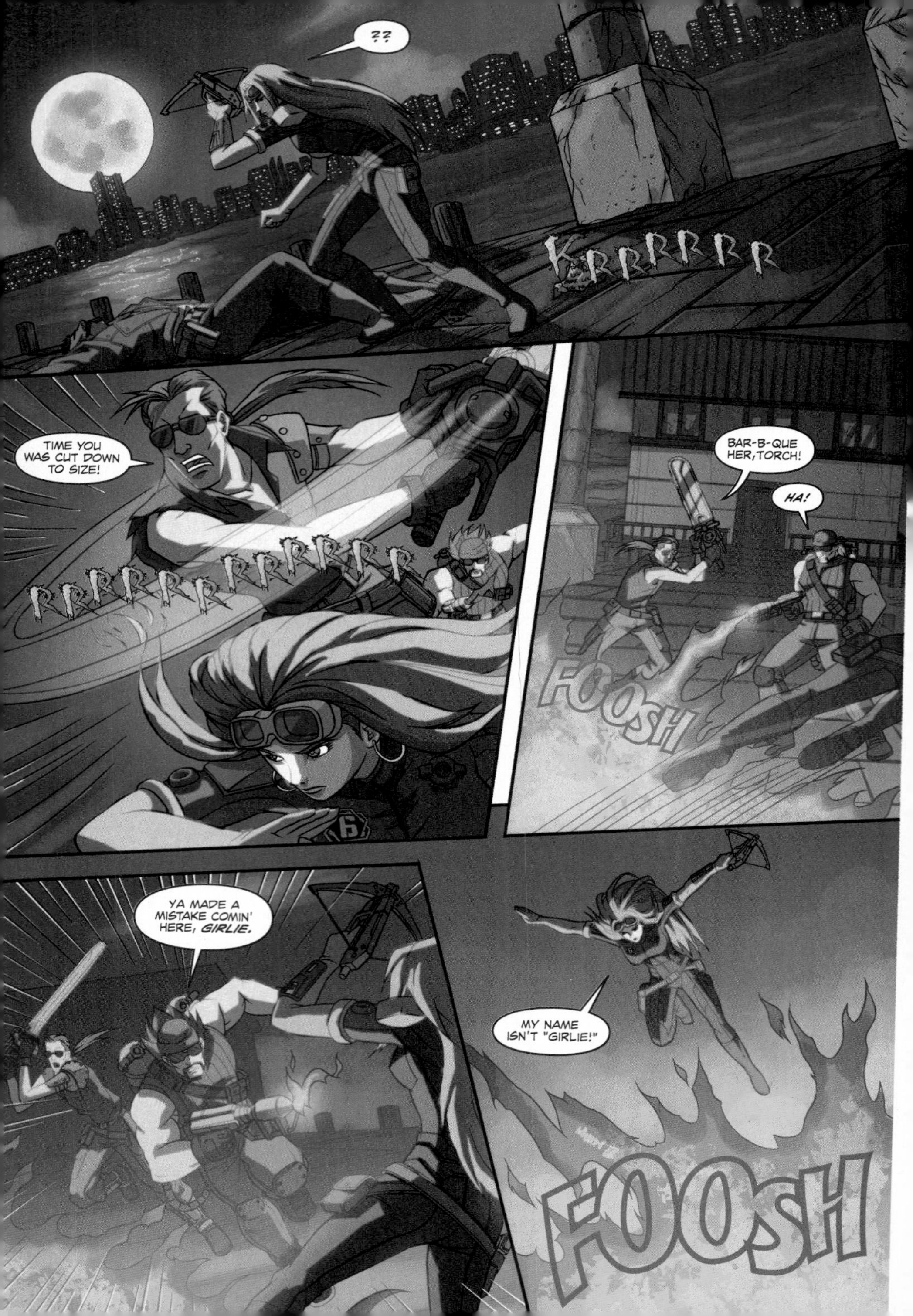
??
KRRRRRRR
TIME YOU WAS CUT DOWN TO SIZE!
RRRRRR RRRRRR
BAR-B-QUE HER, TORCH!
HA!
FOOSH
YA MADE A MISTAKE COMIN' HERE, *GIRLIE.*
MY NAME ISN'T "GIRLIE!"
FOOSH

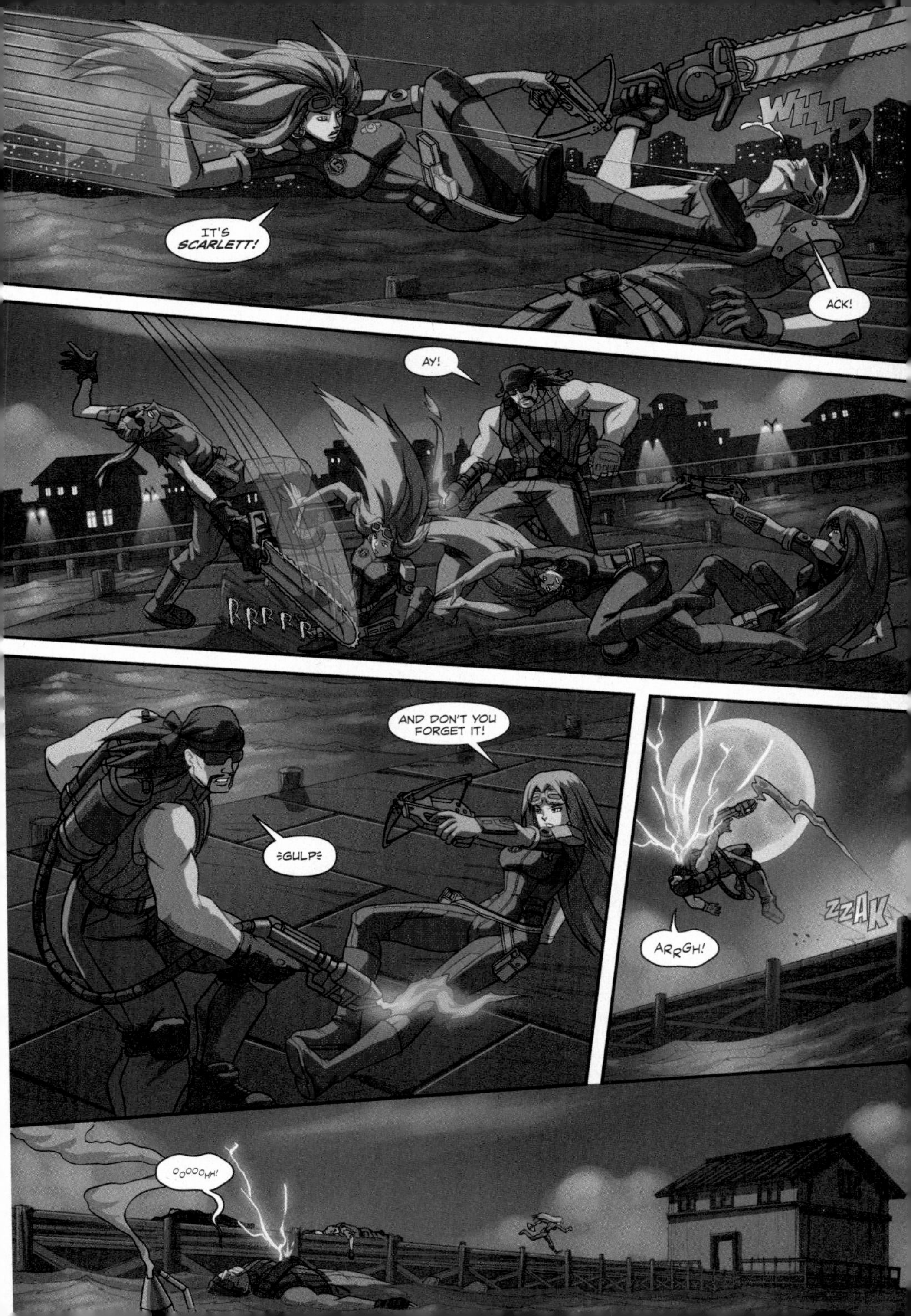
IT'S SCARLETT!
WHUD
ACK!
AY!
RRRRR
AND DON'T YOU FORGET IT!
GULP
ZZAK
ARRGH!
OOOOOHH!

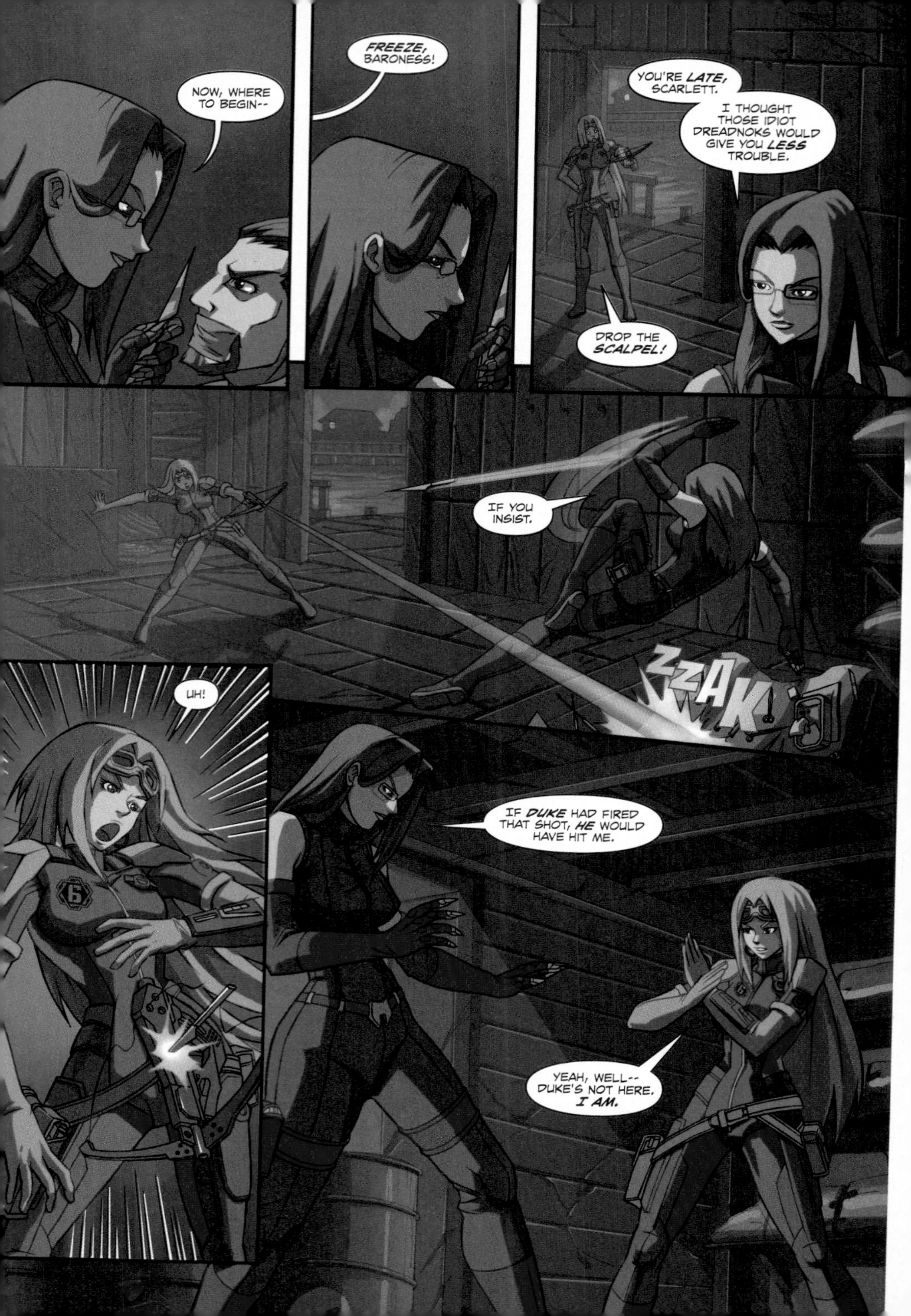
NOW, WHERE TO BEGIN--
FREEZE, BARONESS!
YOU'RE LATE, SCARLETT.
I THOUGHT THOSE IDIOT DREADNOKS WOULD GIVE YOU LESS TROUBLE.
DROP THE SCALPEL!
IF YOU INSIST.
ZZAK!
UH!
IF DUKE HAD FIRED THAT SHOT, HE WOULD HAVE HIT ME.
YEAH, WELL-- DUKE'S NOT HERE. I AM.

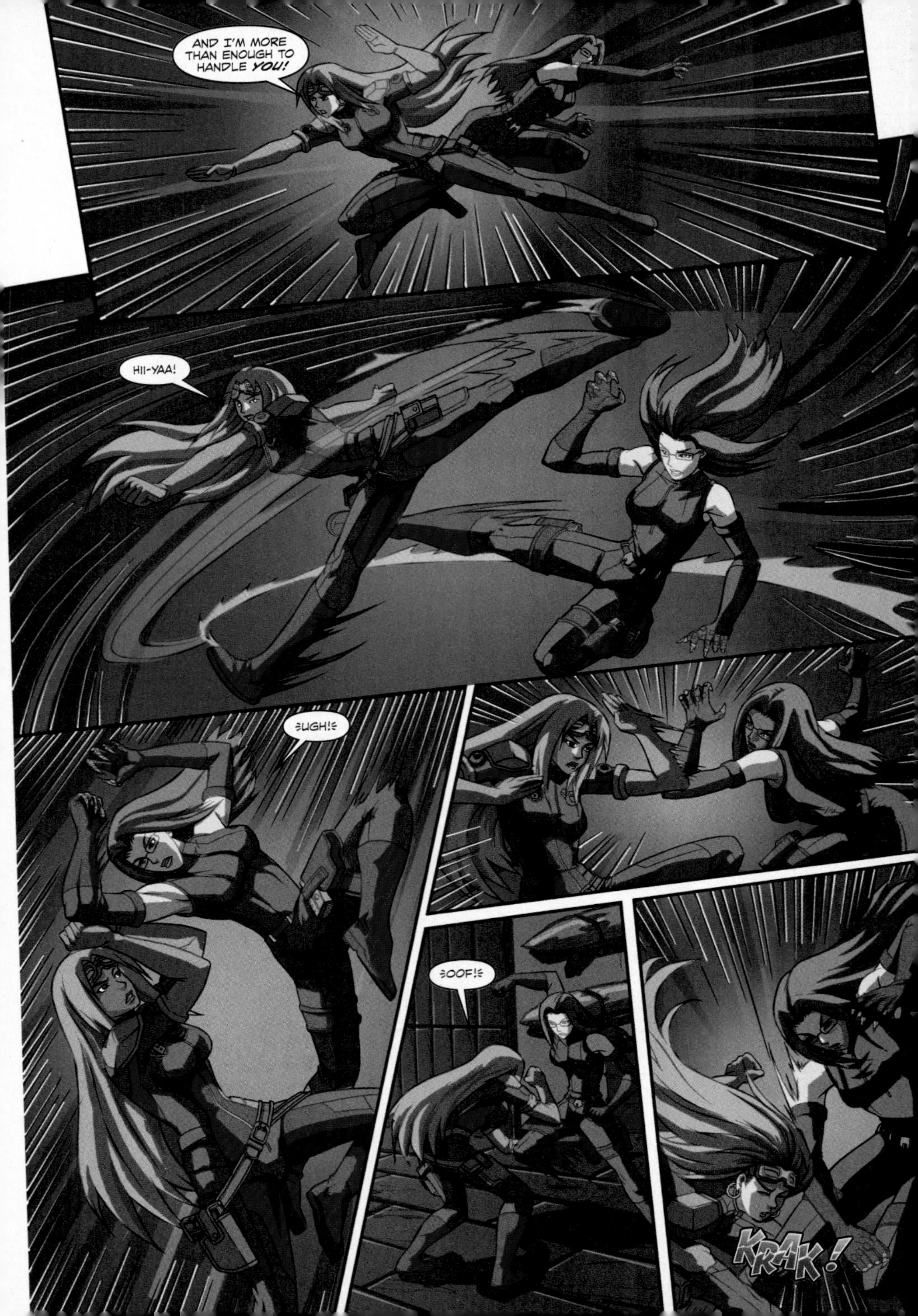
AND I'M MORE THAN ENOUGH TO HANDLE YOU!
HII-YAA!
UGH!
OOF!
KRAK!

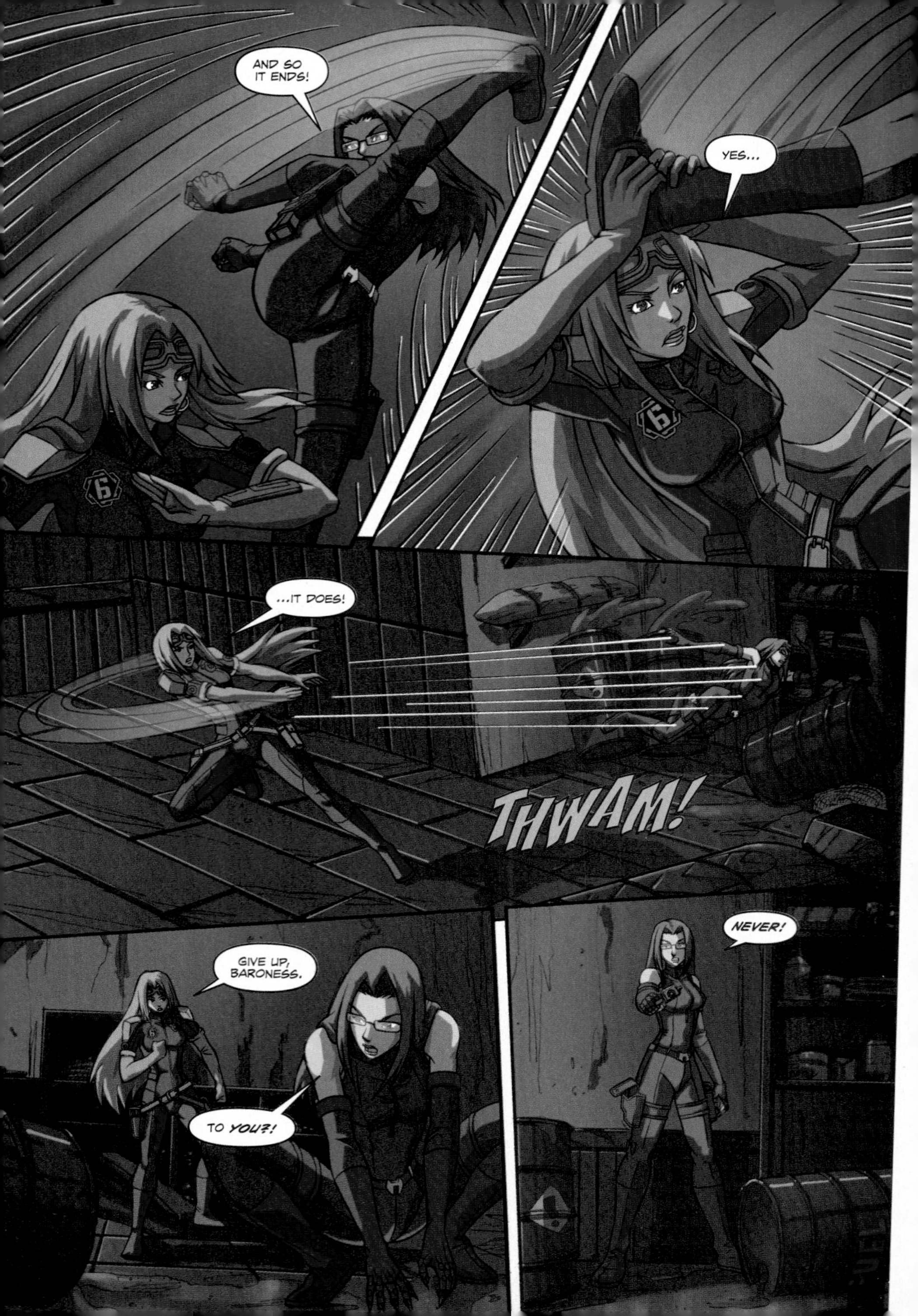
AND SO IT ENDS!
YES...
...IT DOES!
THWAM!
GIVE UP, BARONESS.
TO YOU?!
NEVER!

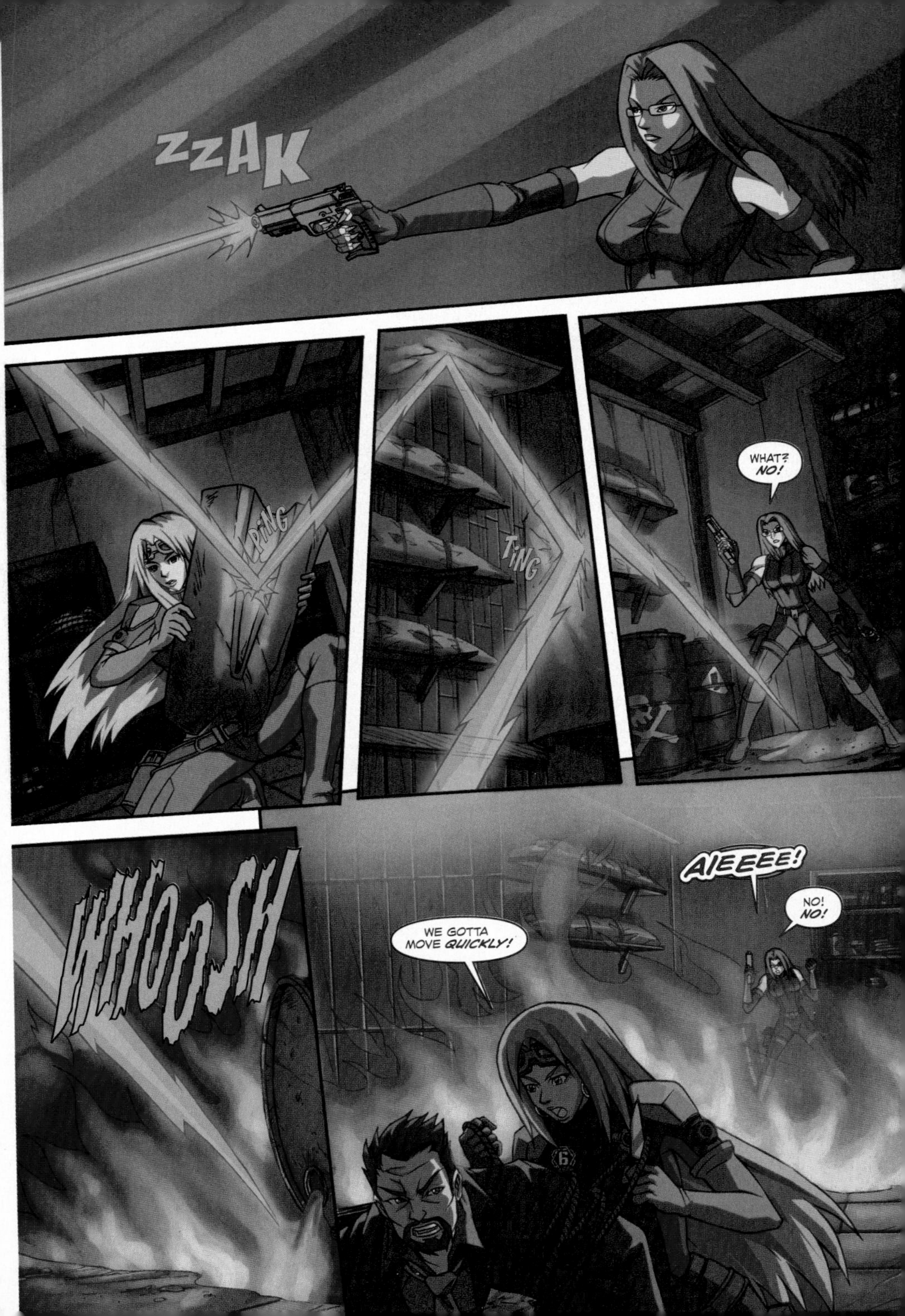
ZZAK
PING
TING
WHAT? NO!
WHOOSH
AIEEEE!
NO! NO!
WE GOTTA MOVE QUICKLY!

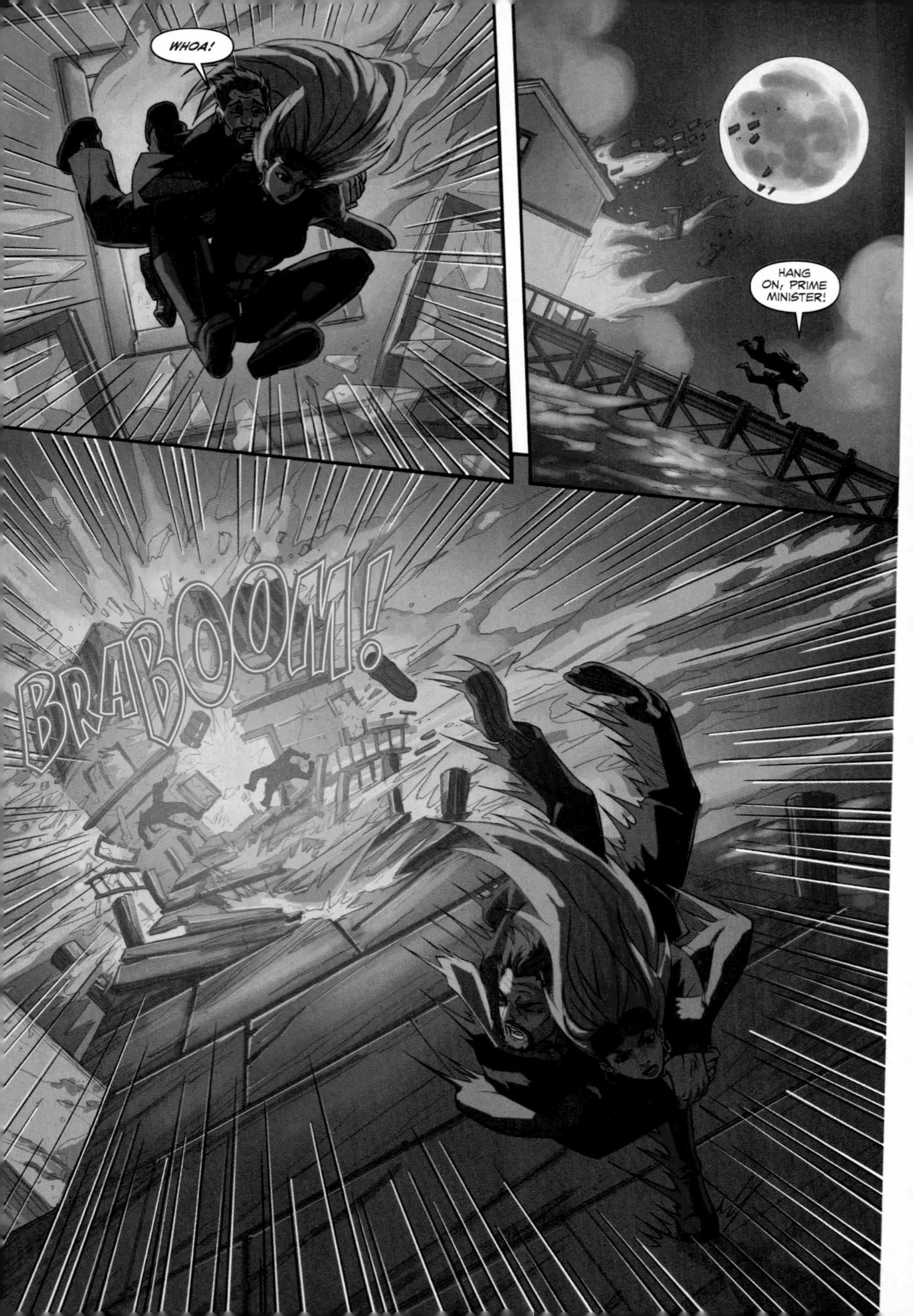
WHOA!
HANG ON, PRIME MINISTER!
BRABOOM!

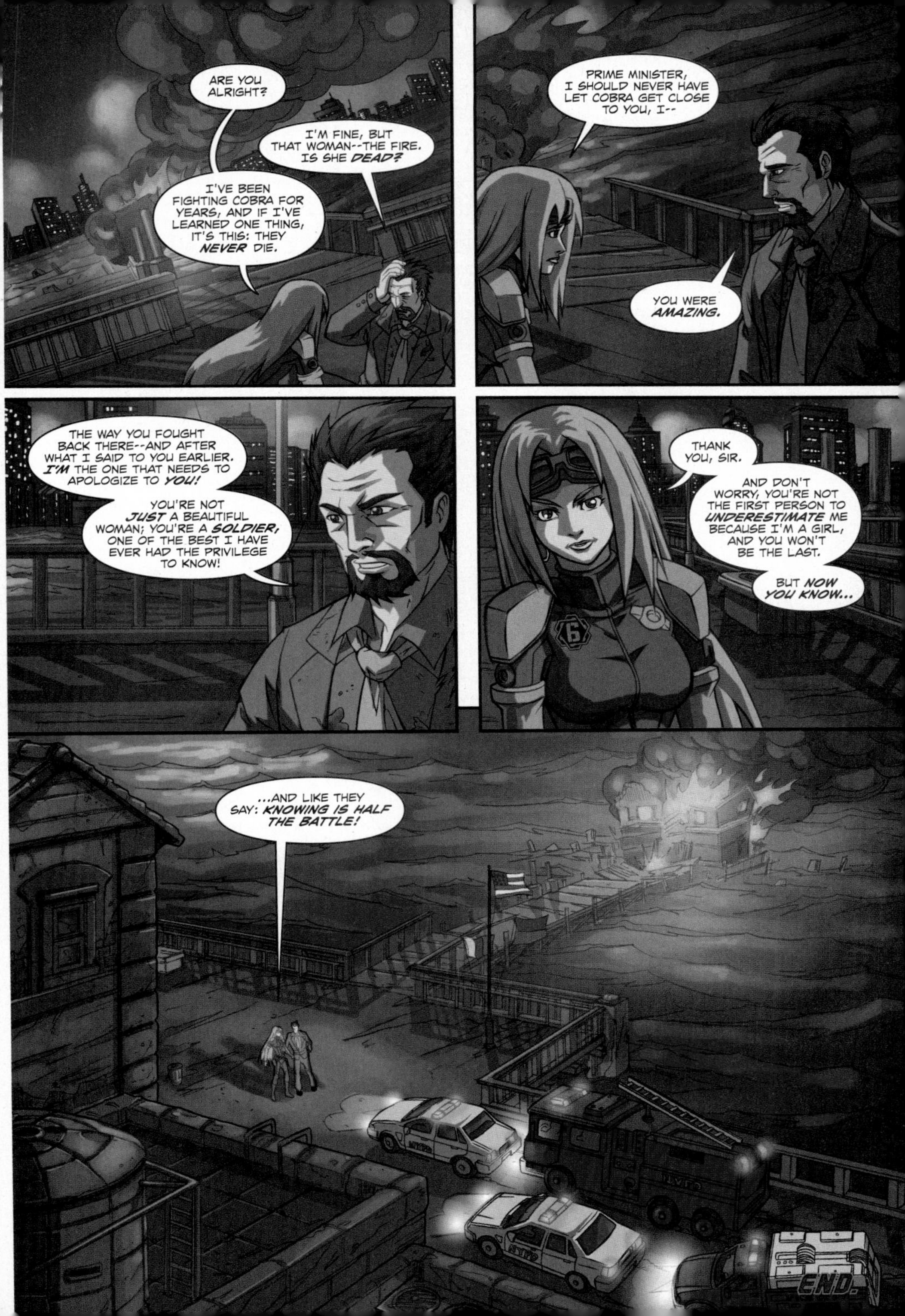
ARE YOU ALRIGHT?
I'M FINE, BUT THAT WOMAN--THE FIRE. IS SHE DEAD?
I'VE BEEN FIGHTING COBRA FOR YEARS, AND IF I'VE LEARNED ONE THING, IT'S THIS: THEY NEVER DIE.
PRIME MINISTER, I SHOULD NEVER HAVE LET COBRA GET CLOSE TO YOU, I--
YOU WERE AMAZING.
THE WAY YOU FOUGHT BACK THERE--AND AFTER WHAT I SAID TO YOU EARLIER. I'M THE ONE THAT NEEDS TO APOLOGIZE TO YOU!
YOU'RE NOT JUST A BEAUTIFUL WOMAN; YOU'RE A SOLDIER, ONE OF THE BEST I HAVE EVER HAD THE PRIVILEGE TO KNOW!
THANK YOU, SIR.
AND DON'T WORRY, YOU'RE NOT THE FIRST PERSON TO UNDERESTIMATE ME BECAUSE I'M A GIRL, AND YOU WON'T BE THE LAST.
BUT NOW YOU KNOW...
...AND LIKE THEY SAY: KNOWING IS HALF THE BATTLE!
END.

SIGMA 6 is the code name for a new group of
capabilities. They use innovative technology and gear designed exclusively for each
their missions. Working against them is the evil COBRA organization, whose goal is t
take control of the world by sabotage, espionage and outright destruction. SIGMA 6 figh
them at every turn and provides a swift solution to critical situations around the glob

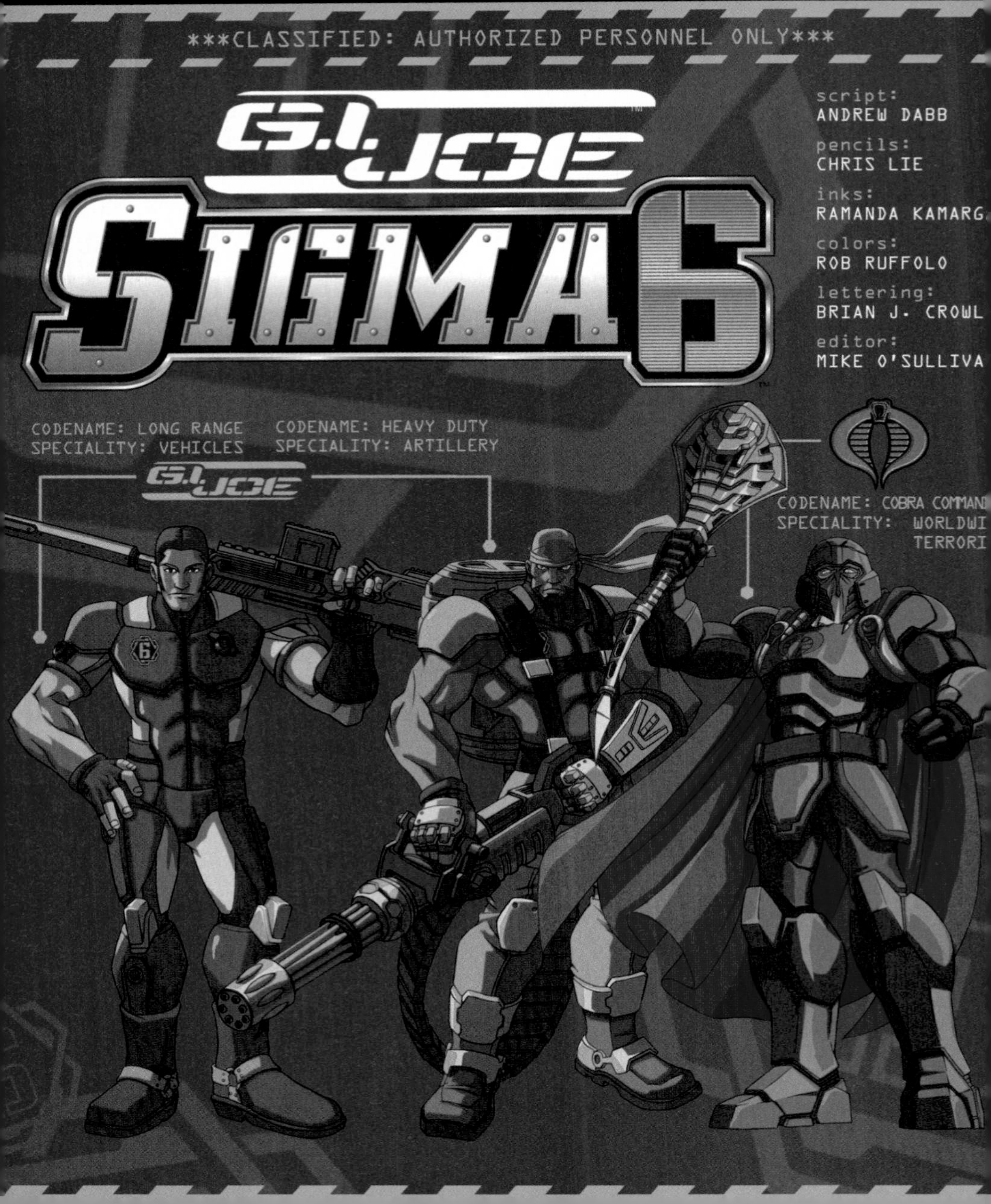

CLASSIFIED: AUTHORIZED PERSONNEL ONLY
G.I. JOE
SIGMA 6
script:
ANDREW DABB
pencils:
CHRIS LIE
inks:
RAMANDA KAMARG
colors:
ROB RUFFOLO
lettering:
BRIAN J. CROWL
editor:
MIKE O'SULLIVA
CODENAME: LONG RANGE
SPECIALITY: VEHICLES
CODENAME: HEAVY DUTY
SPECIALITY: ARTILLERY
G.I. JOE
CODENAME: COBRA COMMAN
SPECIALITY: WORLDWI
TERRORI

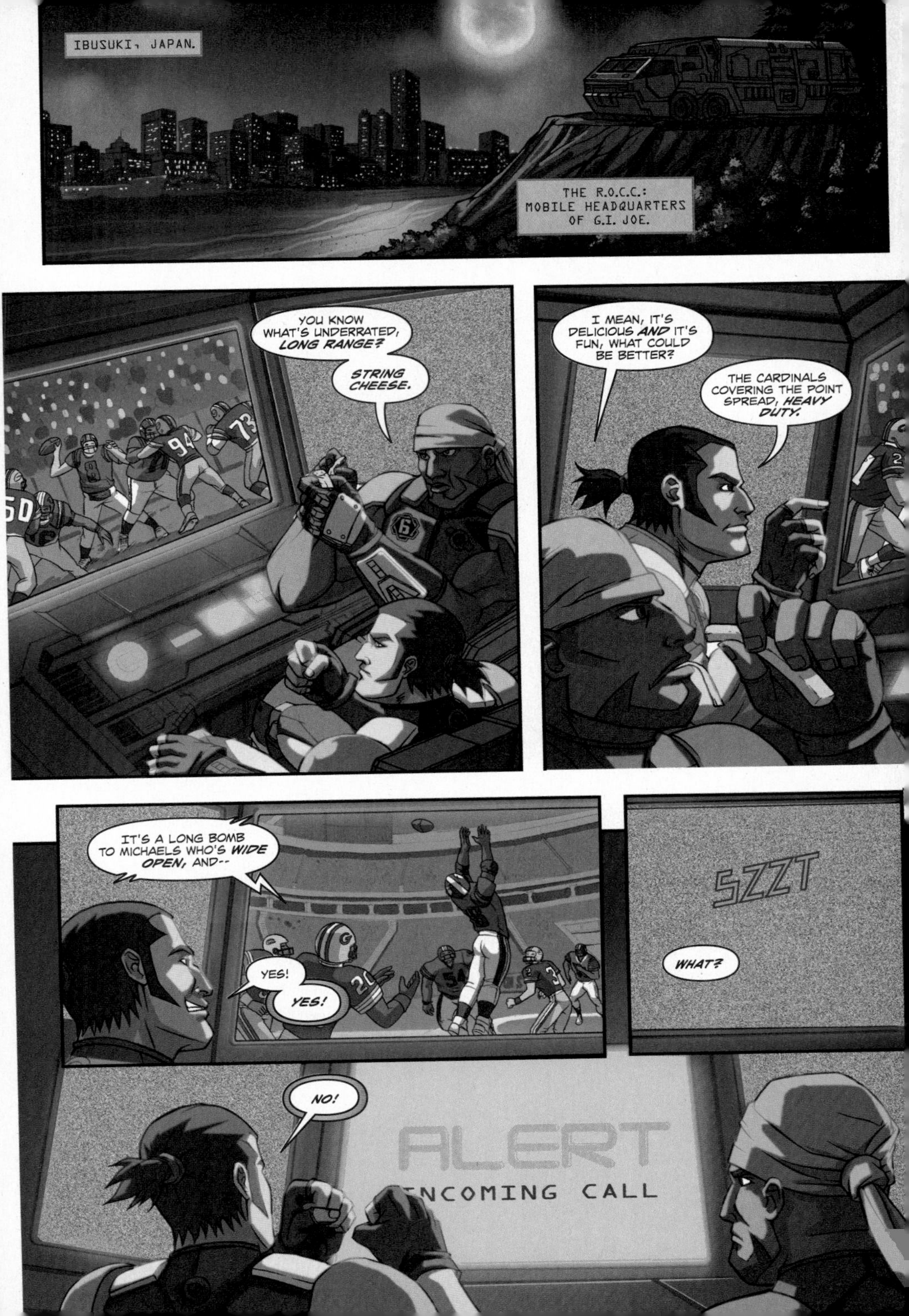
IBUSUKI, JAPAN.
THE R.O.C.C.: MOBILE HEADQUARTERS OF G.I. JOE.
YOU KNOW WHAT'S UNDERRATED, LONG RANGE?
STRING CHEESE.
I MEAN, IT'S DELICIOUS AND IT'S FUN, WHAT COULD BE BETTER?
THE CARDINALS COVERING THE POINT SPREAD, HEAVY DUTY.
IT'S A LONG BOMB TO MICHAELS WHO'S WIDE OPEN, AND--
YES!
YES!
SZZT
WHAT?
NO!
ALERT
INCOMING CALL

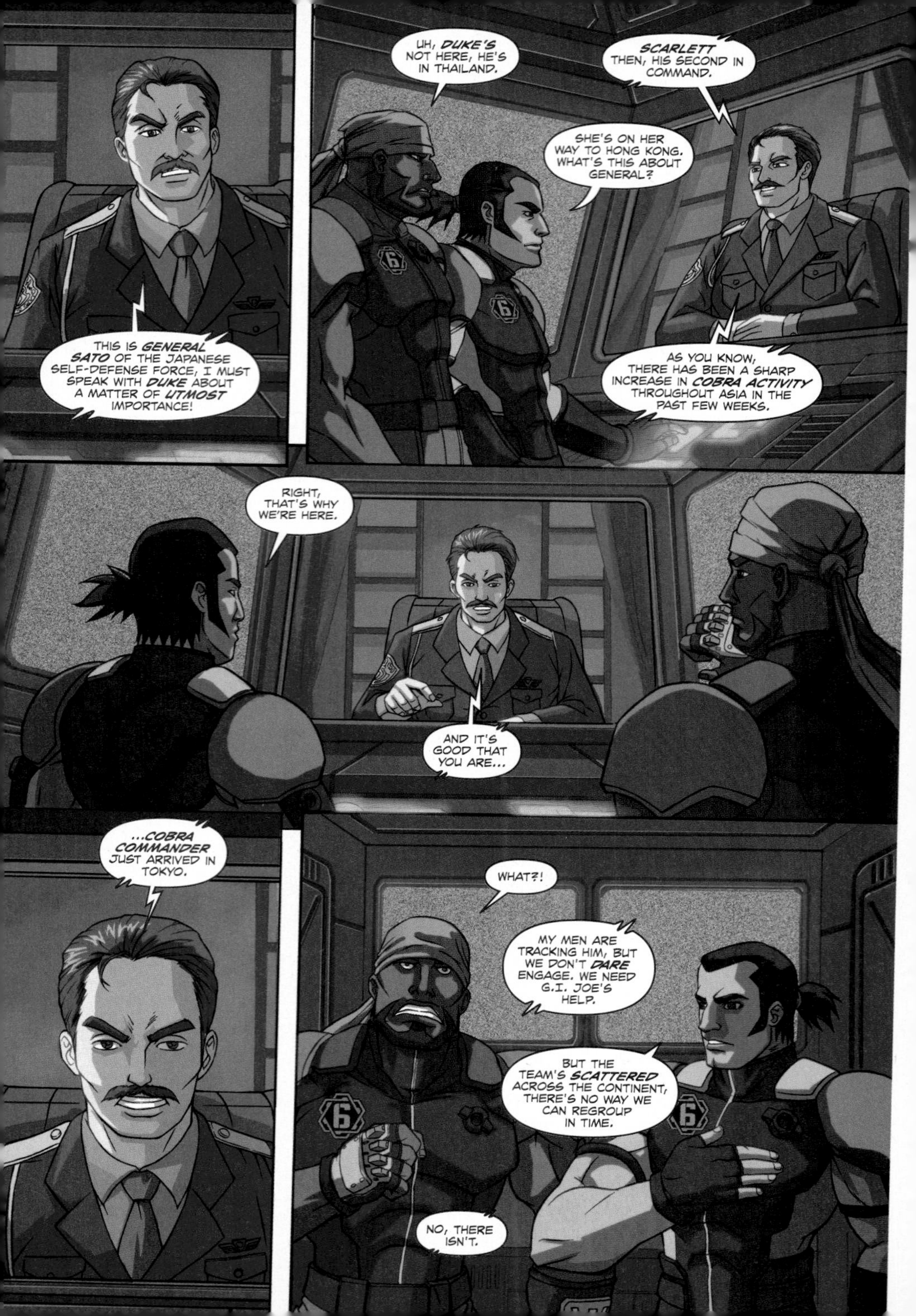

THIS IS GENERAL SATO OF THE JAPANESE SELF-DEFENSE FORCE, I MUST SPEAK WITH DUKE ABOUT A MATTER OF UTMOST IMPORTANCE!
UH, DUKE'S NOT HERE, HE'S IN THAILAND.
SCARLETT THEN, HIS SECOND IN COMMAND.
SHE'S ON HER WAY TO HONG KONG. WHAT'S THIS ABOUT GENERAL?
AS YOU KNOW, THERE HAS BEEN A SHARP INCREASE IN COBRA ACTIVITY THROUGHOUT ASIA IN THE PAST FEW WEEKS.
RIGHT, THAT'S WHY WE'RE HERE.
AND IT'S GOOD THAT YOU ARE...
...COBRA COMMANDER JUST ARRIVED IN TOKYO.
WHAT?!
MY MEN ARE TRACKING HIM, BUT WE DON'T DARE ENGAGE. WE NEED G.I. JOE'S HELP.
BUT THE TEAM'S SCATTERED ACROSS THE CONTINENT, THERE'S NO WAY WE CAN REGROUP IN TIME.
NO, THERE ISN'T.

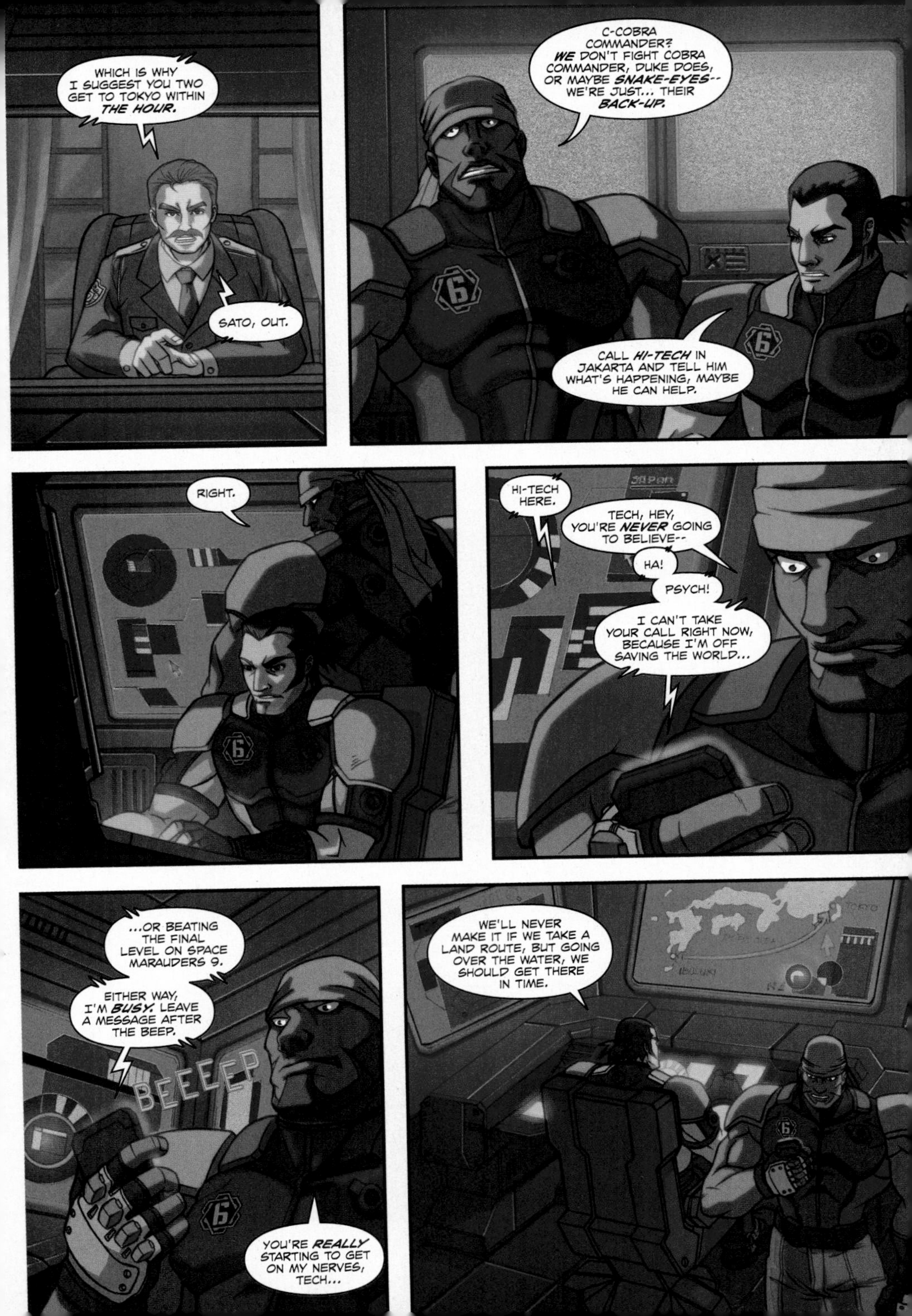
WHICH IS WHY I SUGGEST YOU TWO GET TO TOKYO WITHIN THE HOUR.
SATO, OUT.
C-COBRA COMMANDER? WE DON'T FIGHT COBRA COMMANDER, DUKE DOES, OR MAYBE SNAKE-EYES-- WE'RE JUST... THEIR BACK-UP.
CALL HI-TECH IN JAKARTA AND TELL HIM WHAT'S HAPPENING, MAYBE HE CAN HELP.
RIGHT.
HI-TECH HERE.
TECH, HEY, YOU'RE NEVER GOING TO BELIEVE--
HA!
PSYCH!
I CAN'T TAKE YOUR CALL RIGHT NOW, BECAUSE I'M OFF SAVING THE WORLD...
...OR BEATING THE FINAL LEVEL ON SPACE MARAUDERS 9.
EITHER WAY, I'M BUSY. LEAVE A MESSAGE AFTER THE BEEP.
BEEEEP
YOU'RE REALLY STARTING TO GET ON MY NERVES, TECH...
WE'LL NEVER MAKE IT IF WE TAKE A LAND ROUTE, BUT GOING OVER THE WATER, WE SHOULD GET THERE IN TIME.

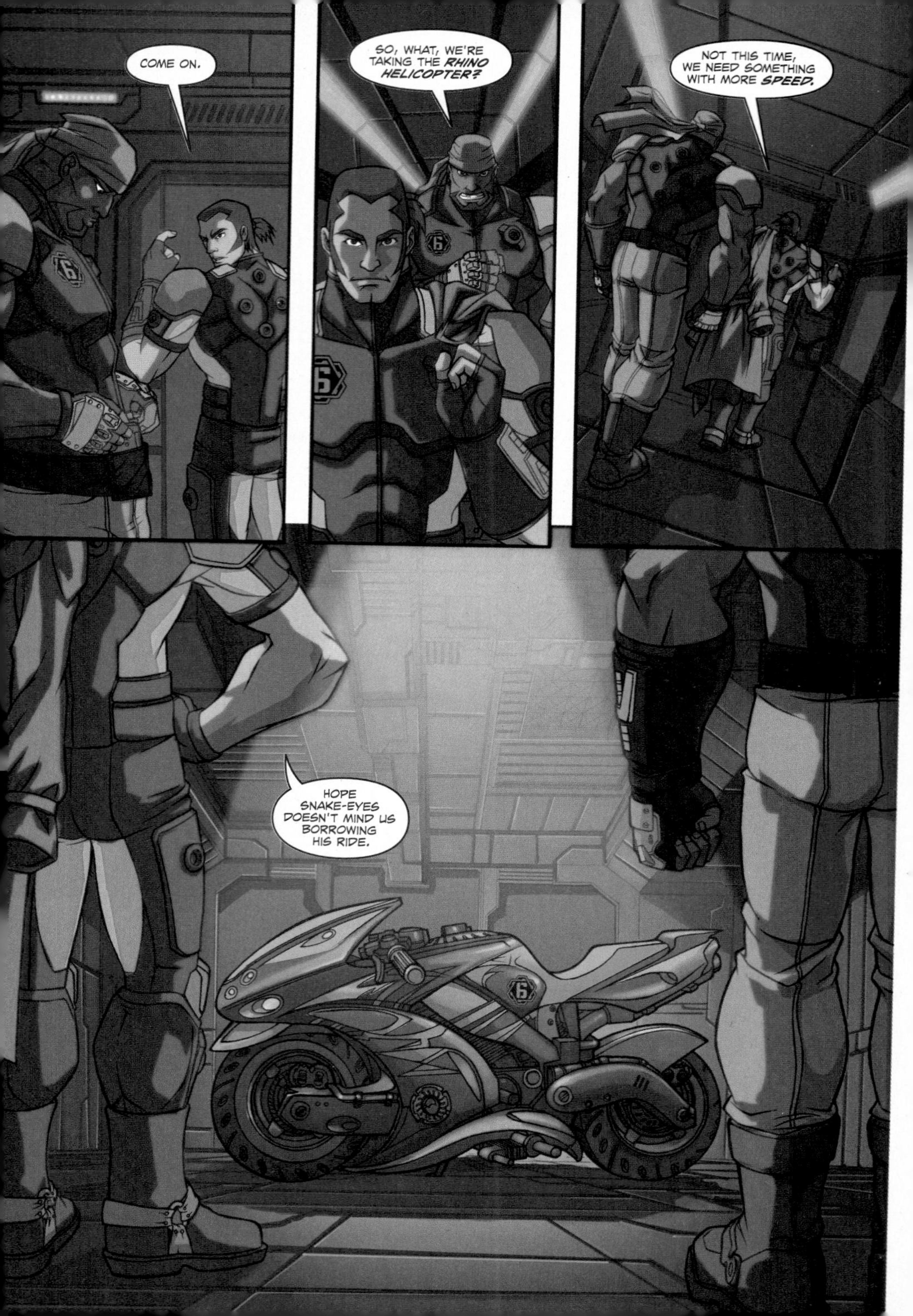
COME ON.
SO, WHAT, WE'RE TAKING THE RHINO HELICOPTER?
NOT THIS TIME, WE NEED SOMETHING WITH MORE SPEED.
HOPE SNAKE-EYES DOESN'T MIND US BORROWING HIS RIDE.

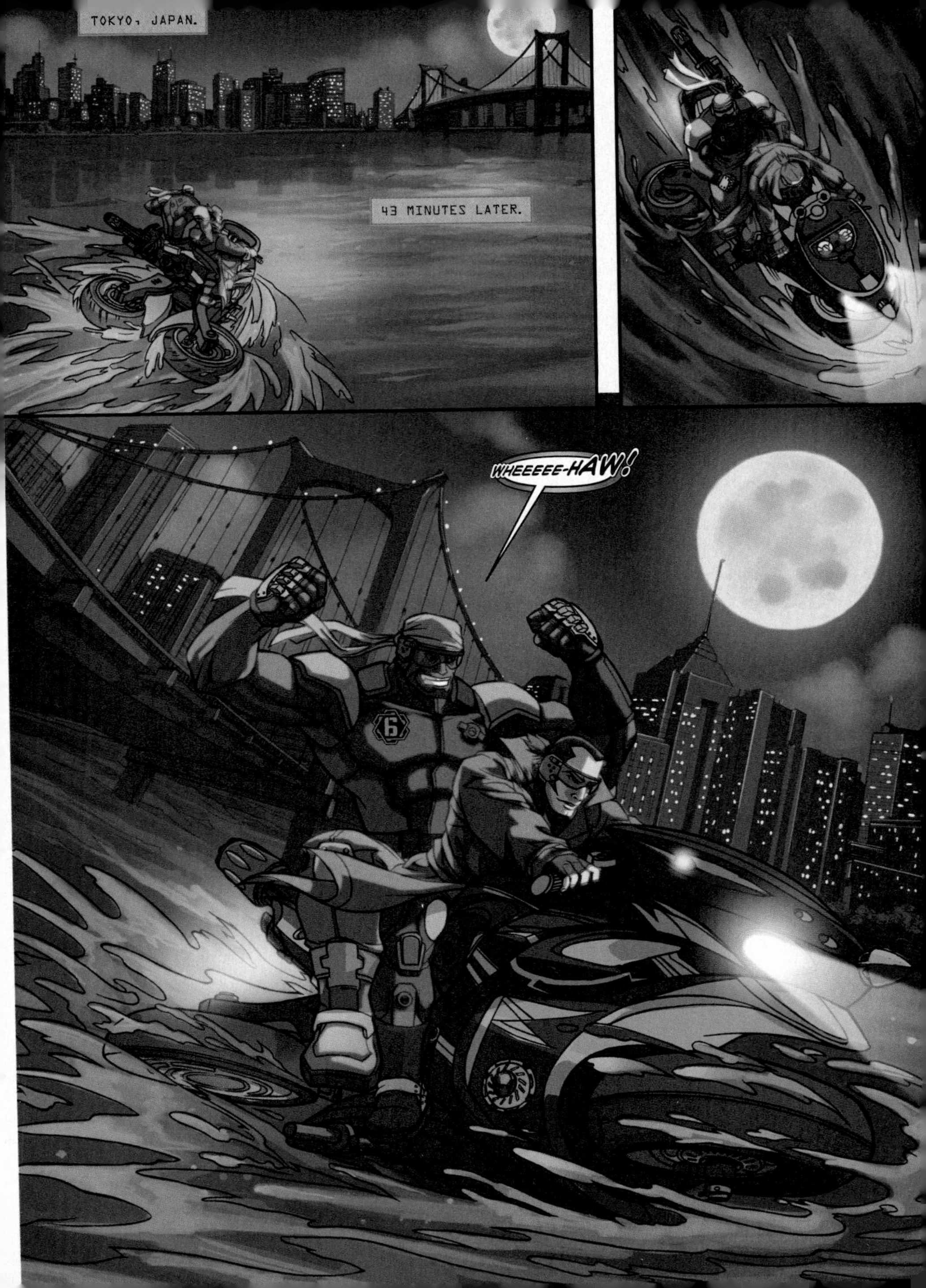
TOKYO, JAPAN.
43 MINUTES LATER.
WHEEEEE-HAW!

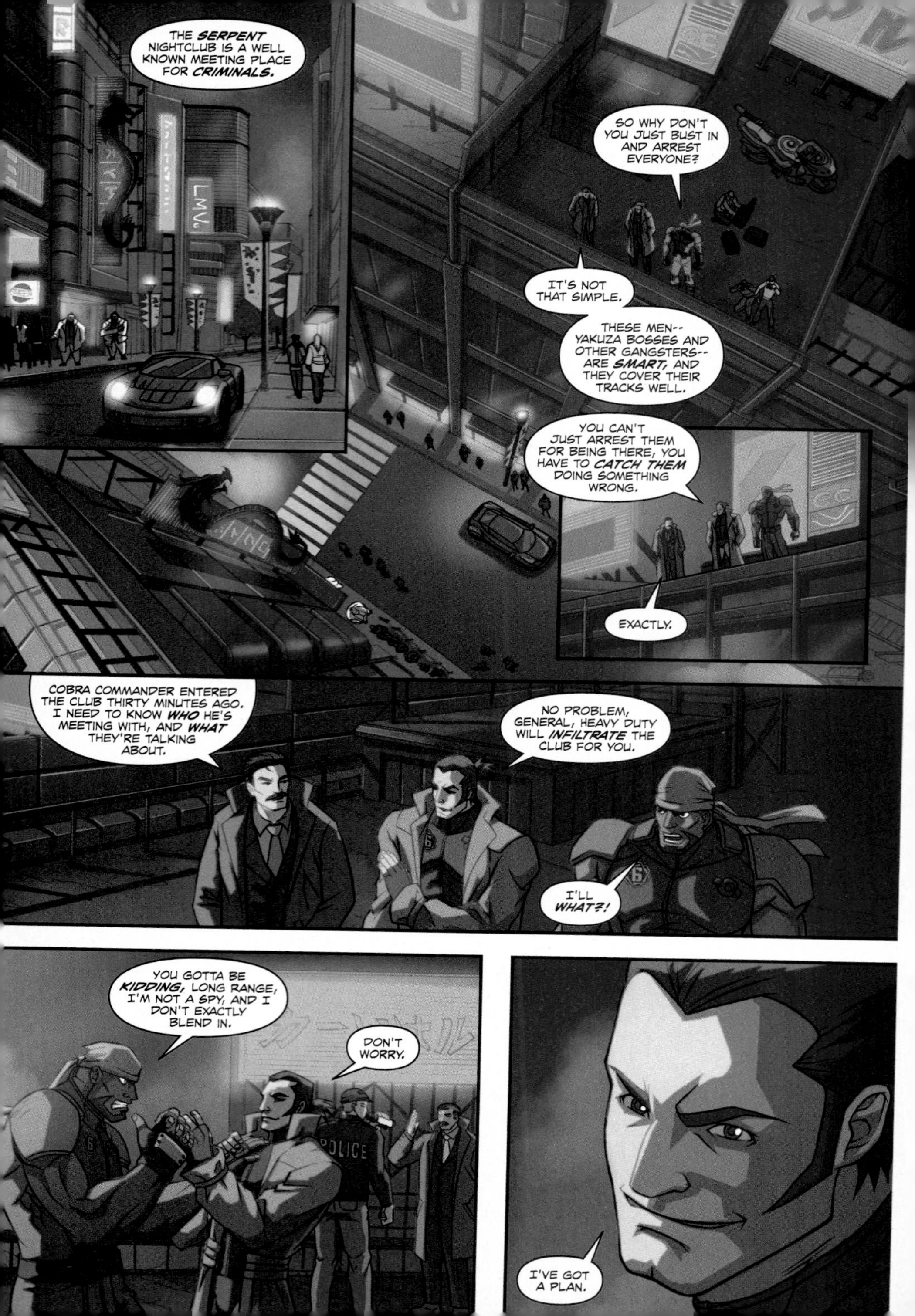
THE SERPENT NIGHTCLUB IS A WELL KNOWN MEETING PLACE FOR CRIMINALS.
SO WHY DON'T YOU JUST BUST IN AND ARREST EVERYONE?
IT'S NOT THAT SIMPLE.
THESE MEN-- YAKUZA BOSSES AND OTHER GANGSTERS-- ARE SMART, AND THEY COVER THEIR TRACKS WELL.
YOU CAN'T JUST ARREST THEM FOR BEING THERE, YOU HAVE TO CATCH THEM DOING SOMETHING WRONG.
EXACTLY.
COBRA COMMANDER ENTERED THE CLUB THIRTY MINUTES AGO. I NEED TO KNOW WHO HE'S MEETING WITH, AND WHAT THEY'RE TALKING ABOUT.
NO PROBLEM, GENERAL, HEAVY DUTY WILL INFILTRATE THE CLUB FOR YOU.
I'LL WHAT?!
YOU GOTTA BE KIDDING, LONG RANGE, I'M NOT A SPY, AND I DON'T EXACTLY BLEND IN.
DON'T WORRY.
POLICE
I'VE GOT A PLAN.

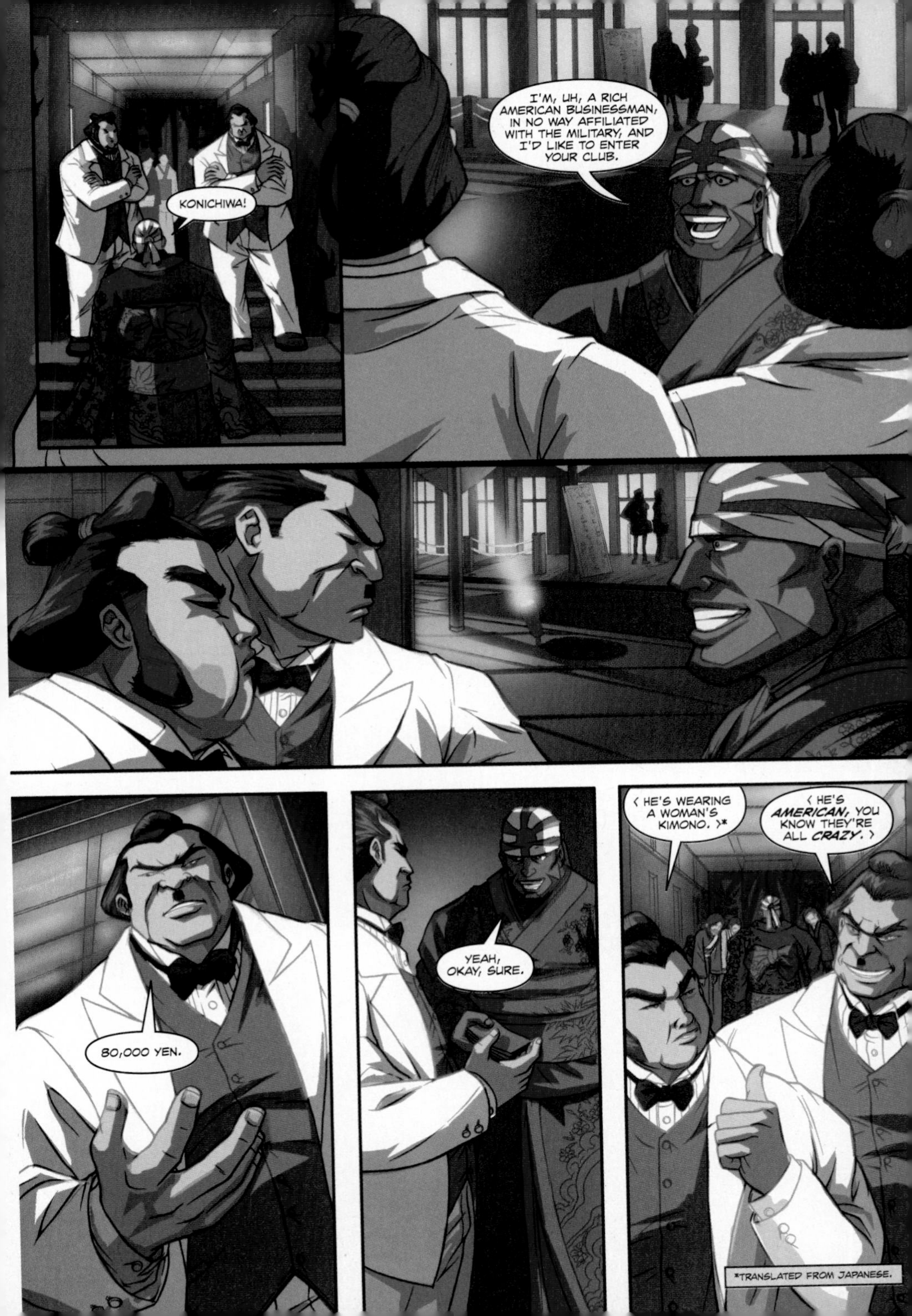
KONICHIWA!
I'M, UH, A RICH AMERICAN BUSINESSMAN, IN NO WAY AFFILIATED WITH THE MILITARY, AND I'D LIKE TO ENTER YOUR CLUB.
80,000 YEN.
YEAH, OKAY, SURE.
‹ HE'S WEARING A WOMAN'S KIMONO. ›*
‹ HE'S *AMERICAN*, YOU KNOW THEY'RE ALL *CRAZY*. ›
*TRANSLATED FROM JAPANESE.

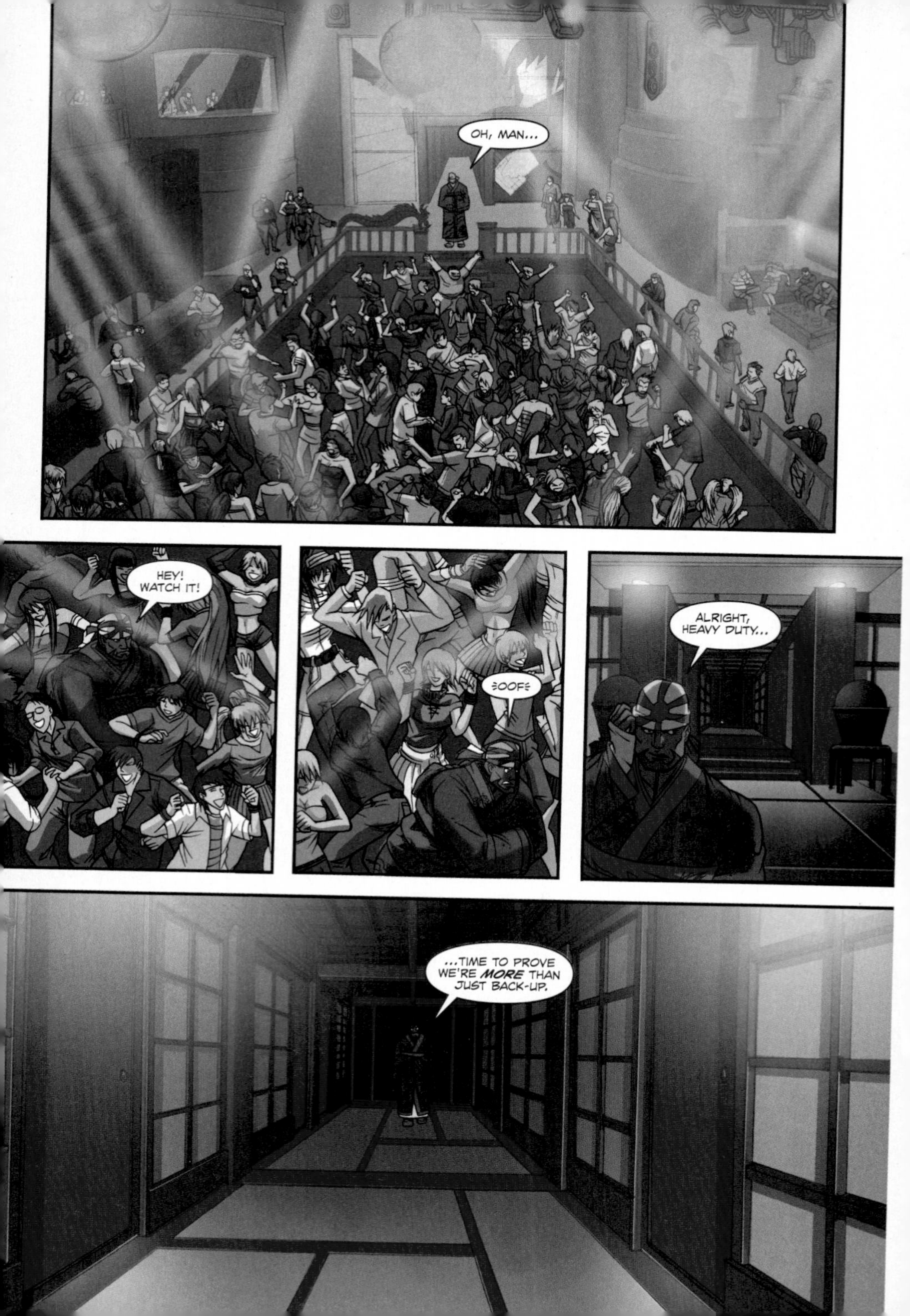
OH, MAN...
HEY! WATCH IT!
OOF
ALRIGHT, HEAVY DUTY...
...TIME TO PROVE WE'RE MORE THAN JUST BACK-UP.

WITH COBRA'S HELP, YOUR MEN WILL CONTROL *ALL OF ASIA* IN SIX MONTHS, AND ALL I ASK FOR IN RETURN IS YOUR *UNDYING LOYALTY!*

THIS BETTER WORK.

KLIK

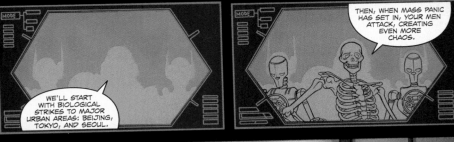

THEN, WHEN MASS PANIC HAS SET IN, YOUR MEN ATTACK, CREATING EVEN MORE CHAOS.

WE'LL START WITH BIOLOGICAL STRIKES TO MAJOR URBAN AREAS: BEIJING, TOKYO, AND SEOUL.

BY THE TIME THE VARIOUS GOVERNMENTS REALIZE WHAT'S HAPPENING, IT WILL BE TOO LATE!

MY B.A.T. ARMIES WILL HAVE MARCHED ON THEIR CAPITALS, AND THE ENTIRE CONTINENT WILL BE OURS!

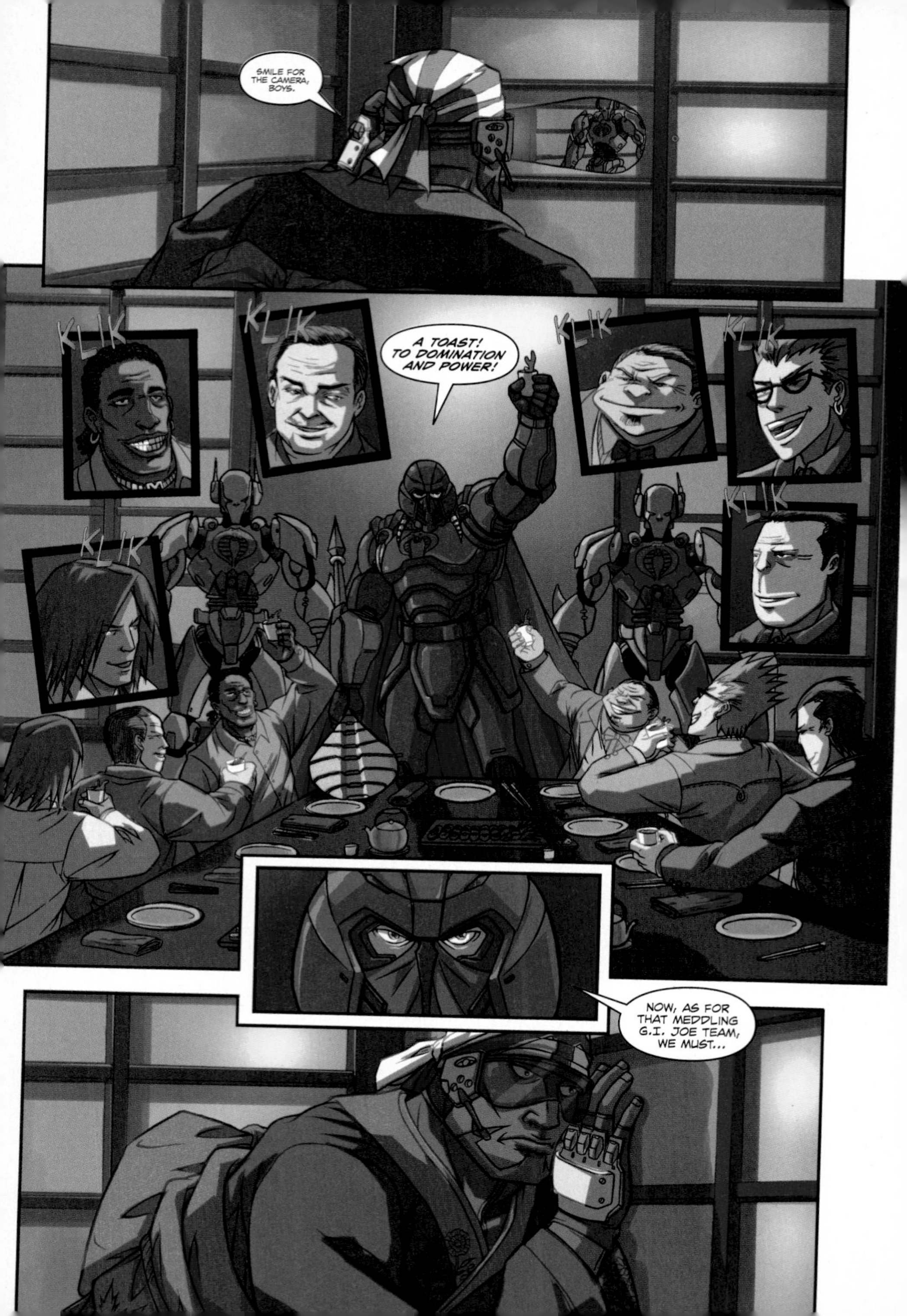
SMILE FOR THE CAMERA, BOYS.
KLIK
KLIK
A TOAST! TO DOMINATION AND POWER!
KLIK
KLIK
KLIK
KLIK
NOW, AS FOR THAT MEDDLING G.I. JOE TEAM, WE MUST...

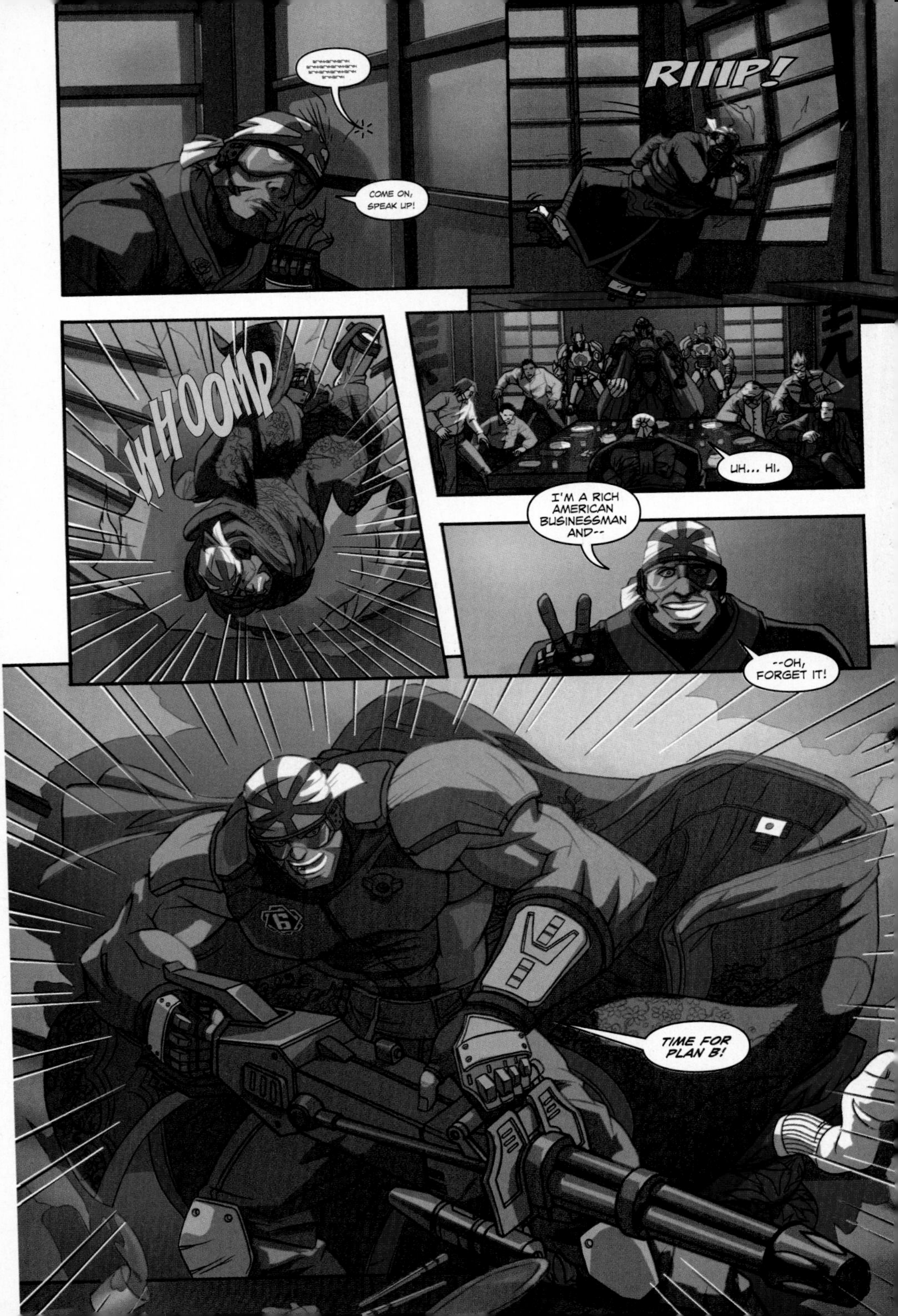
COME ON, SPEAK UP!
RIIIP!
WHOOMP
UH... HI.
I'M A RICH AMERICAN BUSINESSMAN AND--
--OH, FORGET IT!
TIME FOR PLAN B!

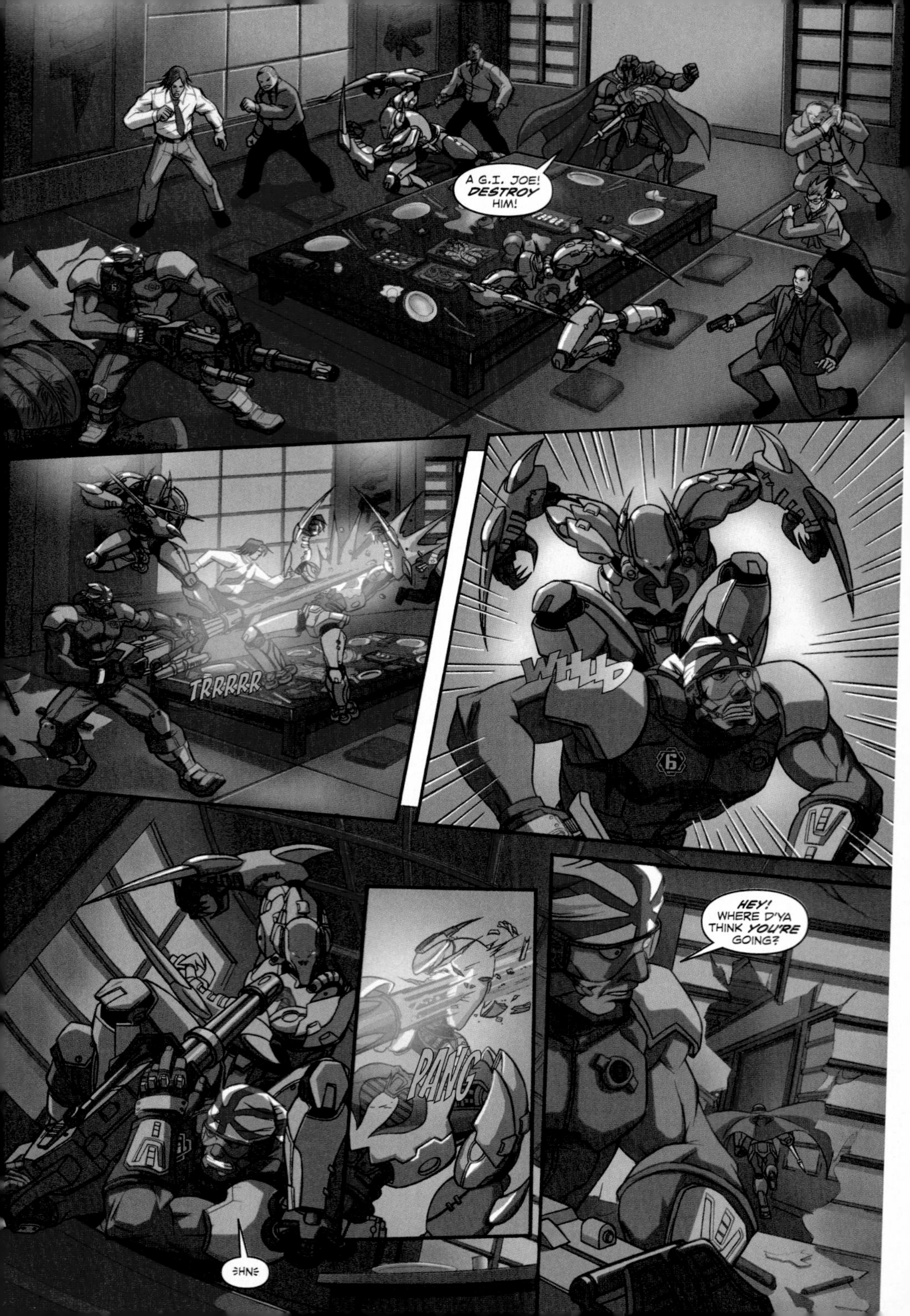

A G.I. JOE! DESTROY HIM!
TRRRRR
WHUD
PANG
=HN=
HEY! WHERE D'YA THINK YOU'RE GOING?

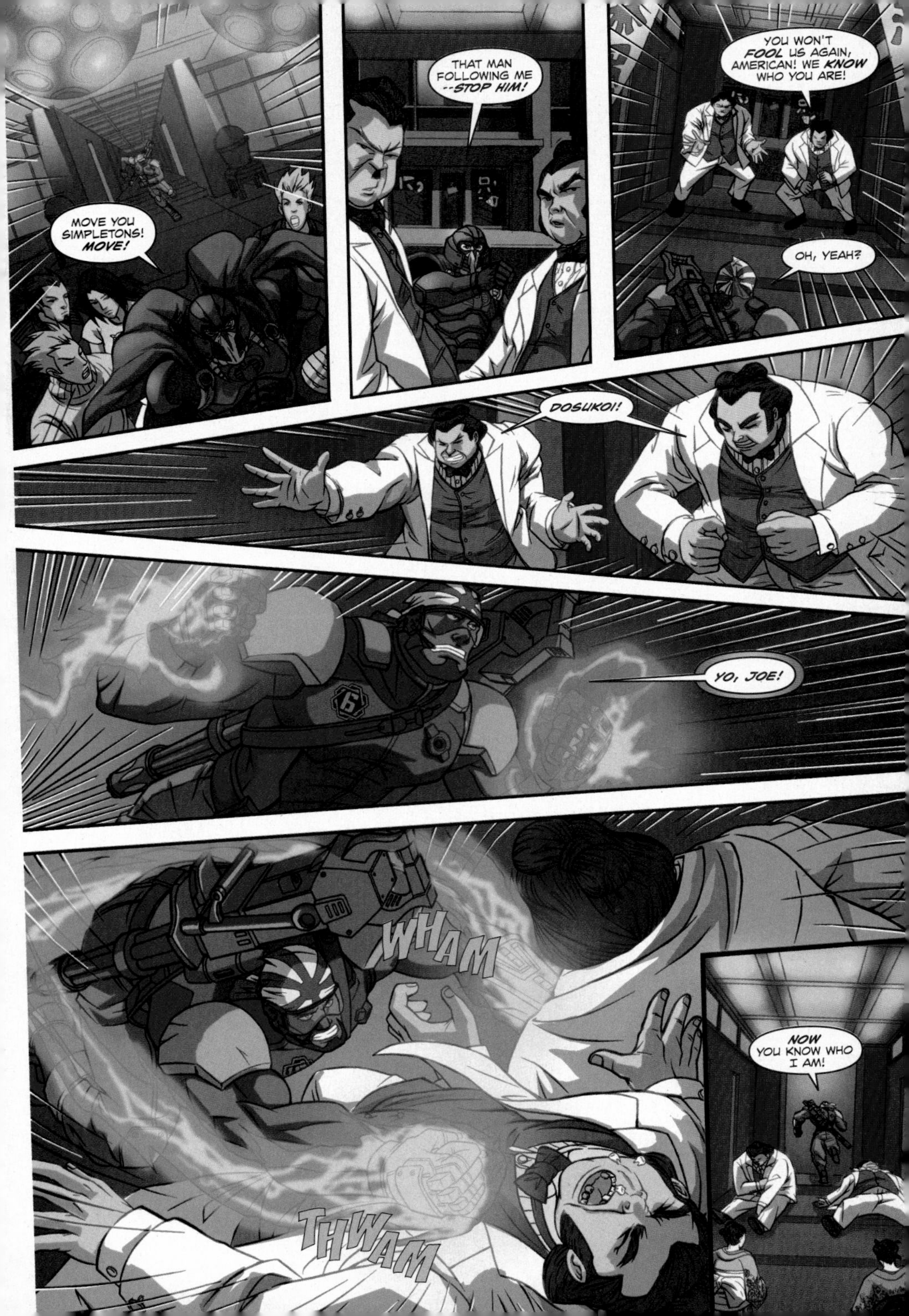

MOVE YOU SIMPLETONS! MOVE!
THAT MAN FOLLOWING ME --STOP HIM!
YOU WON'T FOOL US AGAIN, AMERICAN! WE KNOW WHO YOU ARE!
OH, YEAH?
DOSUKOI!
YO, JOE!
WHAM
THWAM
NOW YOU KNOW WHO I AM!

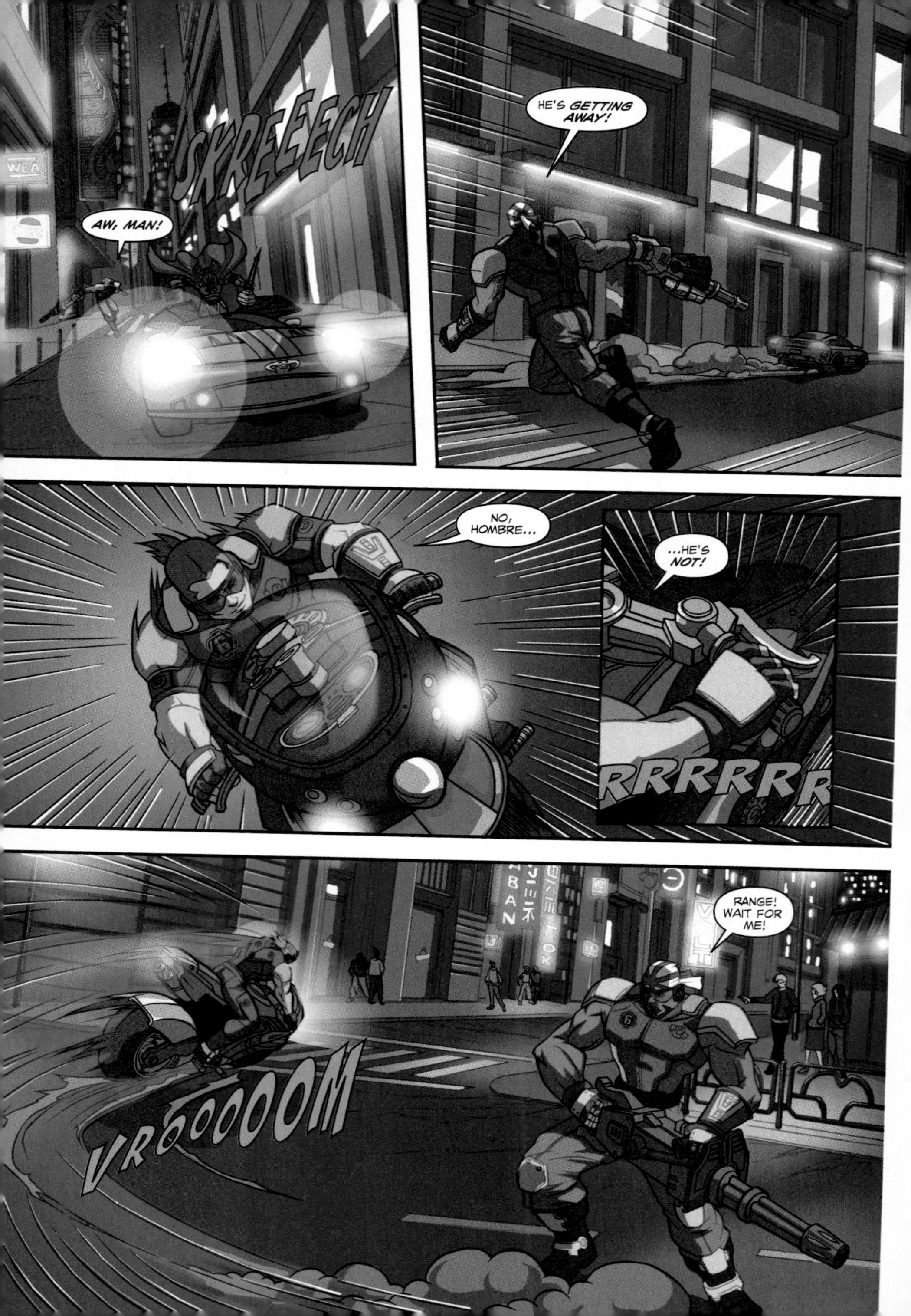
SKREEECH
AW, MAN!
HE'S GETTING AWAY!
NO, HOMBRE...
...HE'S NOT!
RRRRRRR
VROOOOOM
RANGE! WAIT FOR ME!

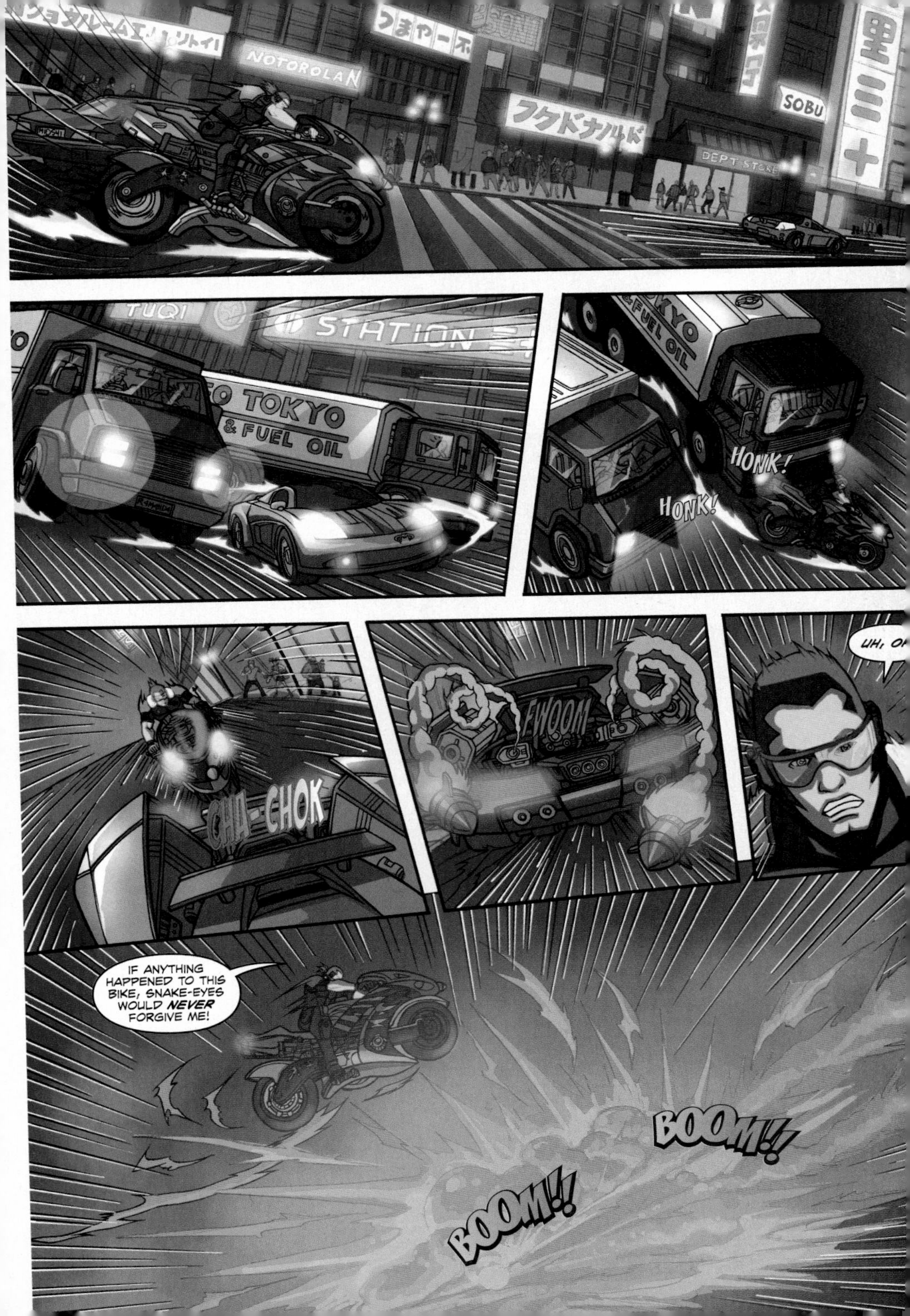
NOTOROLAN
フクドナルド
SOBU
DEPT STORE
TUQI
STATION
TOKYO
& FUEL OIL
HONK!
HONK!
CHA-CHOK
FWOOM
UH, O
IF ANYTHING HAPPENED TO THIS BIKE, SNAKE-EYES WOULD ***NEVER*** FORGIVE ME!
BOOM!!
BOOM!!

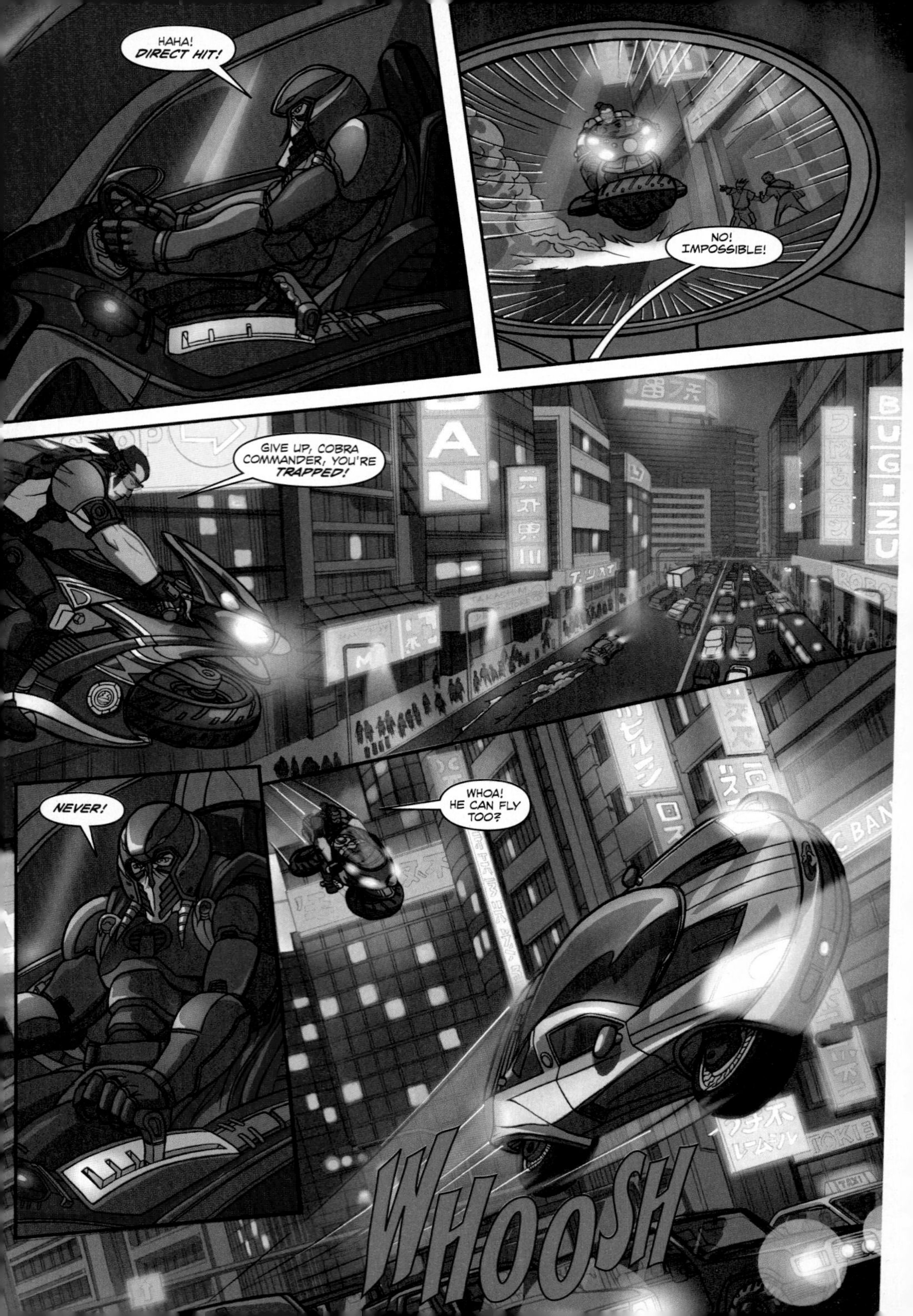
HAHA! DIRECT HIT!
NO! IMPOSSIBLE!
GIVE UP, COBRA COMMANDER, YOU'RE TRAPPED!
NEVER!
WHOA! HE CAN FLY TOO?
WHOOSH

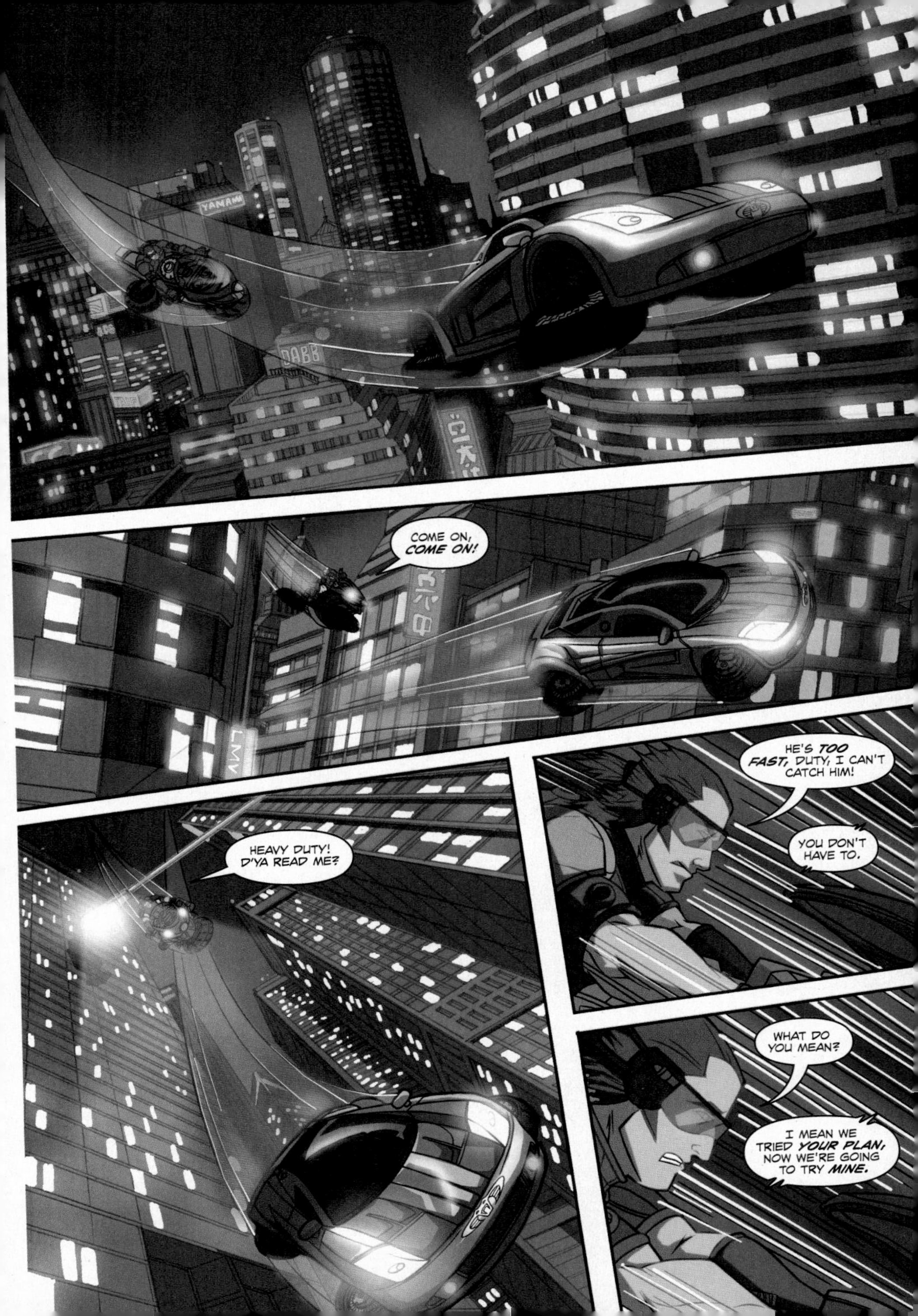
COME ON, *COME ON!*
HE'S *TOO FAST*, DUTY, I CAN'T CATCH HIM!
YOU DON'T HAVE TO.
HEAVY DUTY! D'YA READ ME?
WHAT DO YOU MEAN?
I MEAN WE TRIED *YOUR PLAN*, NOW WE'RE GOING TO TRY *MINE*.

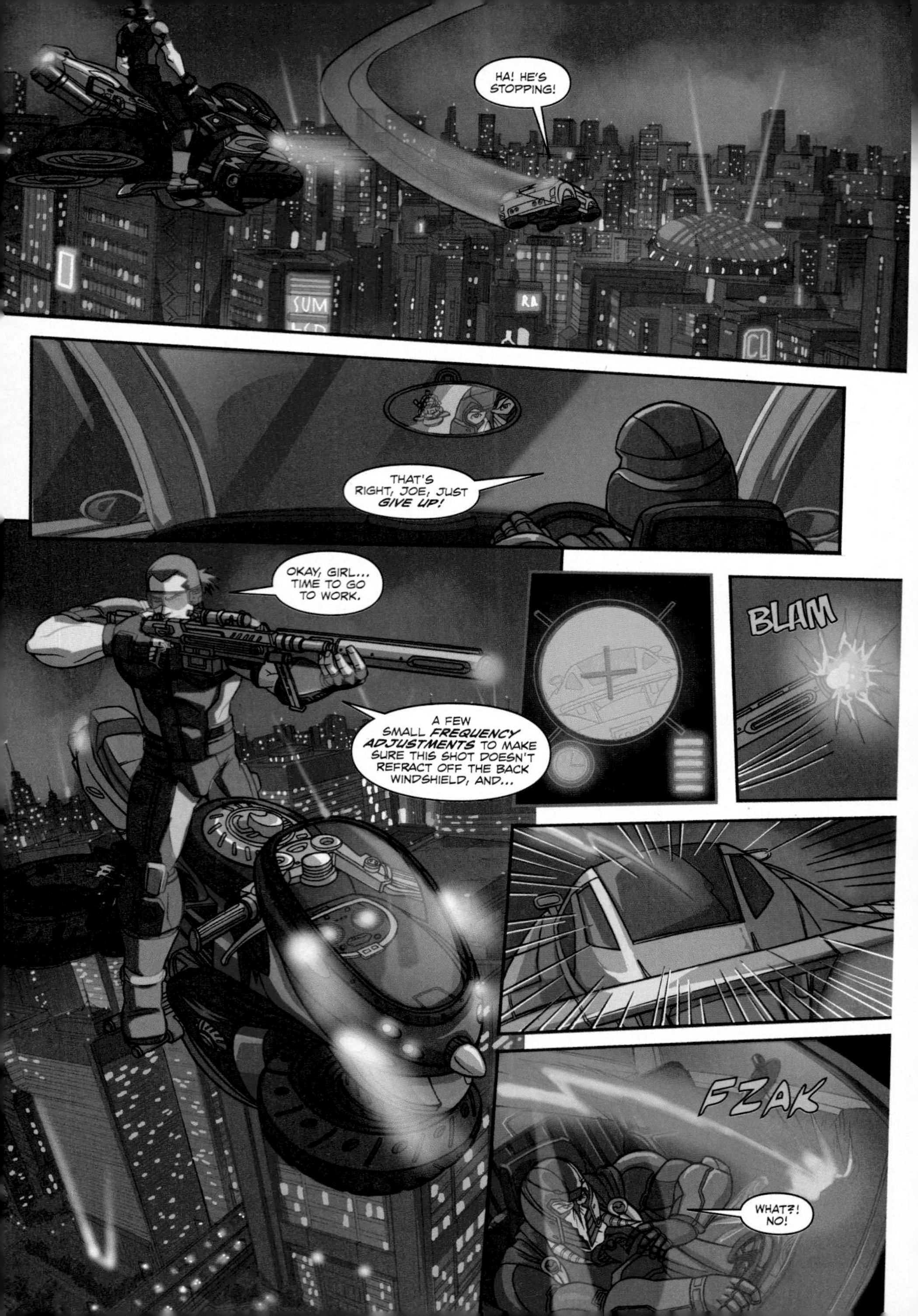
HA! HE'S STOPPING!
SUM
RA
CL
THAT'S RIGHT, JOE, JUST GIVE UP!
OKAY, GIRL... TIME TO GO TO WORK.
A FEW SMALL FREQUENCY ADJUSTMENTS TO MAKE SURE THIS SHOT DOESN'T REFRACT OFF THE BACK WINDSHIELD, AND...
BLAM
FZAK
WHAT?! NO!

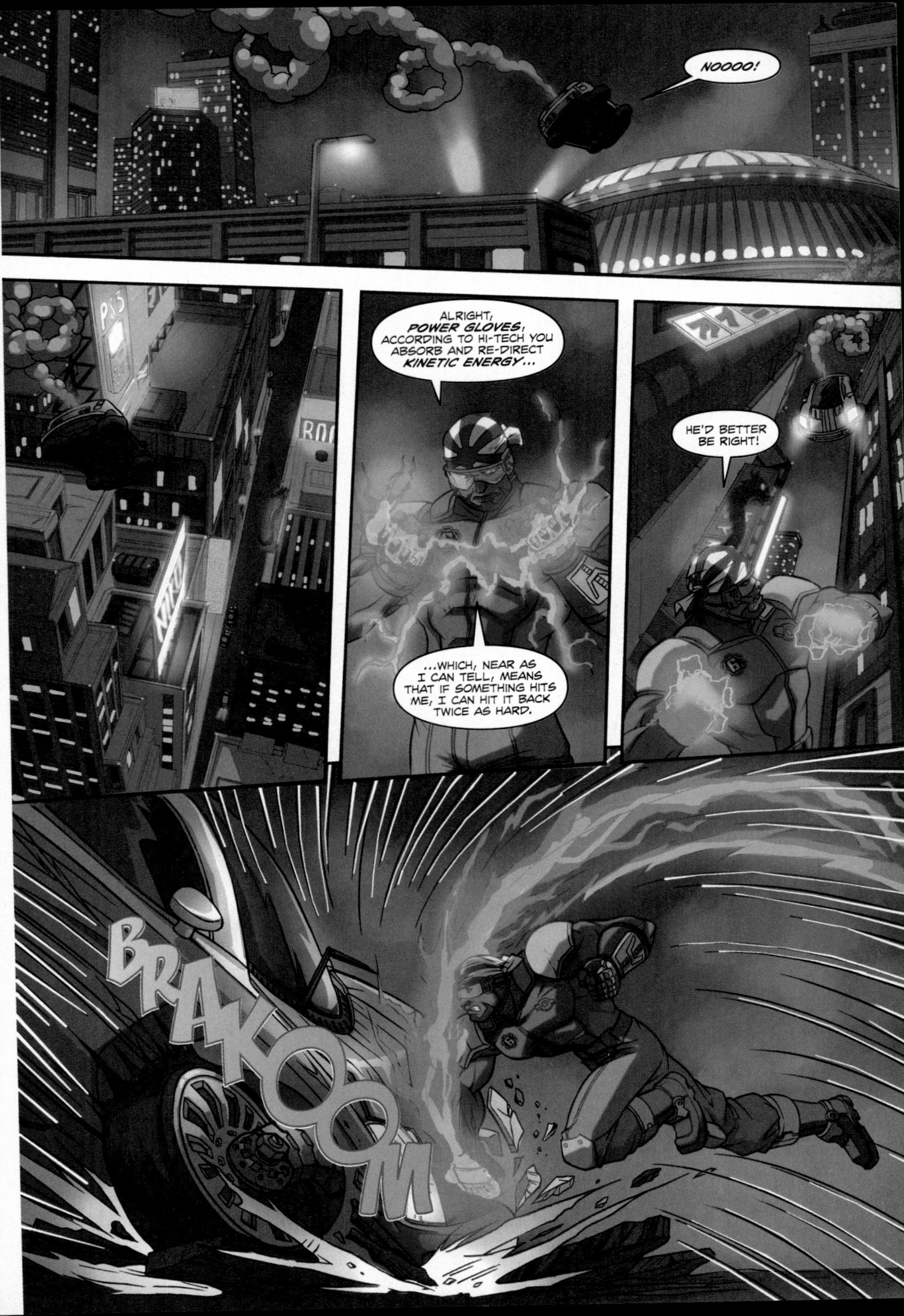
NOOOO!
ALRIGHT, POWER GLOVES, ACCORDING TO HI-TECH YOU ABSORB AND RE-DIRECT KINETIC ENERGY...
...WHICH, NEAR AS I CAN TELL, MEANS THAT IF SOMETHING HITS ME, I CAN HIT IT BACK TWICE AS HARD.
HE'D BETTER BE RIGHT!
BRAKOOOM

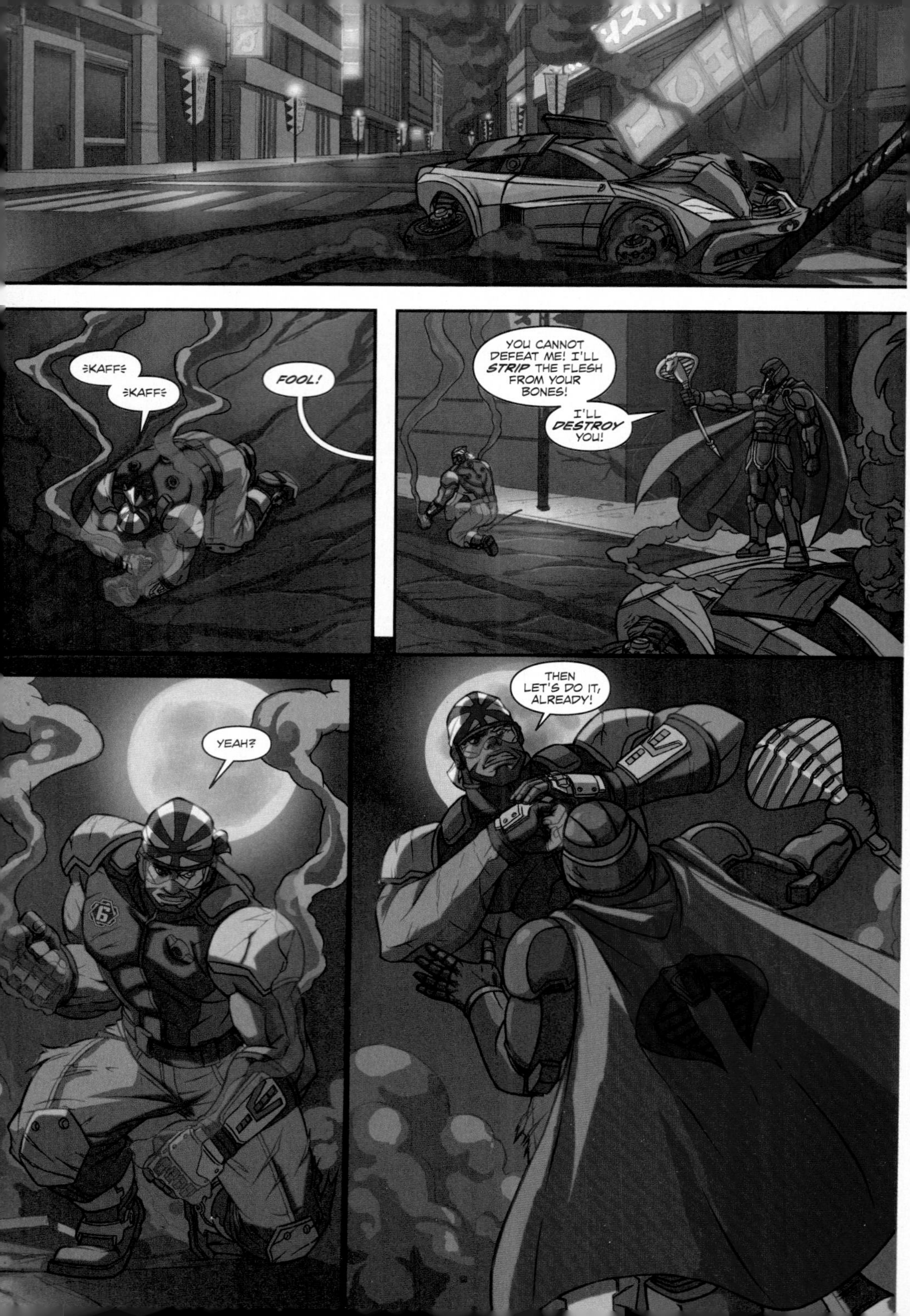

KAFF
KAFF
FOOL!
YOU CANNOT DEFEAT ME! I'LL STRIP THE FLESH FROM YOUR BONES!
I'LL DESTROY YOU!
YEAH?
THEN LET'S DO IT, ALREADY!

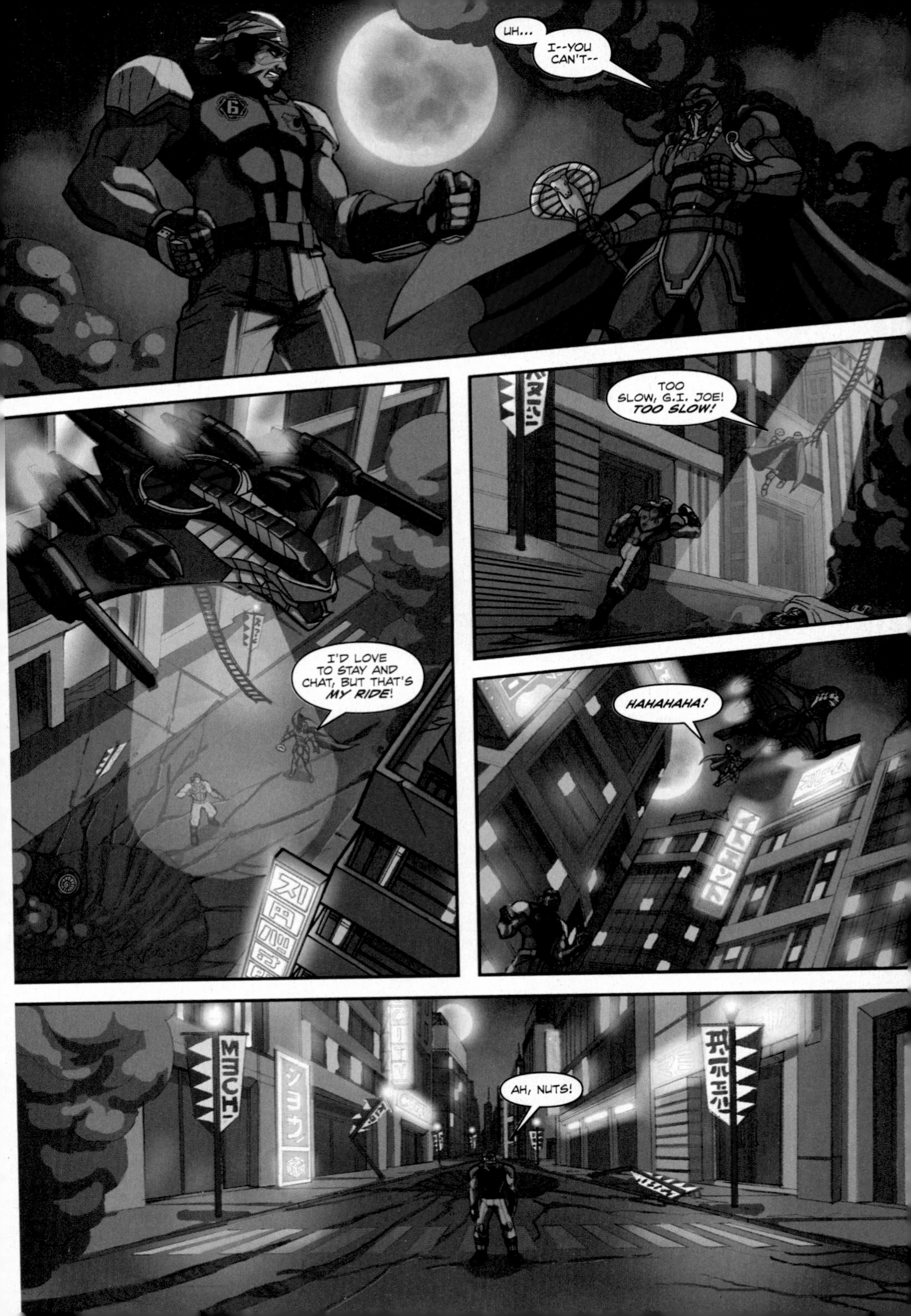
UH...
I--YOU CAN'T--
I'D LOVE TO STAY AND CHAT, BUT THAT'S *MY RIDE*!
TOO SLOW, G.I. JOE! *TOO SLOW!*
HAHAHAHA!
AH, NUTS!

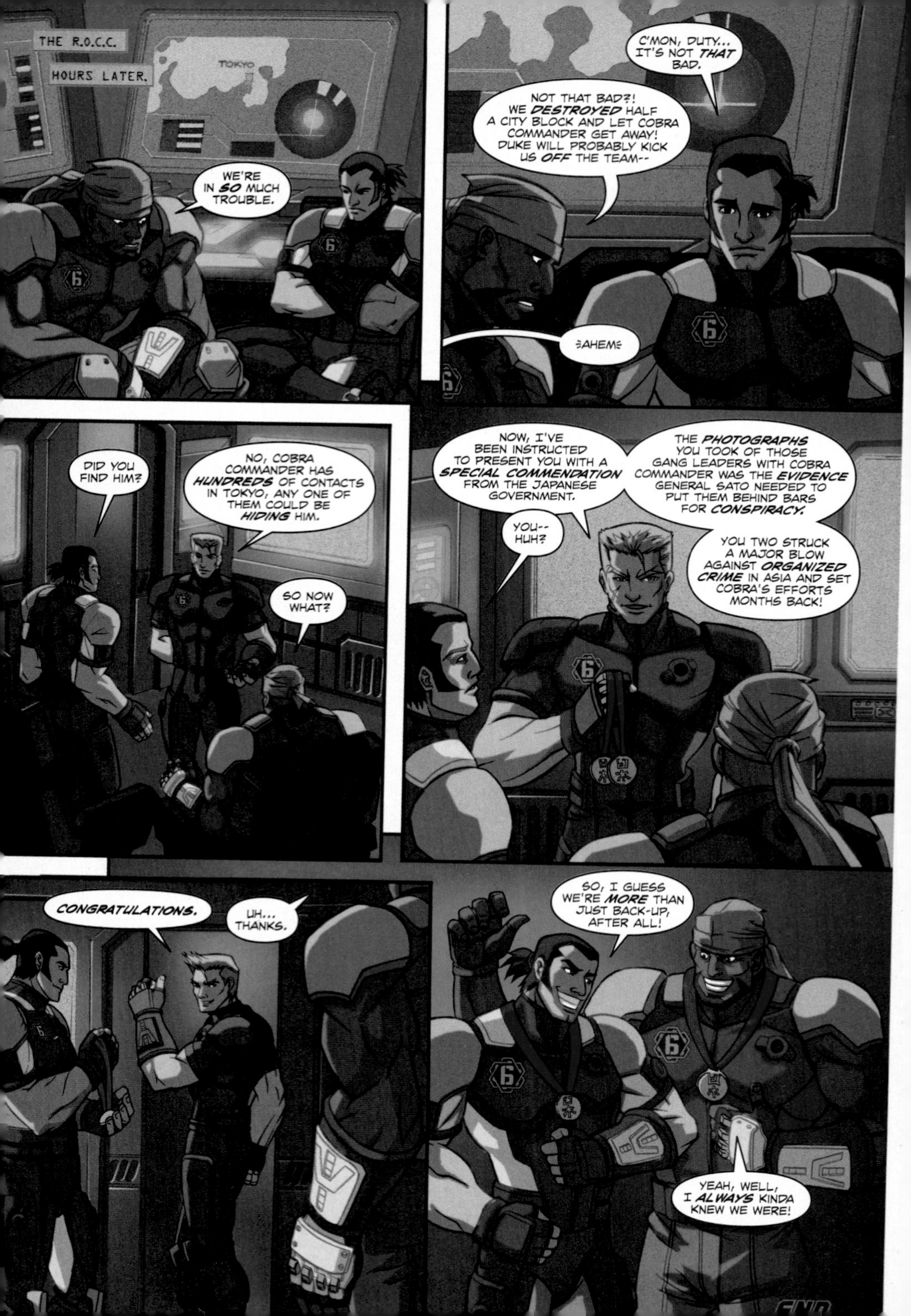
THE R.O.C.C.
HOURS LATER.
TOKYO
WE'RE IN SO MUCH TROUBLE.
C'MON, DUTY... IT'S NOT THAT BAD.
NOT THAT BAD?! WE DESTROYED HALF A CITY BLOCK AND LET COBRA COMMANDER GET AWAY! DUKE WILL PROBABLY KICK US OFF THE TEAM--
AHEM
DID YOU FIND HIM?
NO, COBRA COMMANDER HAS HUNDREDS OF CONTACTS IN TOKYO, ANY ONE OF THEM COULD BE HIDING HIM.
SO NOW WHAT?
NOW, I'VE BEEN INSTRUCTED TO PRESENT YOU WITH A SPECIAL COMMENDATION FROM THE JAPANESE GOVERNMENT.
YOU--HUH?
THE PHOTOGRAPHS YOU TOOK OF THOSE GANG LEADERS WITH COBRA COMMANDER WAS THE EVIDENCE GENERAL SATO NEEDED TO PUT THEM BEHIND BARS FOR CONSPIRACY.
YOU TWO STRUCK A MAJOR BLOW AGAINST ORGANIZED CRIME IN ASIA AND SET COBRA'S EFFORTS MONTHS BACK!
CONGRATULATIONS.
UH... THANKS.
SO, I GUESS WE'RE MORE THAN JUST BACK-UP, AFTER ALL!
YEAH, WELL, I ALWAYS KINDA KNEW WE WERE!

SIGMA 6 is the code name for a new group of covert G.I. JOE operatives with highly specialized capabilities. They use innovative technology and gear designed exclusively for each of their missions. Working against them is the evil COBRA organization, whose goal is to take control of the world by sabotage, espionage and outright destruction. SIGMA 6 fights them at every turn and provides a swift solution to critical situations around the globe.

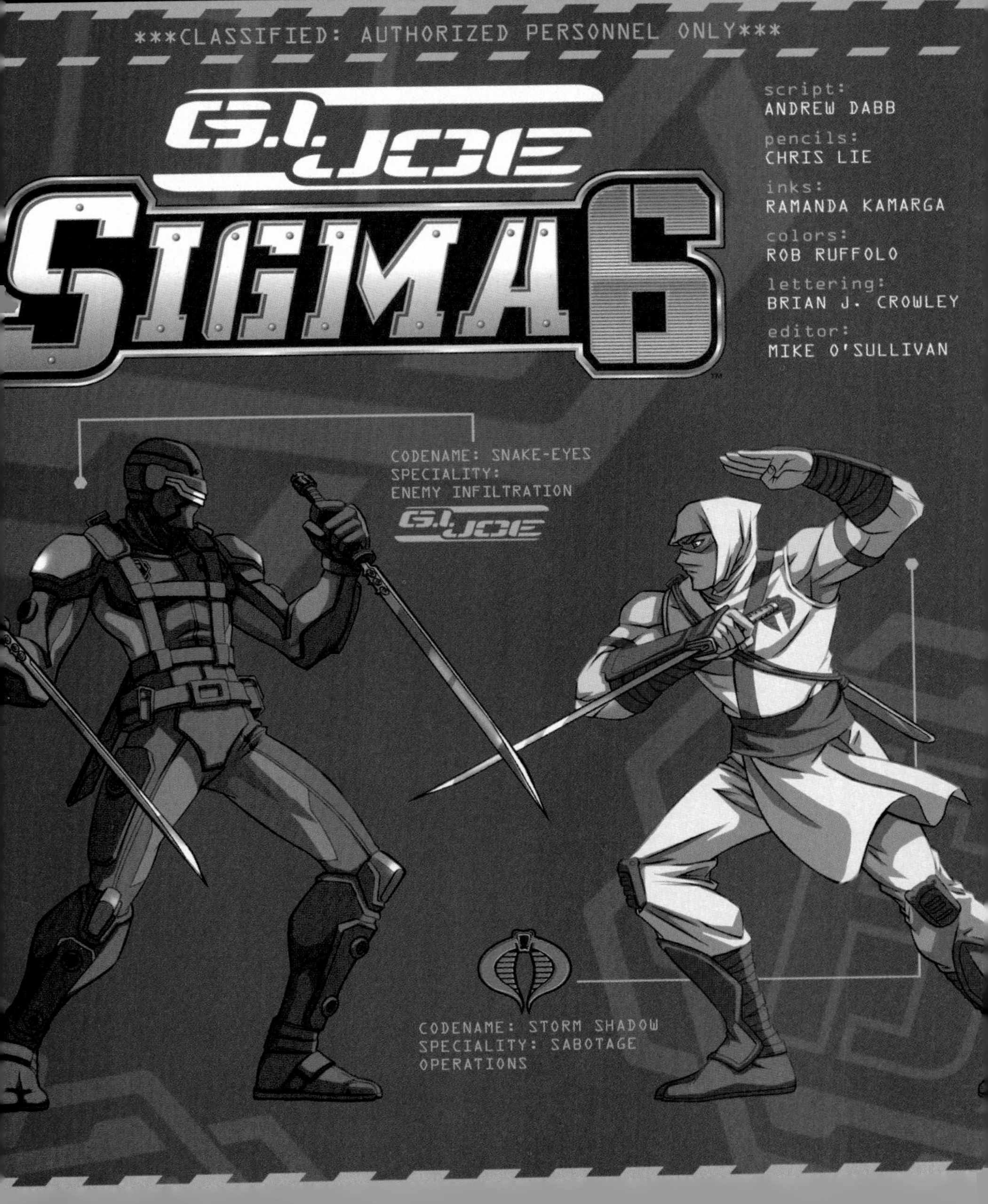

CLASSIFIED: AUTHORIZED PERSONNEL ONLY
G.I. JOE
SIGMA 6
script:
ANDREW DABB
pencils:
CHRIS LIE
inks:
RAMANDA KAMARGA
colors:
ROB RUFFOLO
lettering:
BRIAN J. CROWLEY
editor:
MIKE O'SULLIVAN
CODENAME: SNAKE-EYES
SPECIALITY:
ENEMY INFILTRATION
G.I. JOE
CODENAME: STORM SHADOW
SPECIALITY: SABOTAGE
OPERATIONS

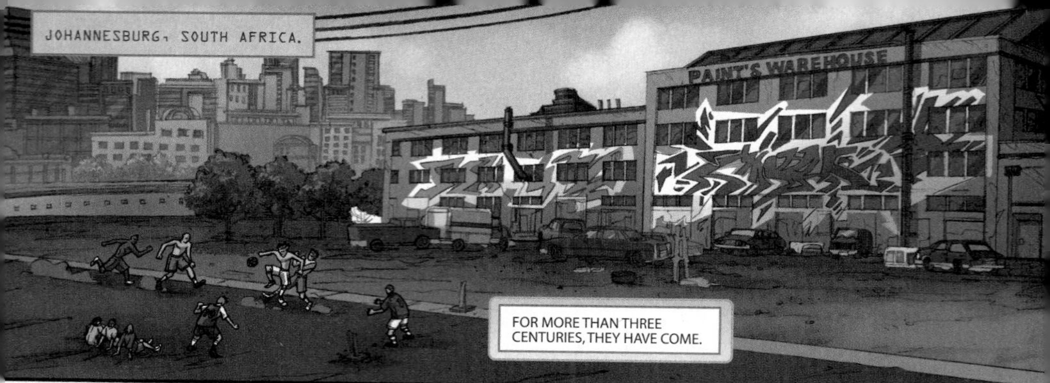
JOHANNESBURG, SOUTH AFRICA.
PAINT'S WAREHOUSE
FOR MORE THAN THREE CENTURIES, THEY HAVE COME.

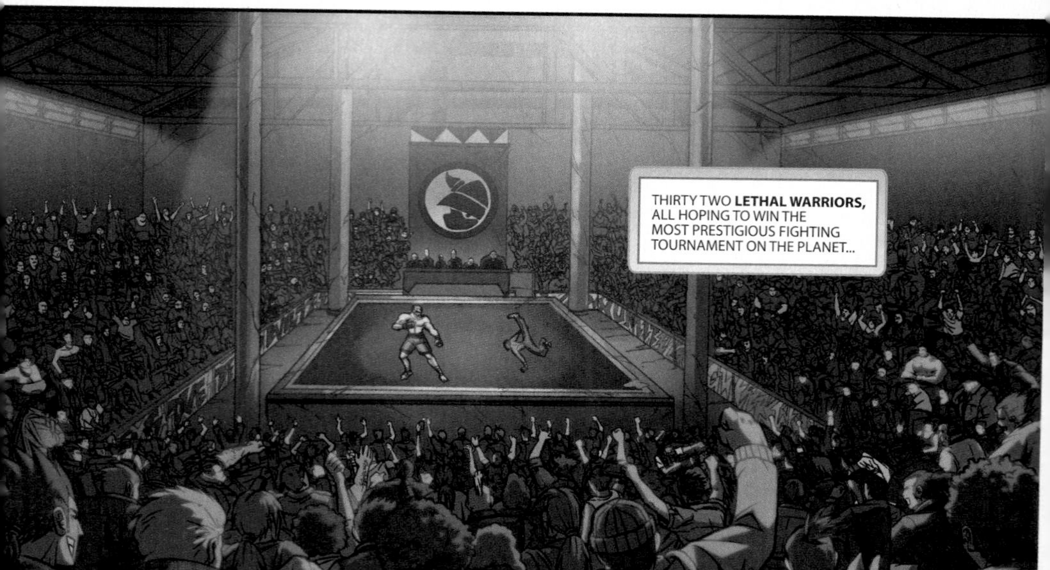
THIRTY TWO **LETHAL WARRIORS,** ALL HOPING TO WIN THE MOST PRESTIGIOUS FIGHTING TOURNAMENT ON THE PLANET...

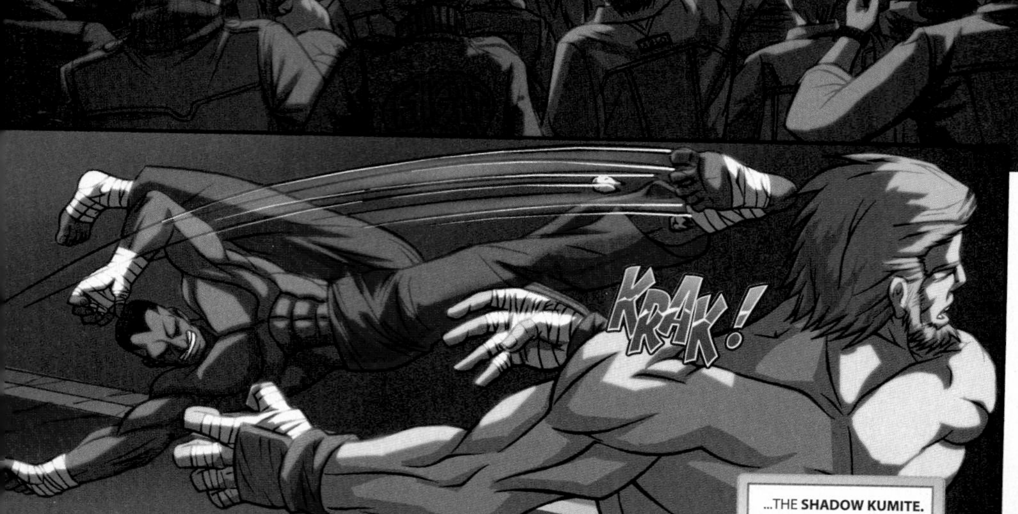
KRAK!
...THE **SHADOW KUMITE.**

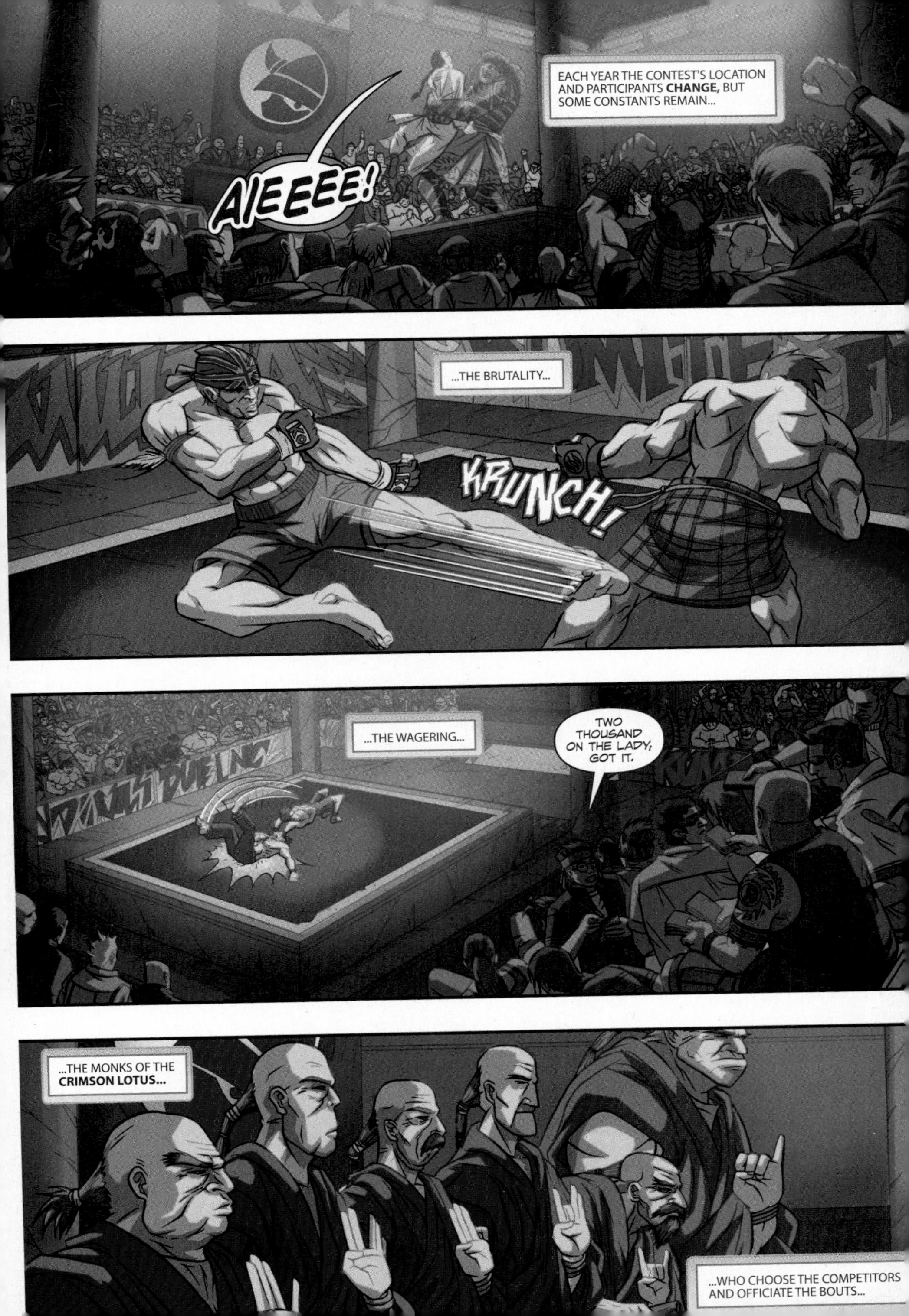
EACH YEAR THE CONTEST'S LOCATION AND PARTICIPANTS **CHANGE,** BUT SOME CONSTANTS REMAIN...
AIEEEEE!
...THE BRUTALITY...
KRUNCH!
...THE WAGERING...
TWO THOUSAND ON THE LADY, GOT IT.
...THE MONKS OF THE **CRIMSON LOTUS...**
...WHO CHOOSE THE COMPETITORS AND OFFICIATE THE BOUTS...

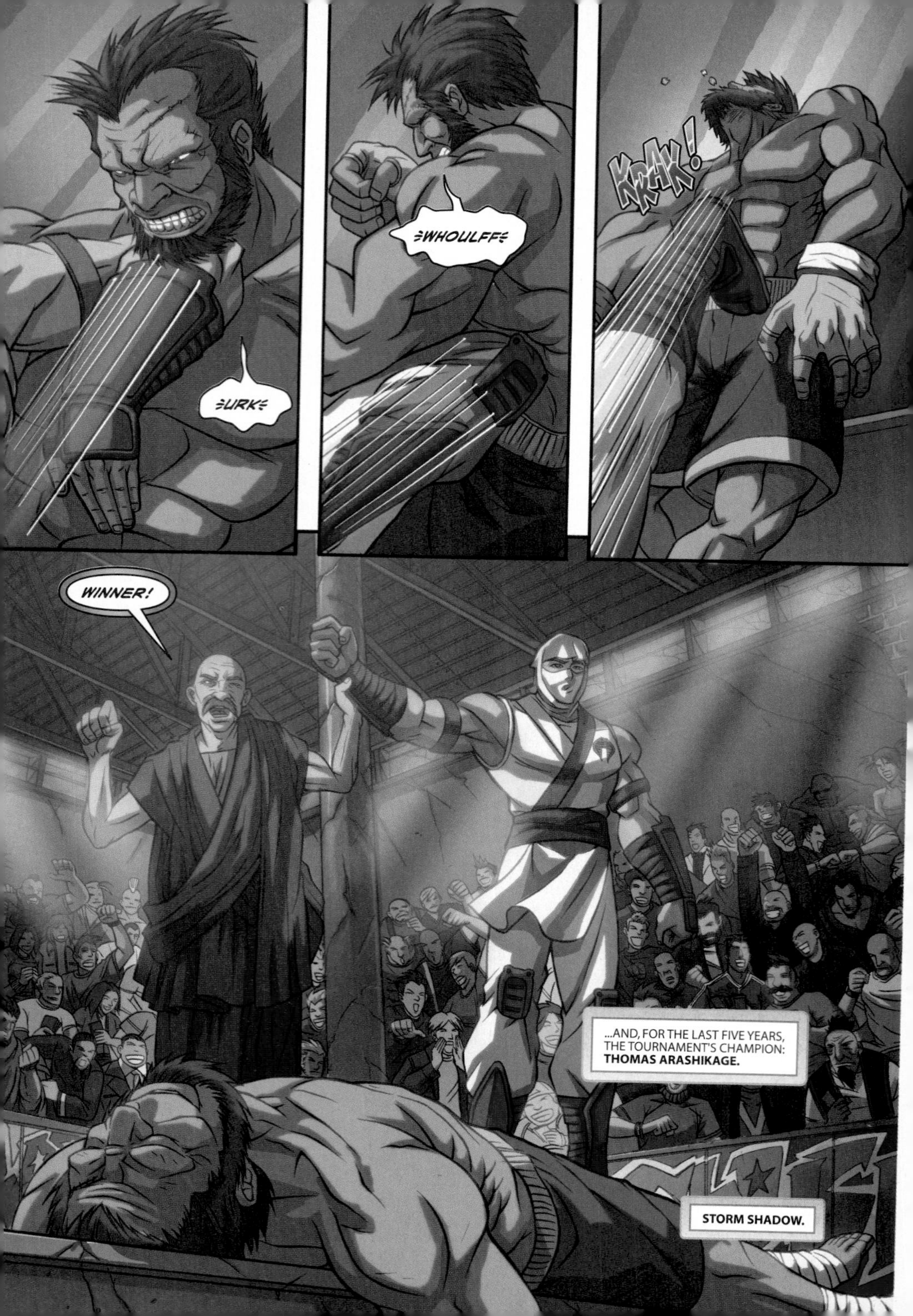
URK
WHOULFF
KRAK!
WINNER!
...AND, FOR THE LAST FIVE YEARS, THE TOURNAMENT'S CHAMPION: **THOMAS ARASHIKAGE.**
STORM SHADOW.

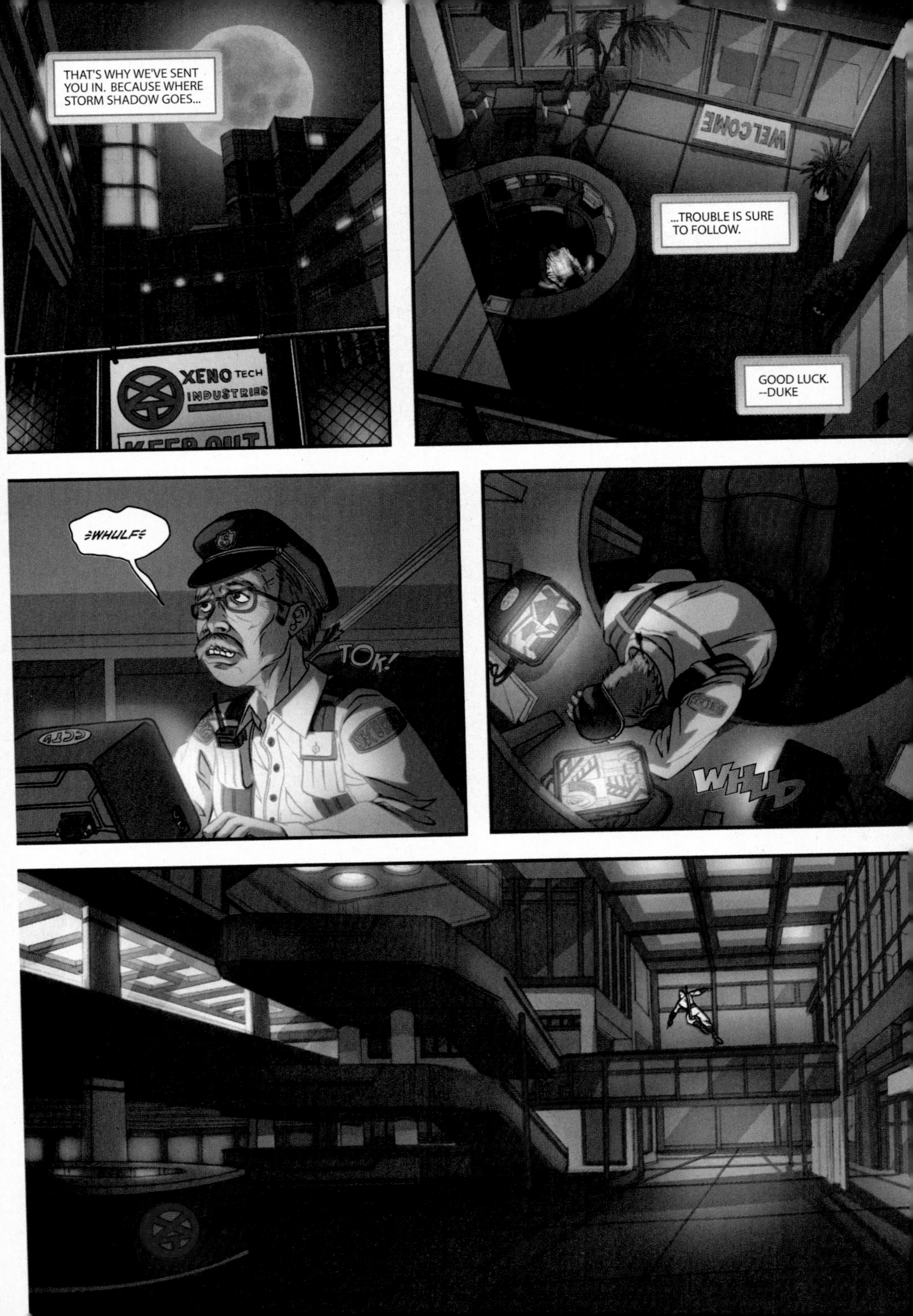
THAT'S WHY WE'VE SENT YOU IN. BECAUSE WHERE STORM SHADOW GOES...
XENO TECH INDUSTRIES
KEEP OUT
WELCOME
...TROUBLE IS SURE TO FOLLOW.
GOOD LUCK. --DUKE
WHULF
TOK!
WHUM

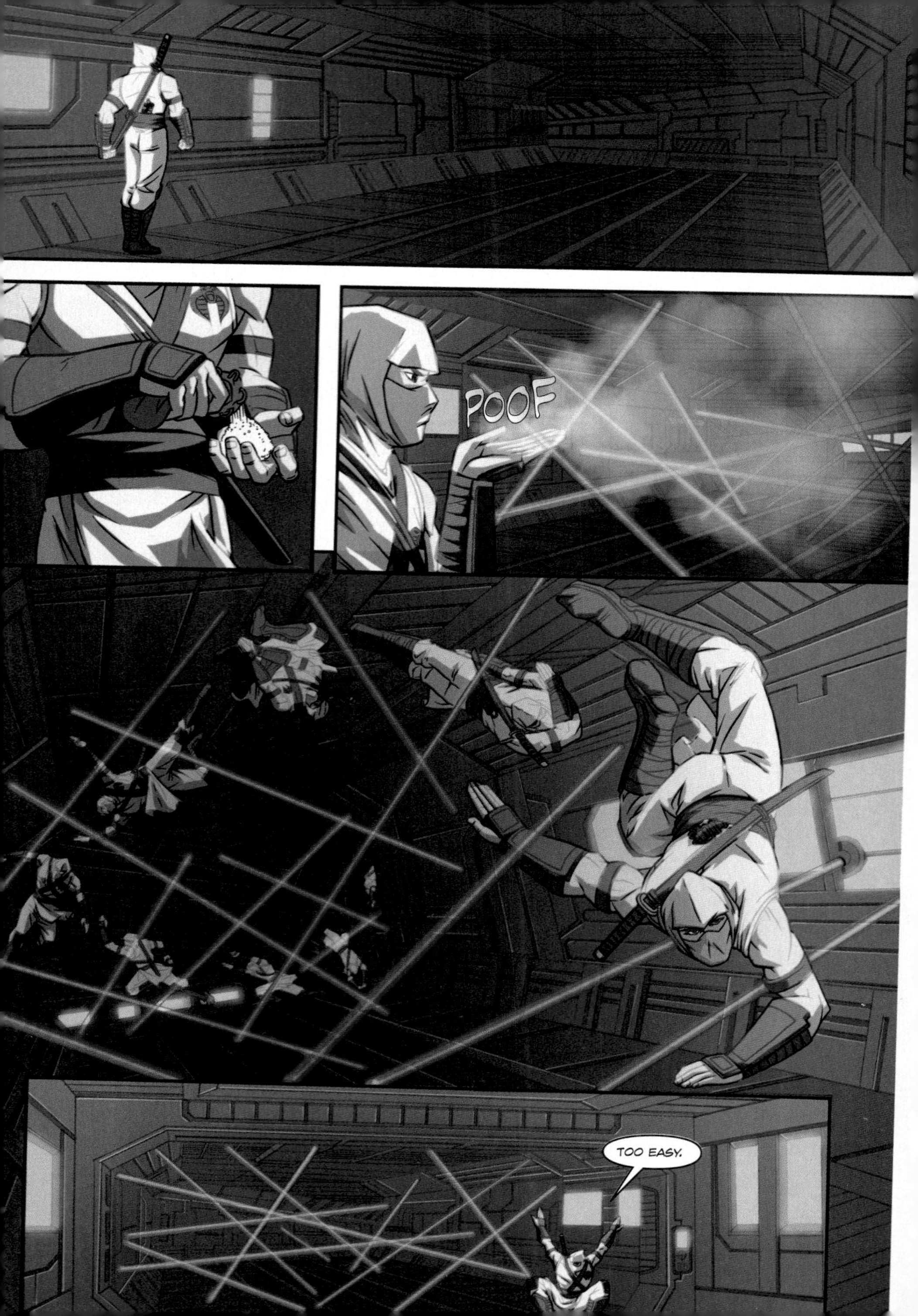
POOF
TOO EASY.

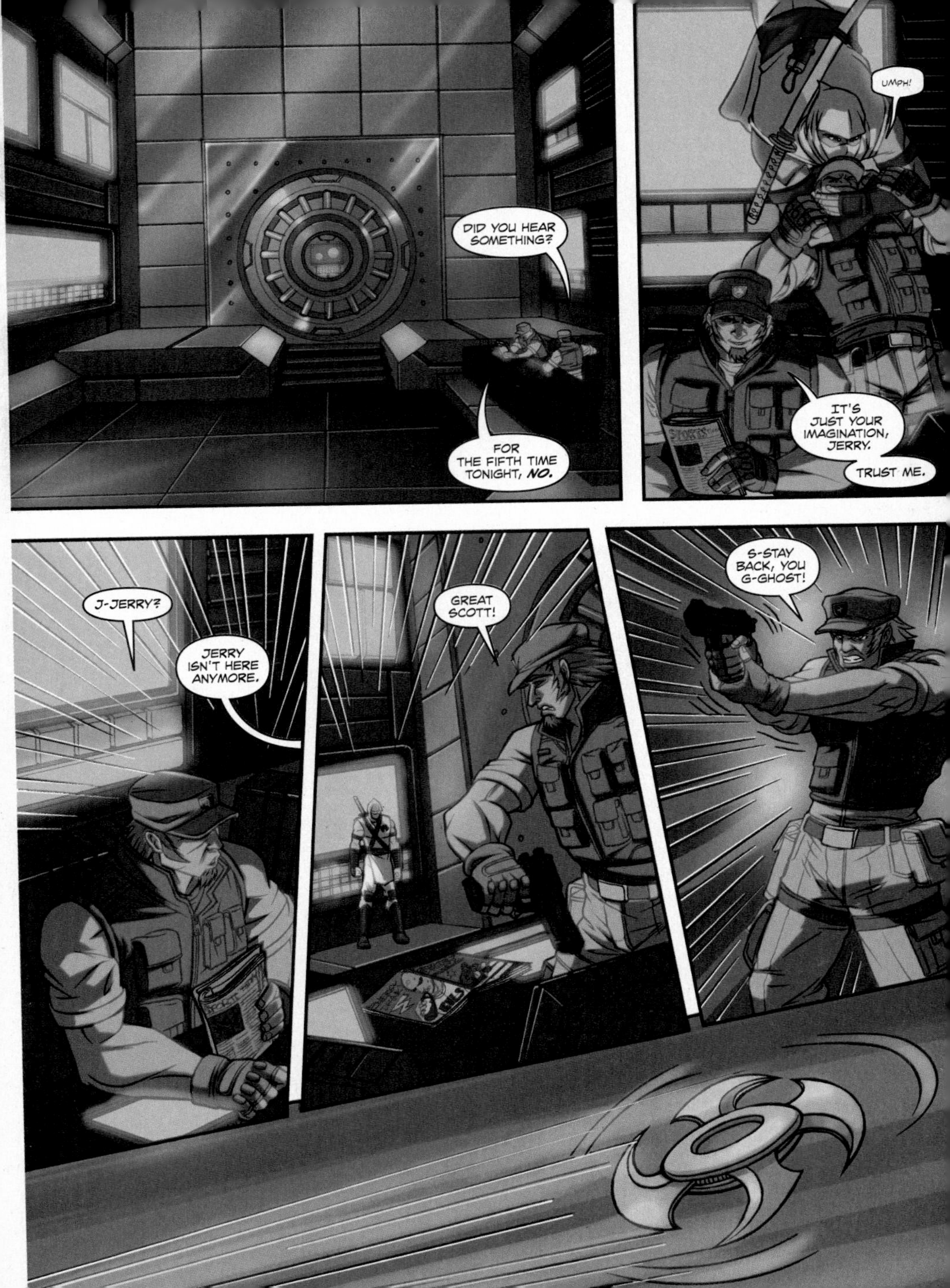
DID YOU HEAR SOMETHING?
FOR THE FIFTH TIME TONIGHT, NO.
UMPH!
IT'S JUST YOUR IMAGINATION, JERRY.
TRUST ME.
J-JERRY?
JERRY ISN'T HERE ANYMORE.
GREAT SCOTT!
S-STAY BACK, YOU G-GHOST!

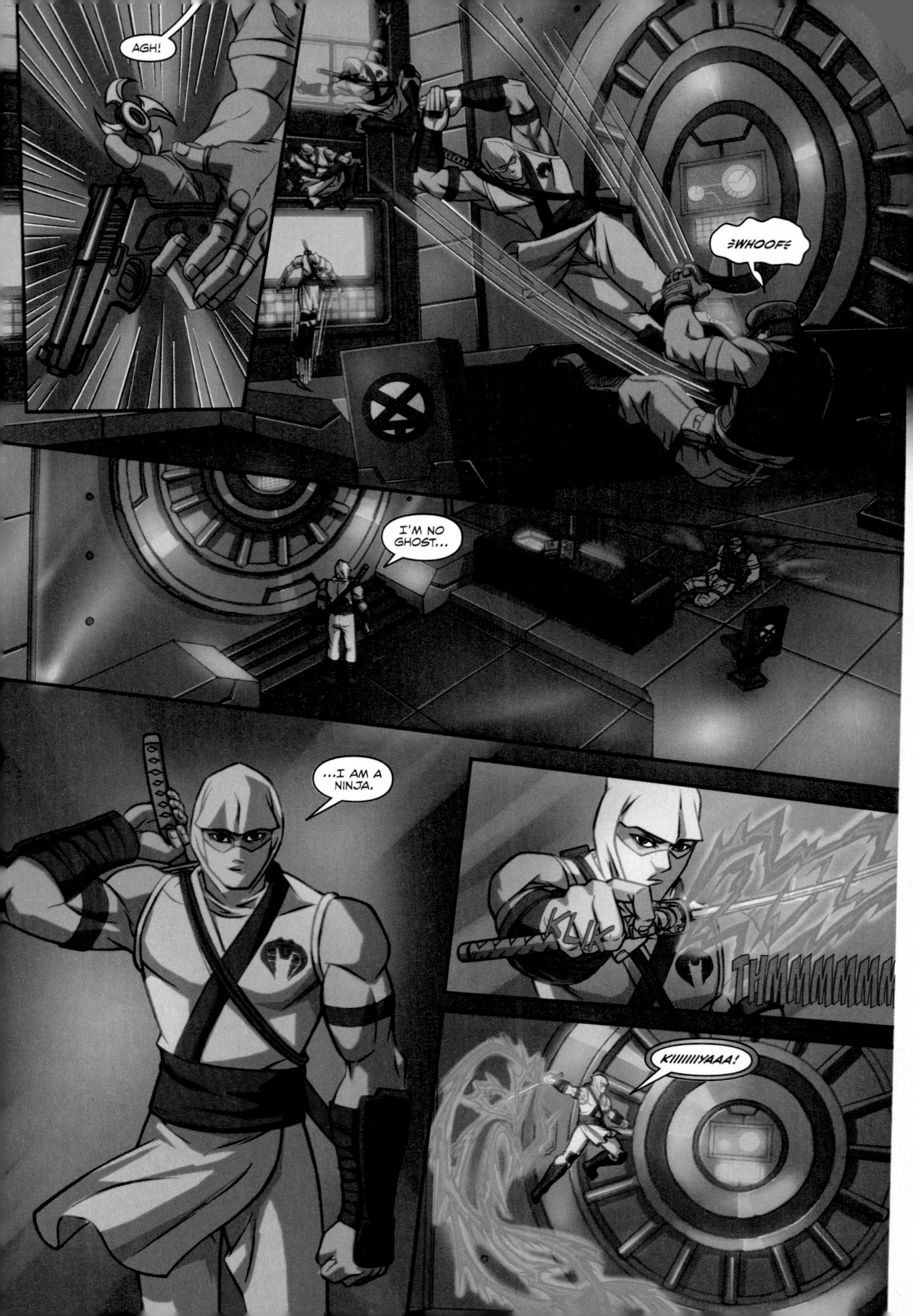
AGH!
WHOOF
I'M NO GHOST...
...I AM A NINJA.
KLIK
THMMMMMMM
KIIIIIIYAAA!

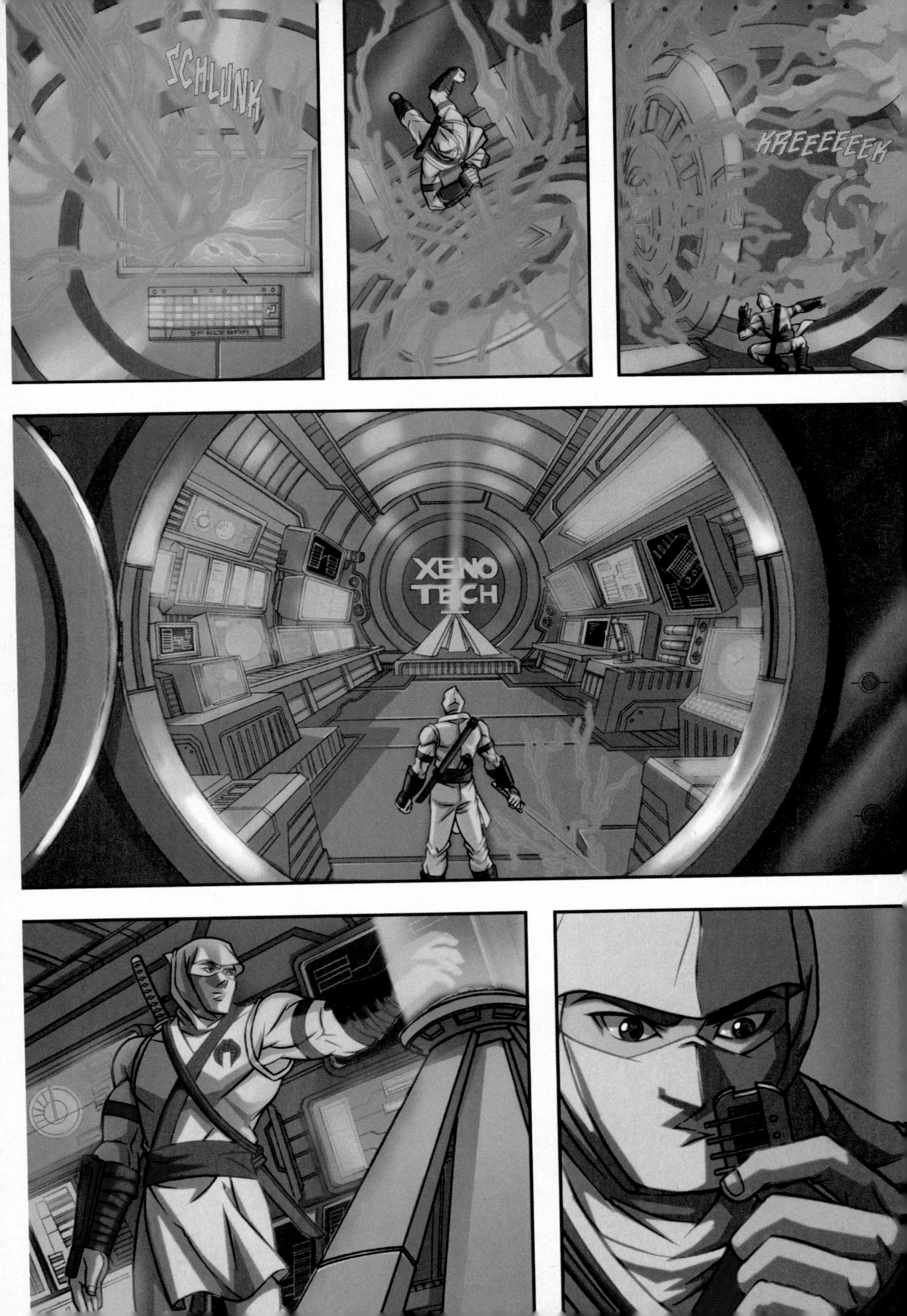
SCHLUNK
SPACEBAR
KREEEEEEK
XENO
TECH

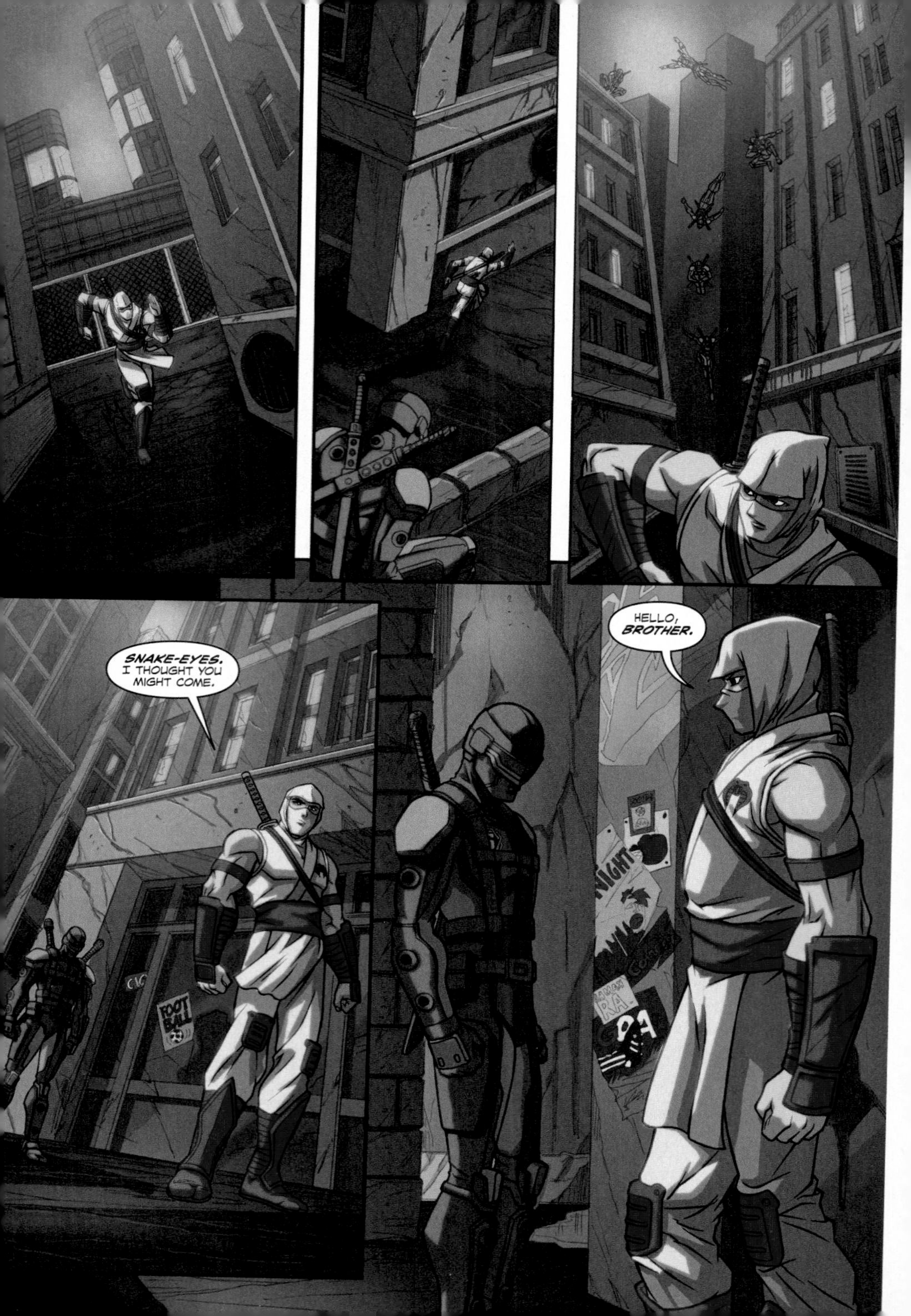

SNAKE-EYES. I THOUGHT YOU MIGHT COME.
HELLO, BROTHER.

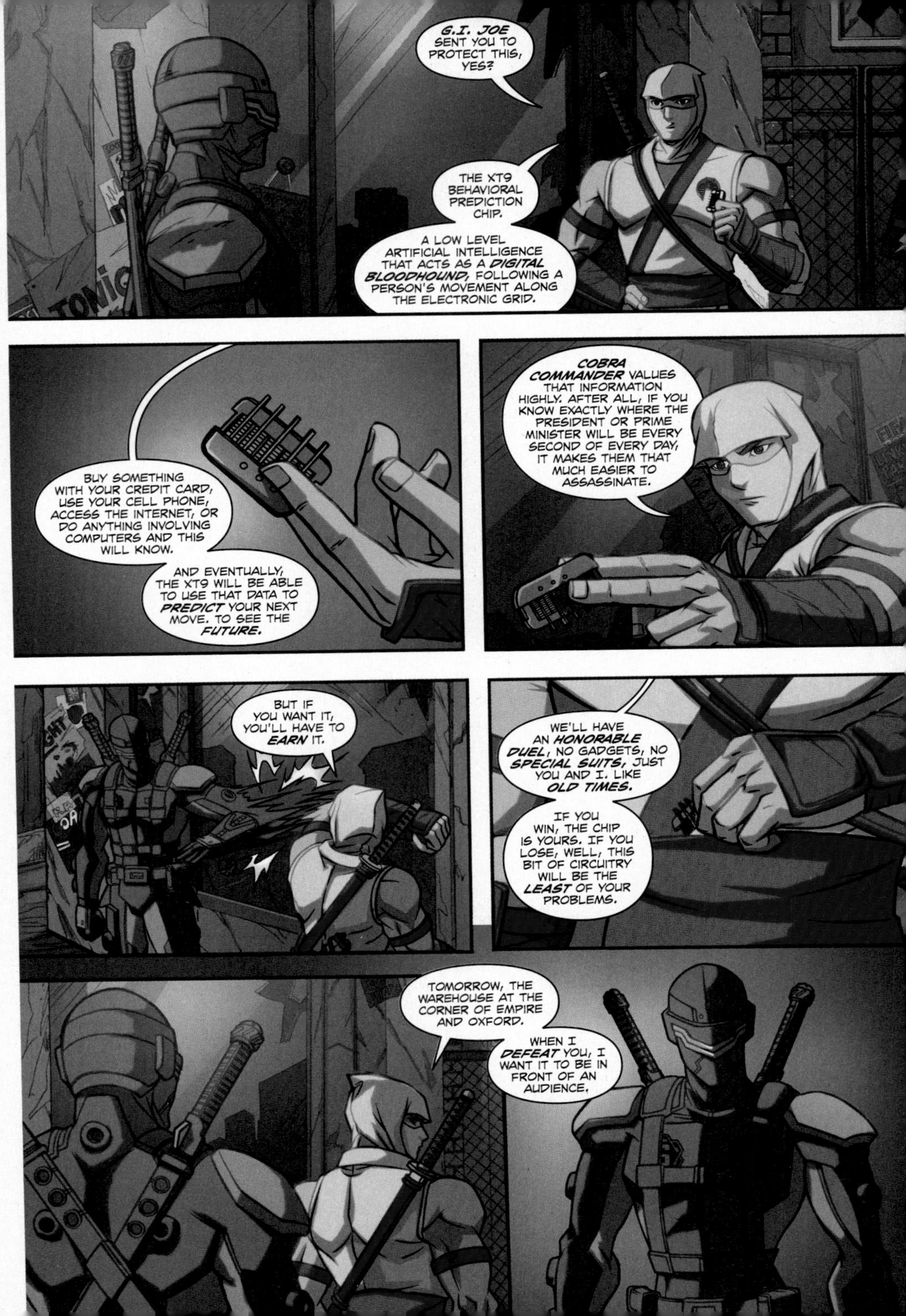
G.I. JOE SENT YOU TO PROTECT THIS, YES?
THE XT9 BEHAVIORAL PREDICTION CHIP.
A LOW LEVEL ARTIFICIAL INTELLIGENCE THAT ACTS AS A DIGITAL BLOODHOUND, FOLLOWING A PERSON'S MOVEMENT ALONG THE ELECTRONIC GRID.
BUY SOMETHING WITH YOUR CREDIT CARD, USE YOUR CELL PHONE, ACCESS THE INTERNET, OR DO ANYTHING INVOLVING COMPUTERS AND THIS WILL KNOW.
AND EVENTUALLY, THE XT9 WILL BE ABLE TO USE THAT DATA TO PREDICT YOUR NEXT MOVE. TO SEE THE FUTURE.
COBRA COMMANDER VALUES THAT INFORMATION HIGHLY. AFTER ALL, IF YOU KNOW EXACTLY WHERE THE PRESIDENT OR PRIME MINISTER WILL BE EVERY SECOND OF EVERY DAY, IT MAKES THEM THAT MUCH EASIER TO ASSASSINATE.
BUT IF YOU WANT IT, YOU'LL HAVE TO EARN IT.
WE'LL HAVE AN HONORABLE DUEL, NO GADGETS, NO SPECIAL SUITS, JUST YOU AND I. LIKE OLD TIMES.
IF YOU WIN, THE CHIP IS YOURS. IF YOU LOSE, WELL, THIS BIT OF CIRCUITRY WILL BE THE LEAST OF YOUR PROBLEMS.
TOMORROW, THE WAREHOUSE AT THE CORNER OF EMPIRE AND OXFORD.
WHEN I DEFEAT YOU, I WANT IT TO BE IN FRONT OF AN AUDIENCE.

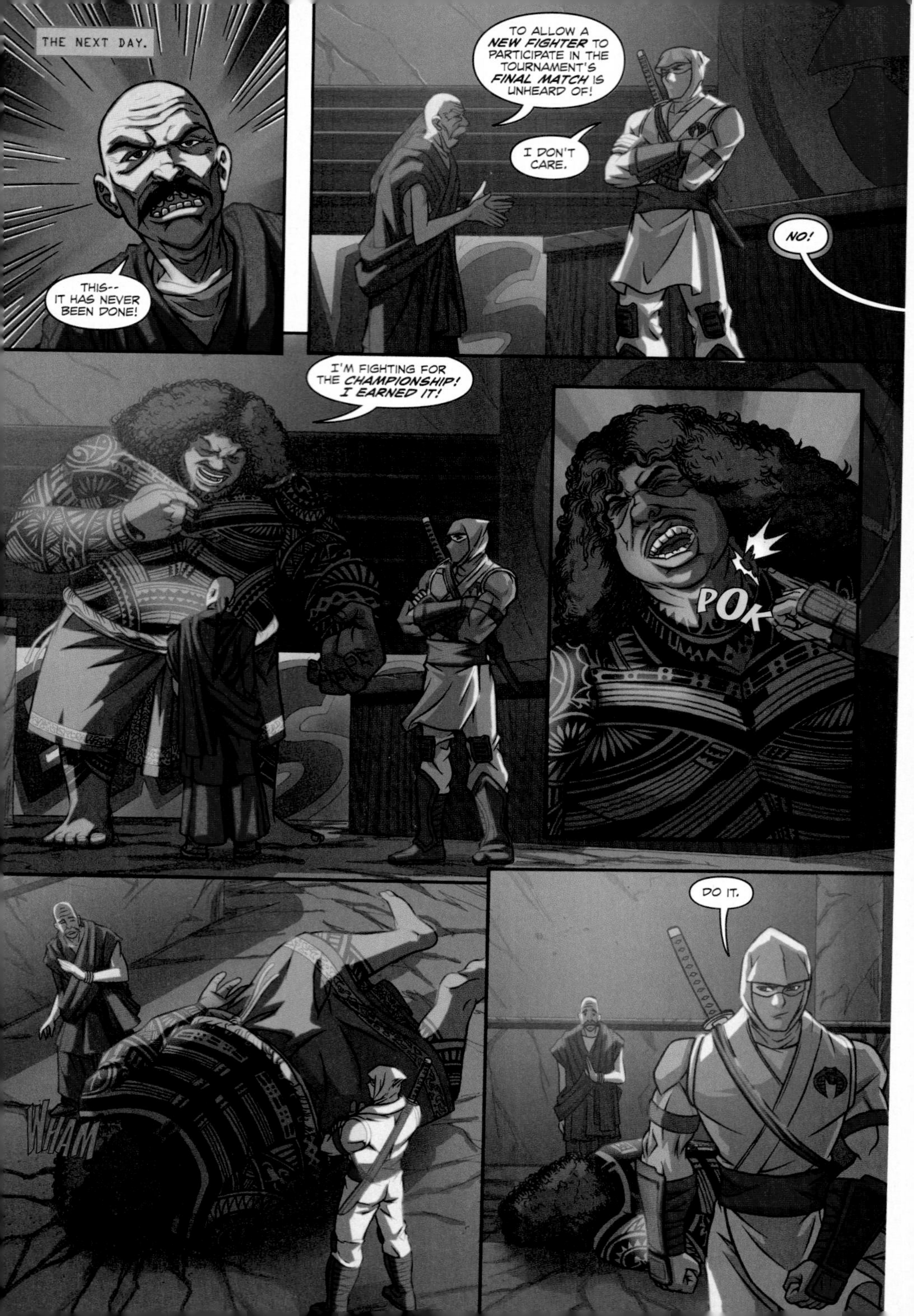
THE NEXT DAY.
THIS--
IT HAS NEVER BEEN DONE!
TO ALLOW A NEW FIGHTER TO PARTICIPATE IN THE TOURNAMENT'S FINAL MATCH IS UNHEARD OF!
I DON'T CARE.
NO!
I'M FIGHTING FOR THE CHAMPIONSHIP! I EARNED IT!
POK
WHAM
DO IT.

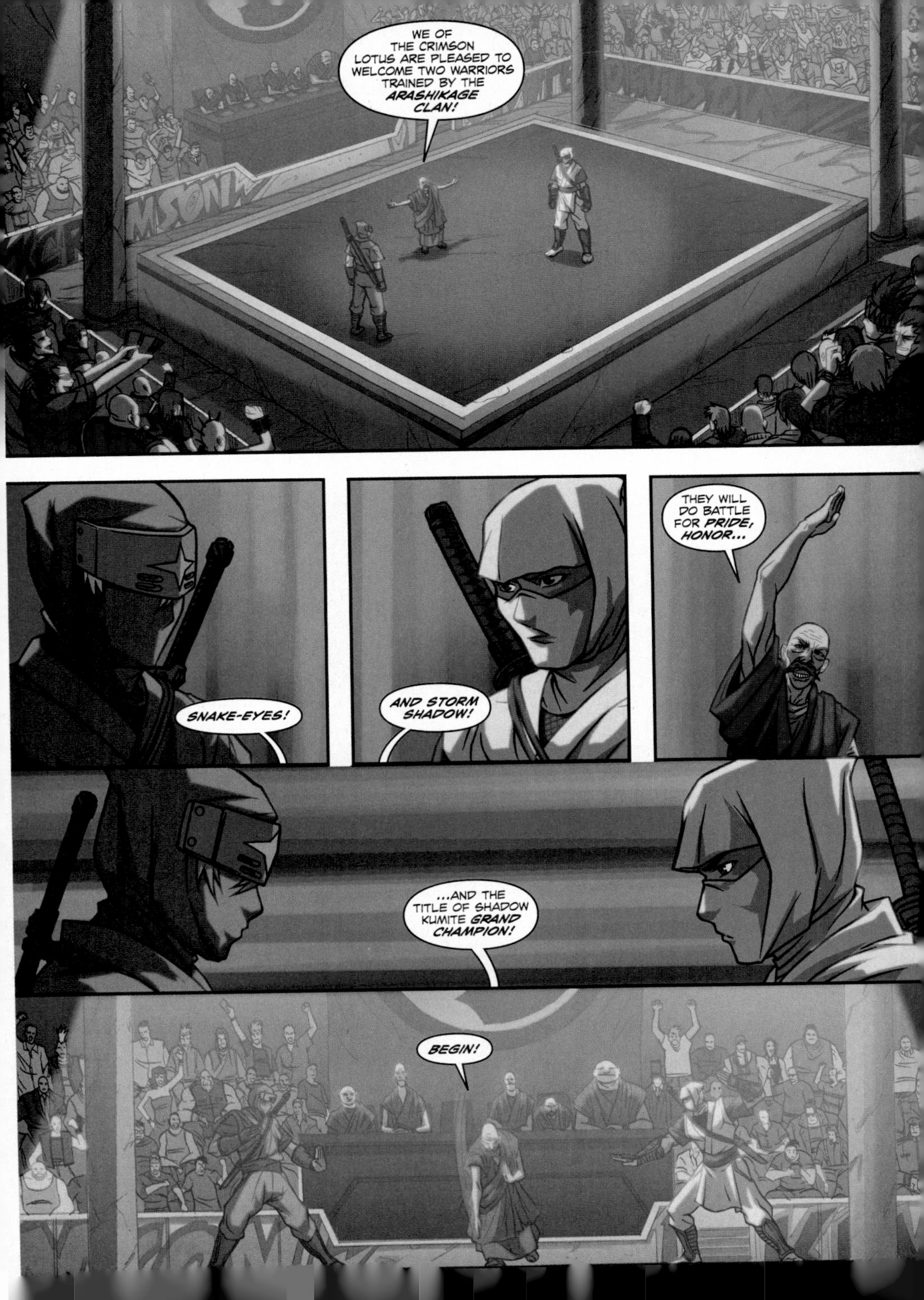
WE OF THE CRIMSON LOTUS ARE PLEASED TO WELCOME TWO WARRIORS TRAINED BY THE *ARASHIKAGE CLAN!*
SNAKE-EYES!
AND STORM SHADOW!
THEY WILL DO BATTLE FOR *PRIDE, HONOR...*
...AND THE TITLE OF SHADOW KUMITE *GRAND CHAMPION!*
BEGIN!

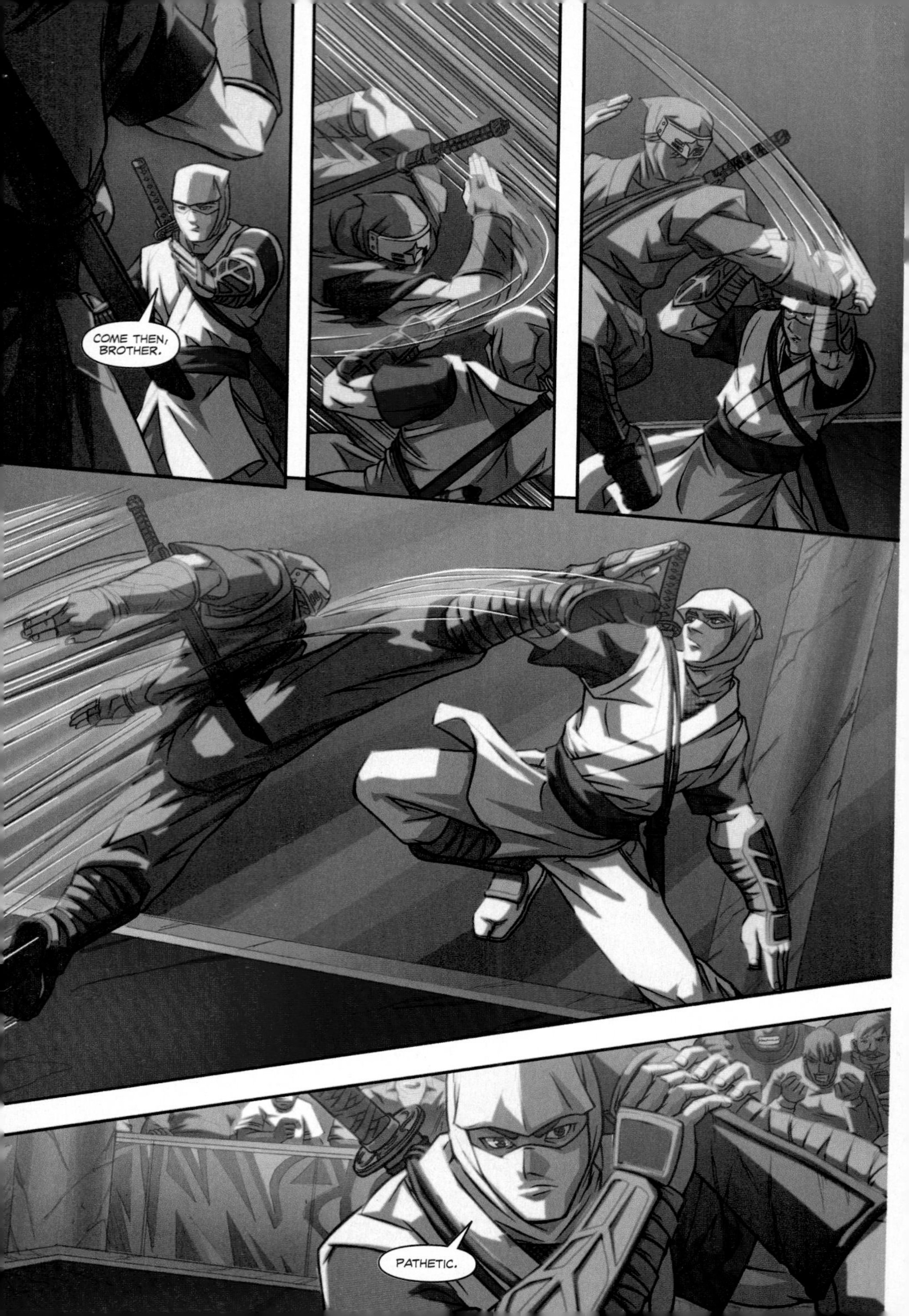
COME THEN, BROTHER.
PATHETIC.

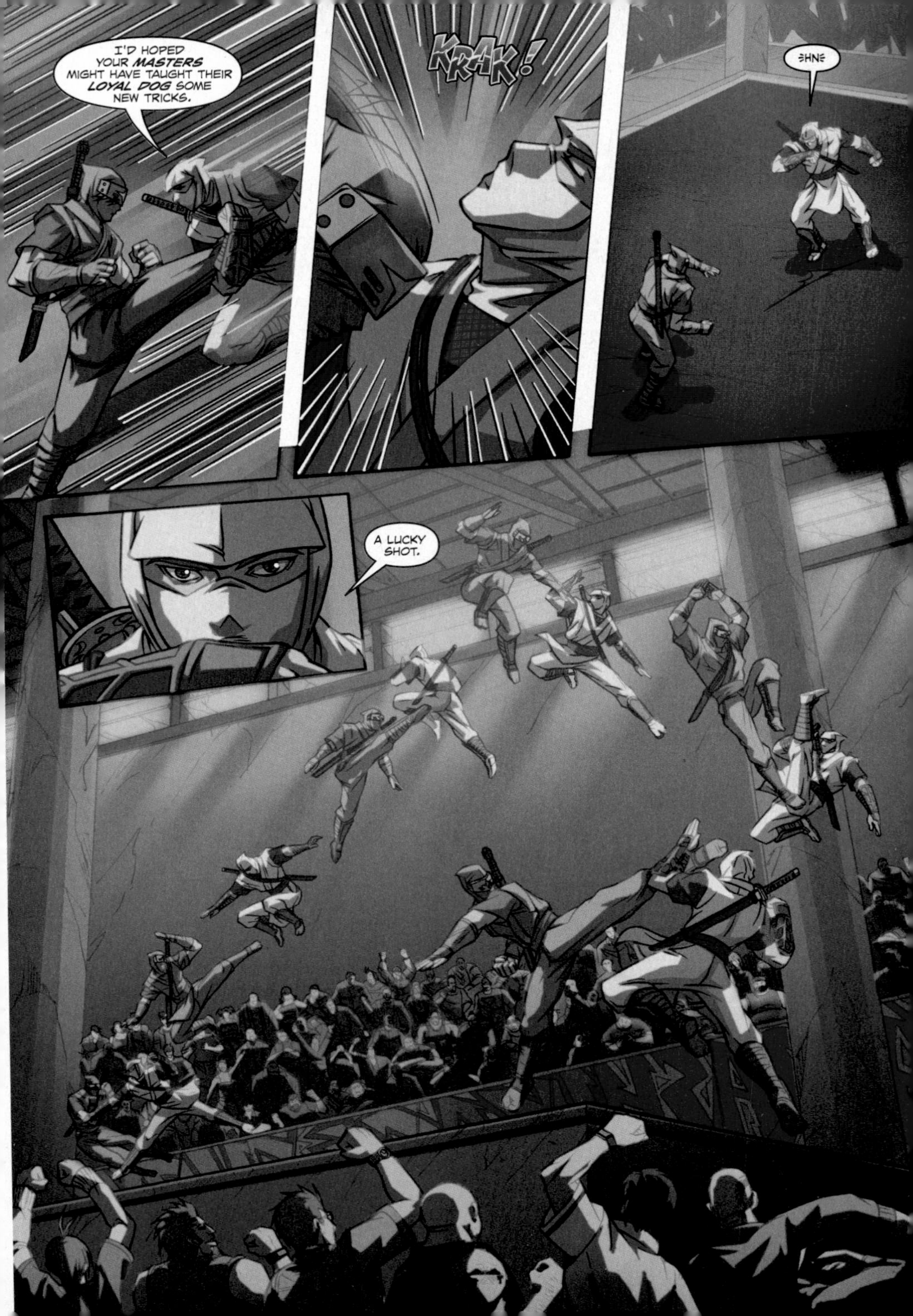
I'D HOPED YOUR MASTERS MIGHT HAVE TAUGHT THEIR LOYAL DOG SOME NEW TRICKS.
KRAK!
HN
A LUCKY SHOT.

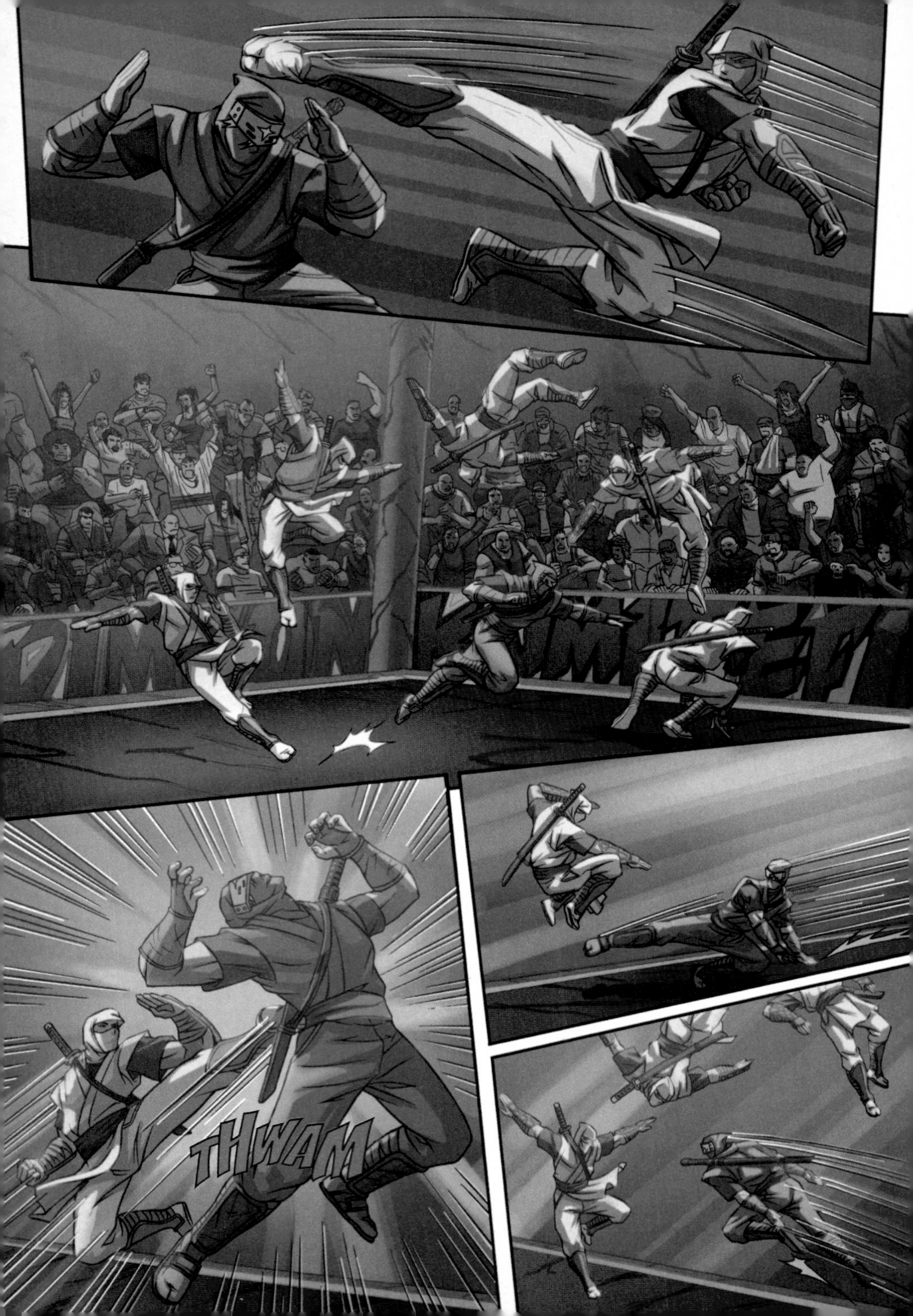
THWAM

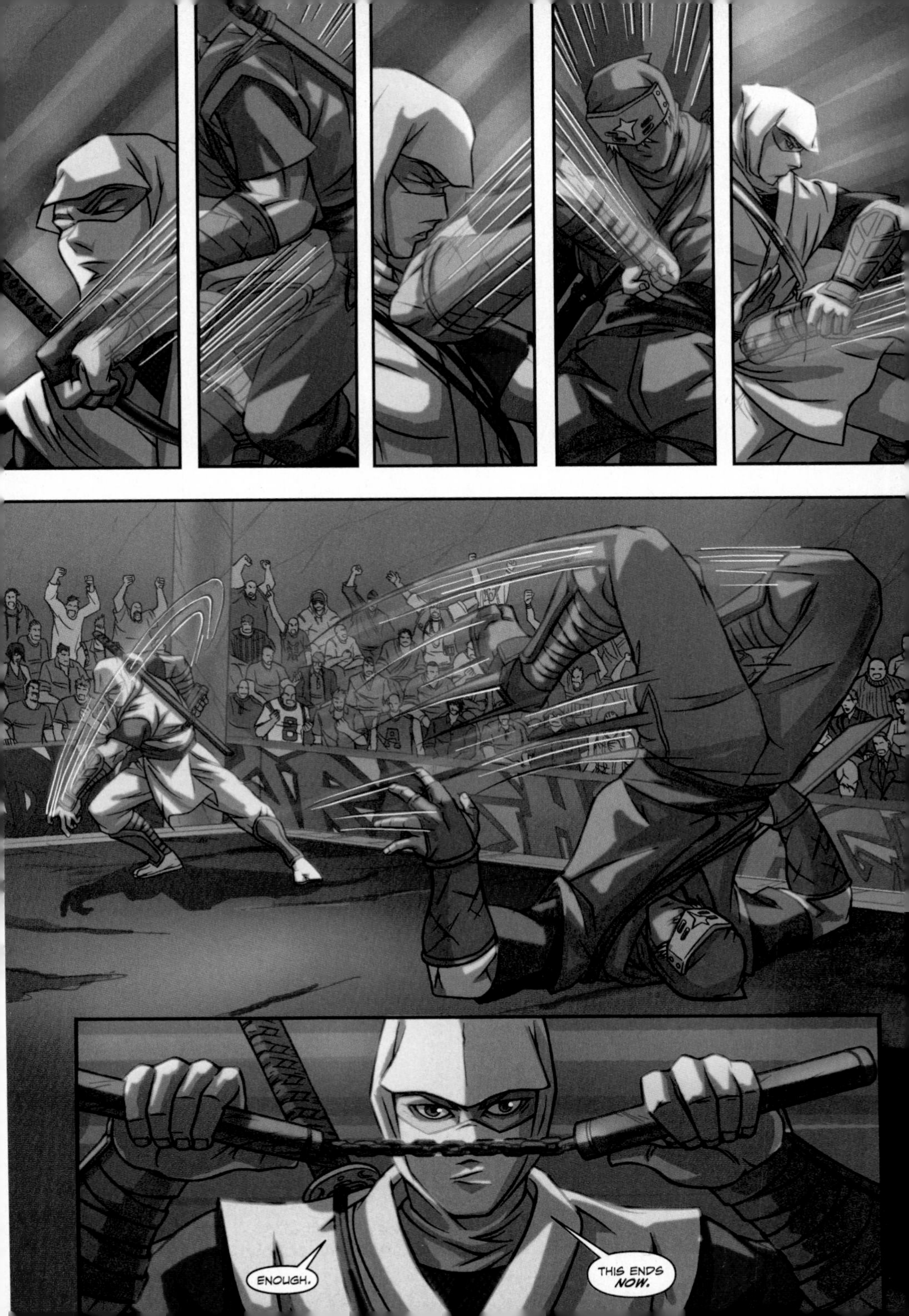
ENOUGH.
THIS ENDS NOW.

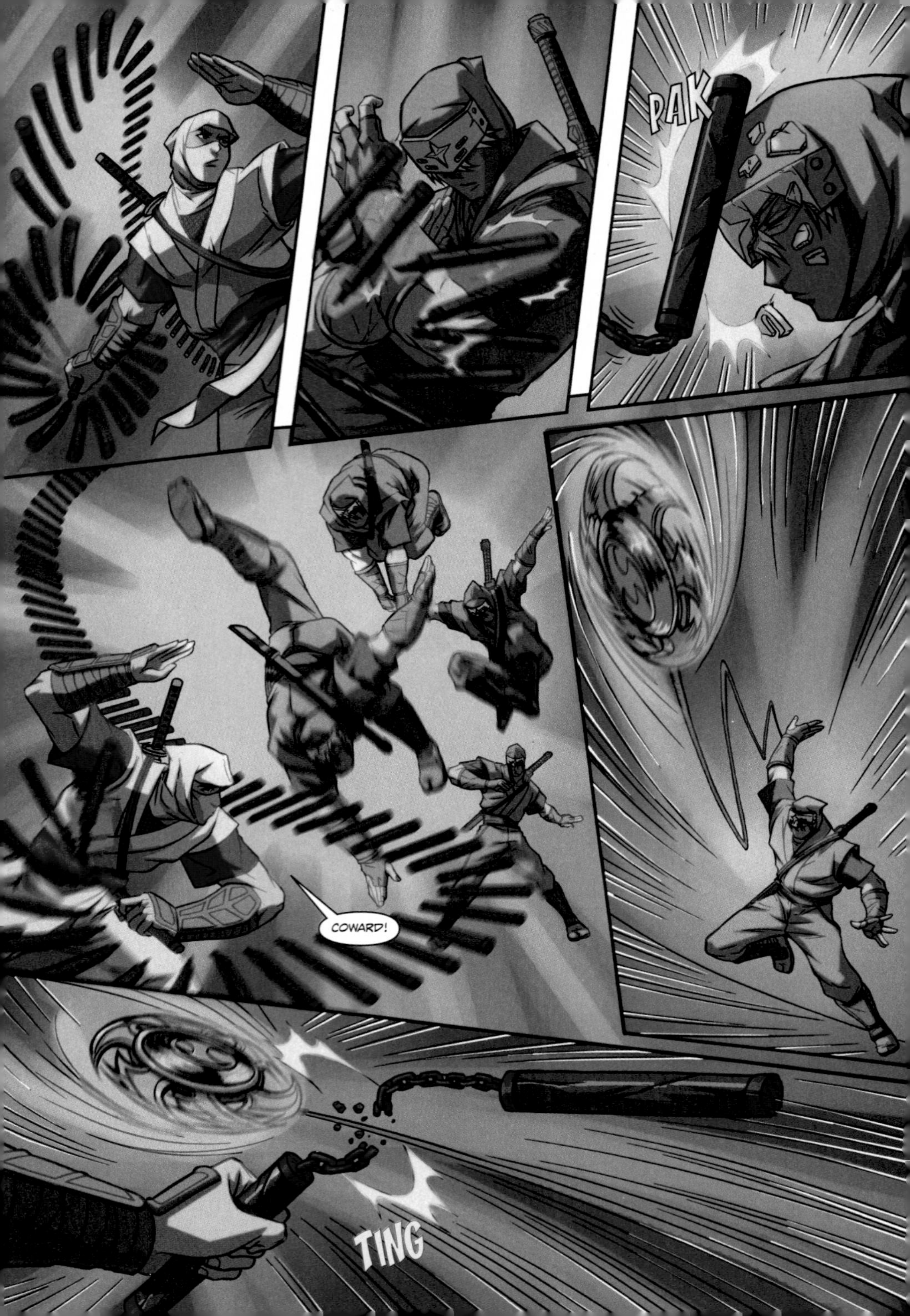
PAK
COWARD!
TING

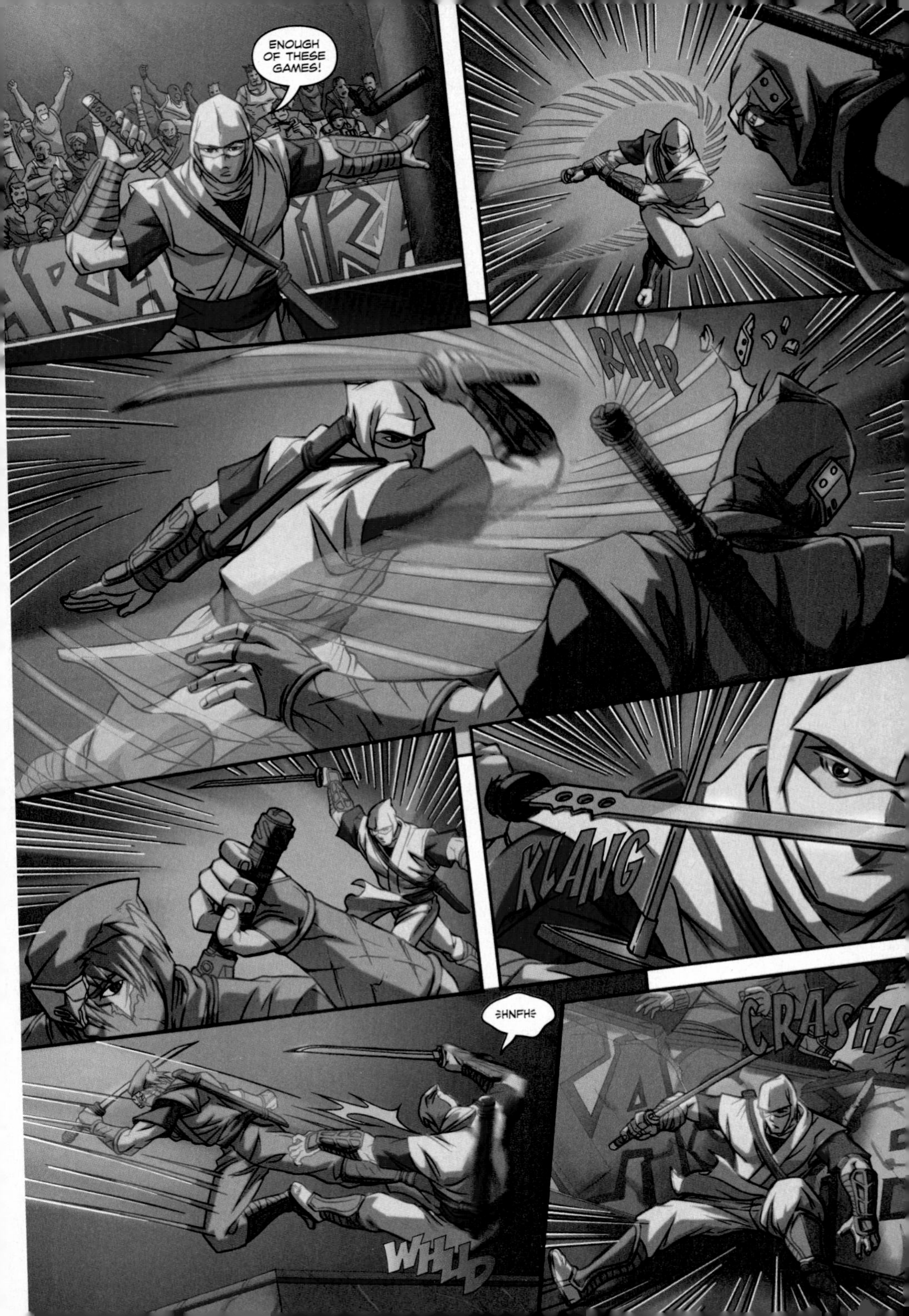
ENOUGH OF THESE GAMES!
RIIIP
KLANG
HNFH
CRASH!
WHUD

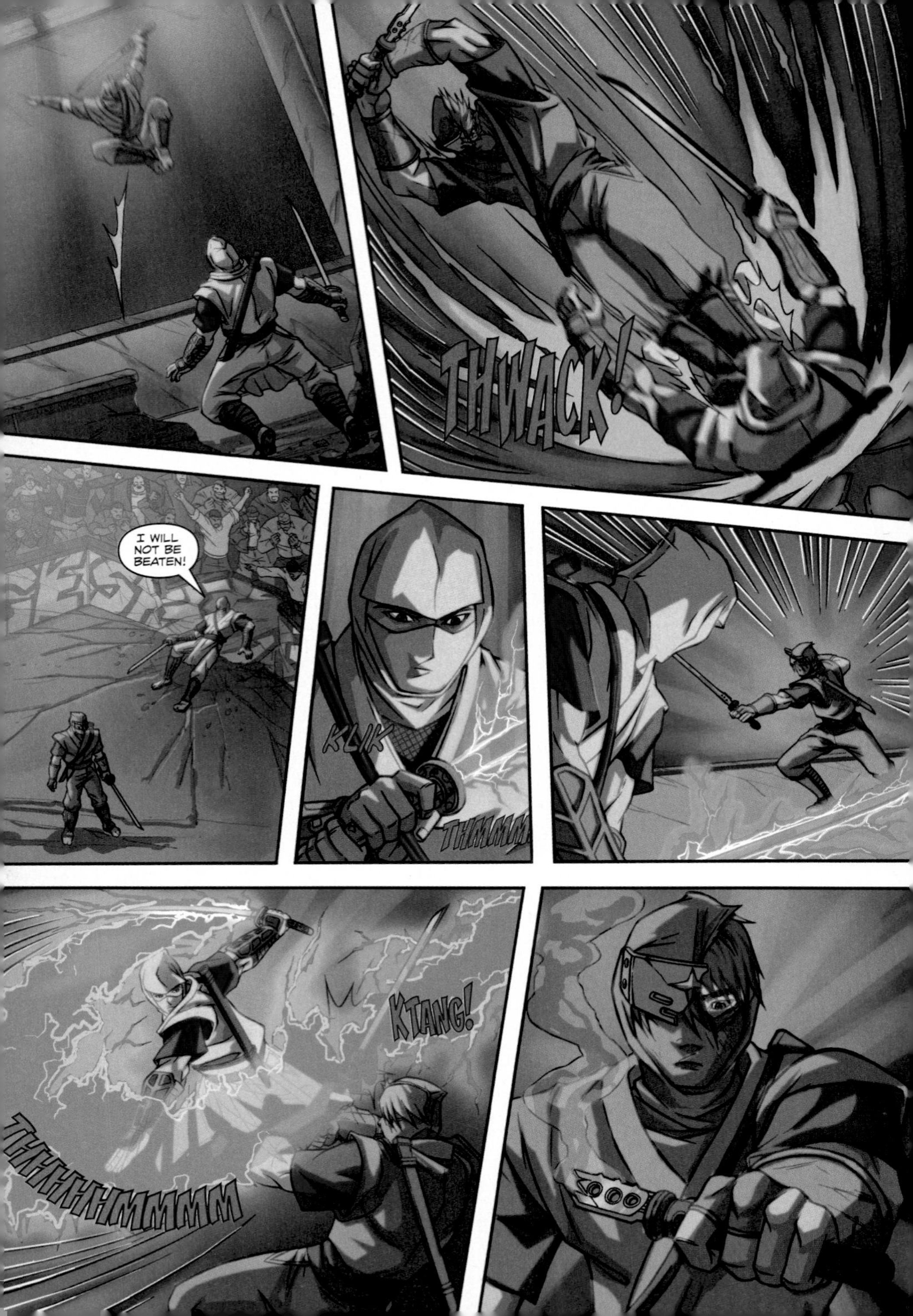
THWACK!
I WILL NOT BE BEATEN!
KLIK
THMMMM
KTANG!
THHHHHMMMMM

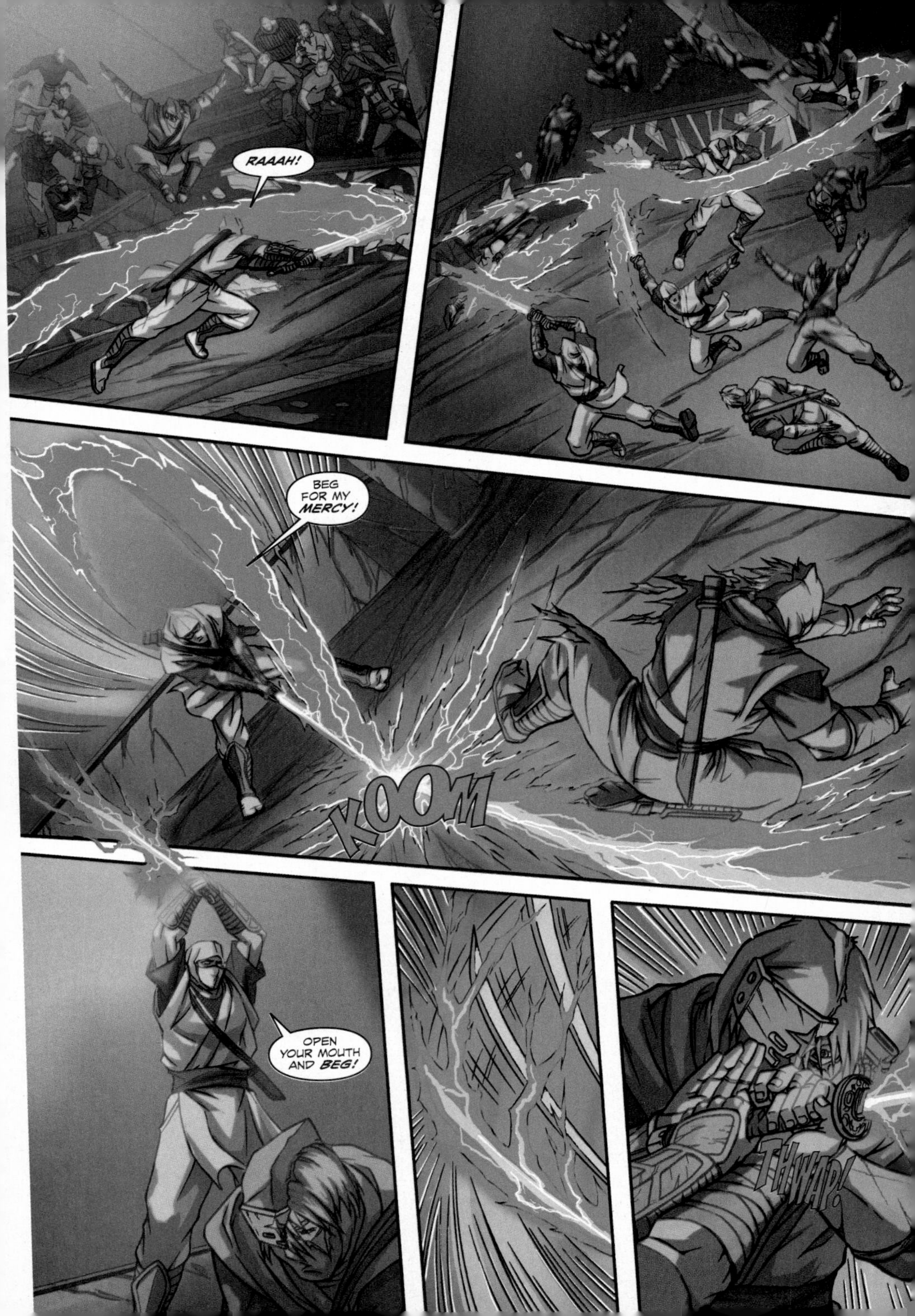
RAAAH!
BEG FOR MY *MERCY!*
KOOM
OPEN YOUR MOUTH AND *BEG!*
THWAP!

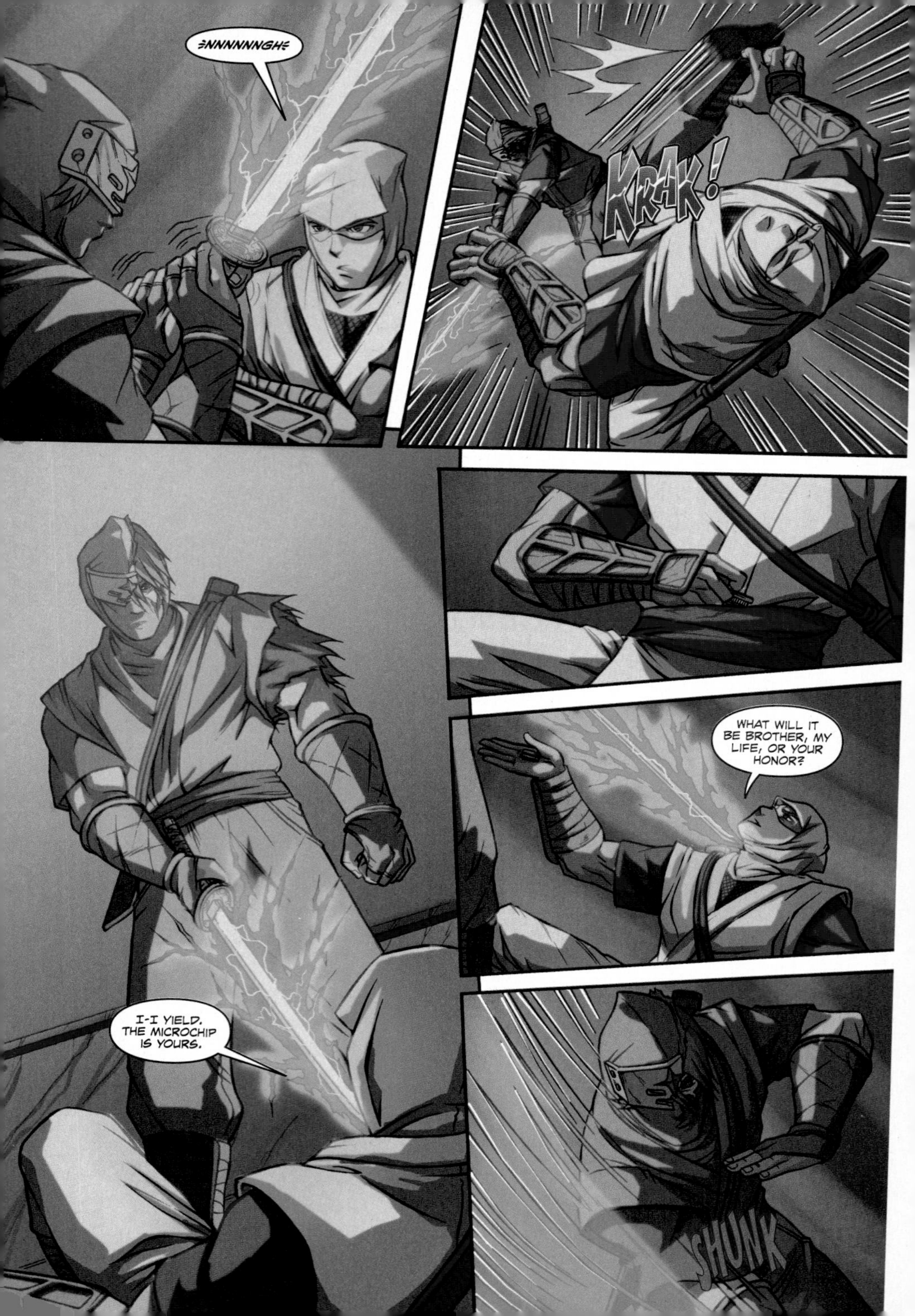

NNNNNNGH
KRAK!
WHAT WILL IT BE BROTHER, MY LIFE, OR YOUR HONOR?
I-I YIELD. THE MICROCHIP IS YOURS.
SHUNK

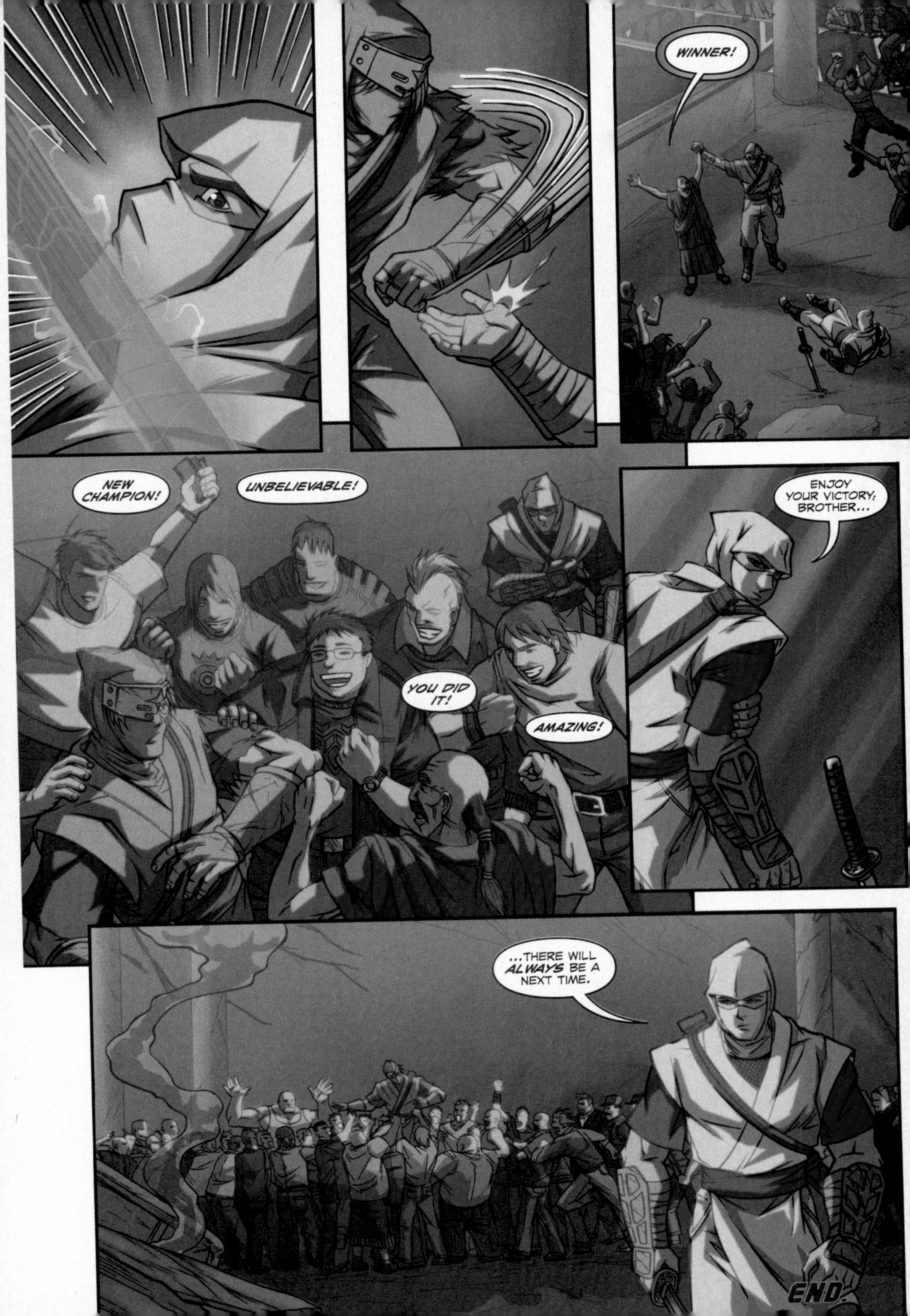
WINNER!
NEW CHAMPION!
UNBELIEVABLE!
YOU DID IT!
AMAZING!
ENJOY YOUR VICTORY, BROTHER...
...THERE WILL ALWAYS BE A NEXT TIME.
END.

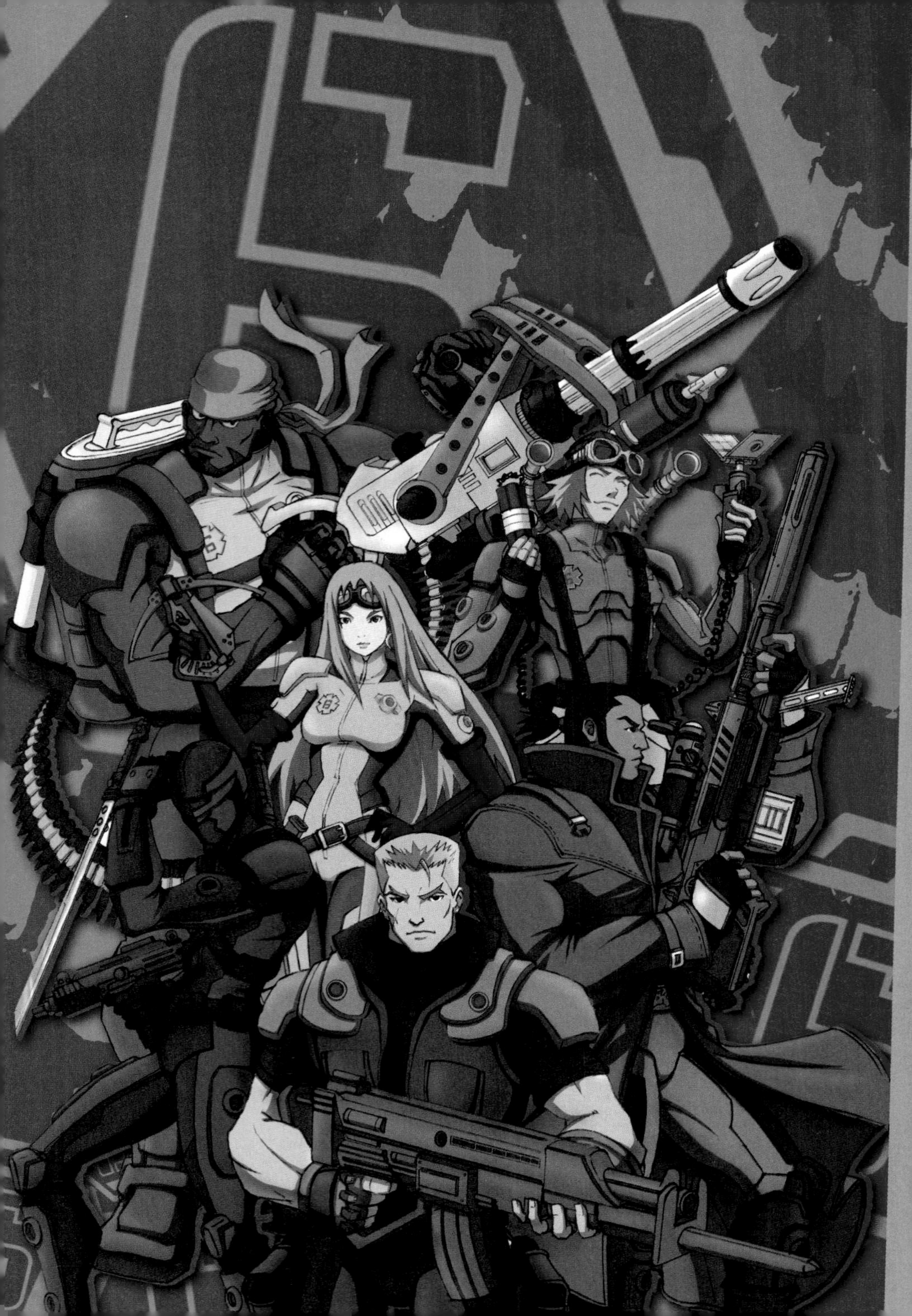

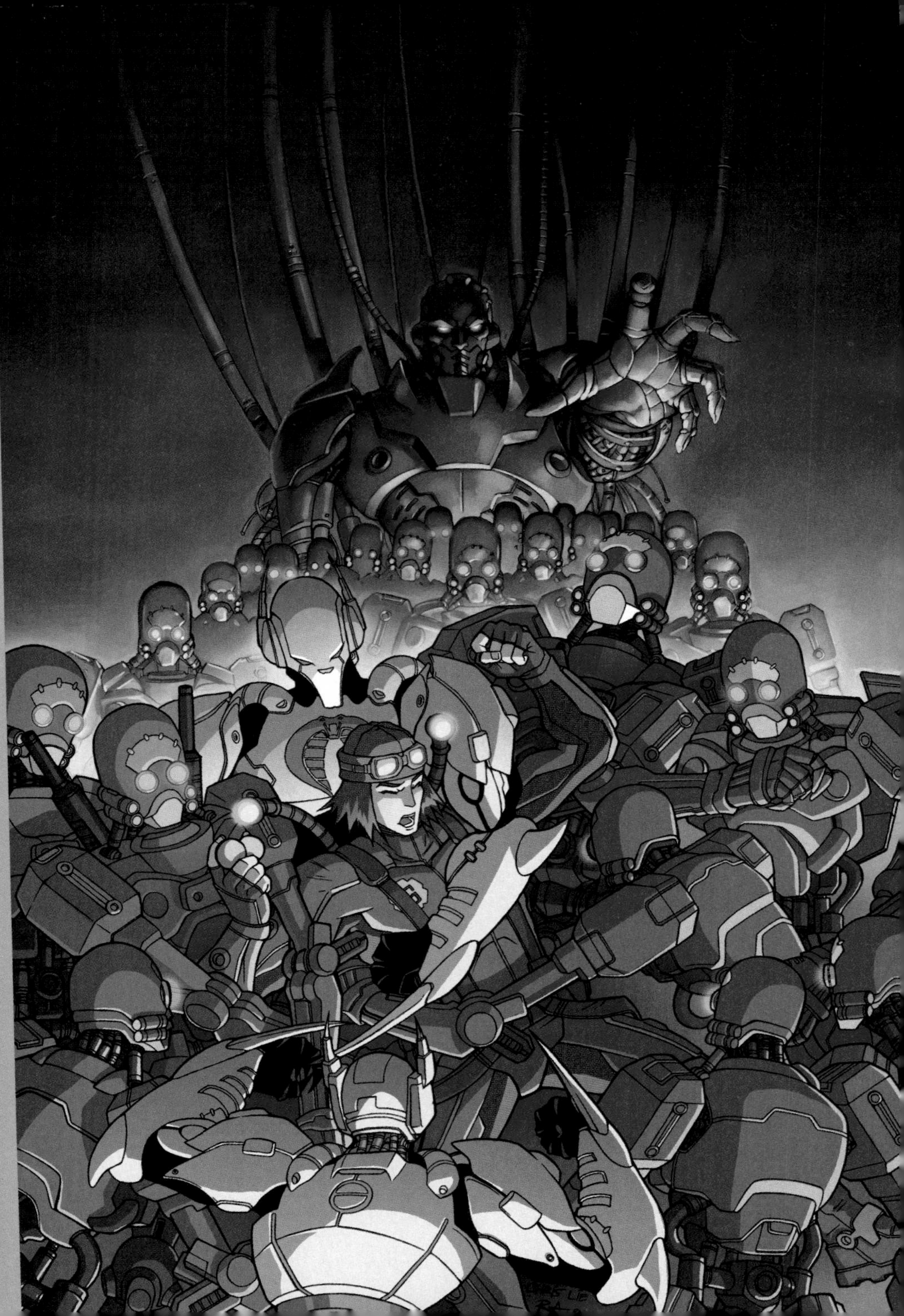

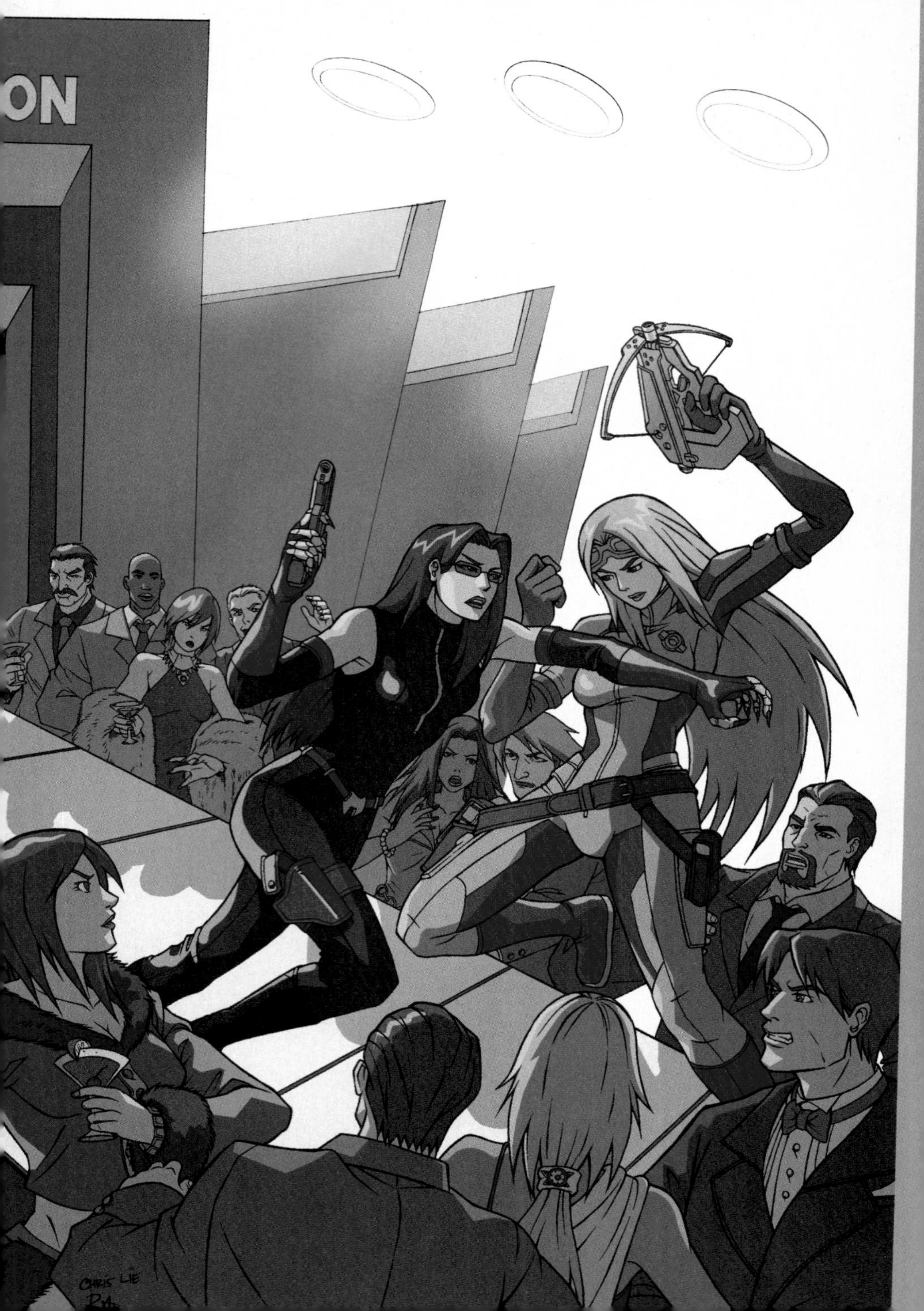
ON
CHRIS LIE

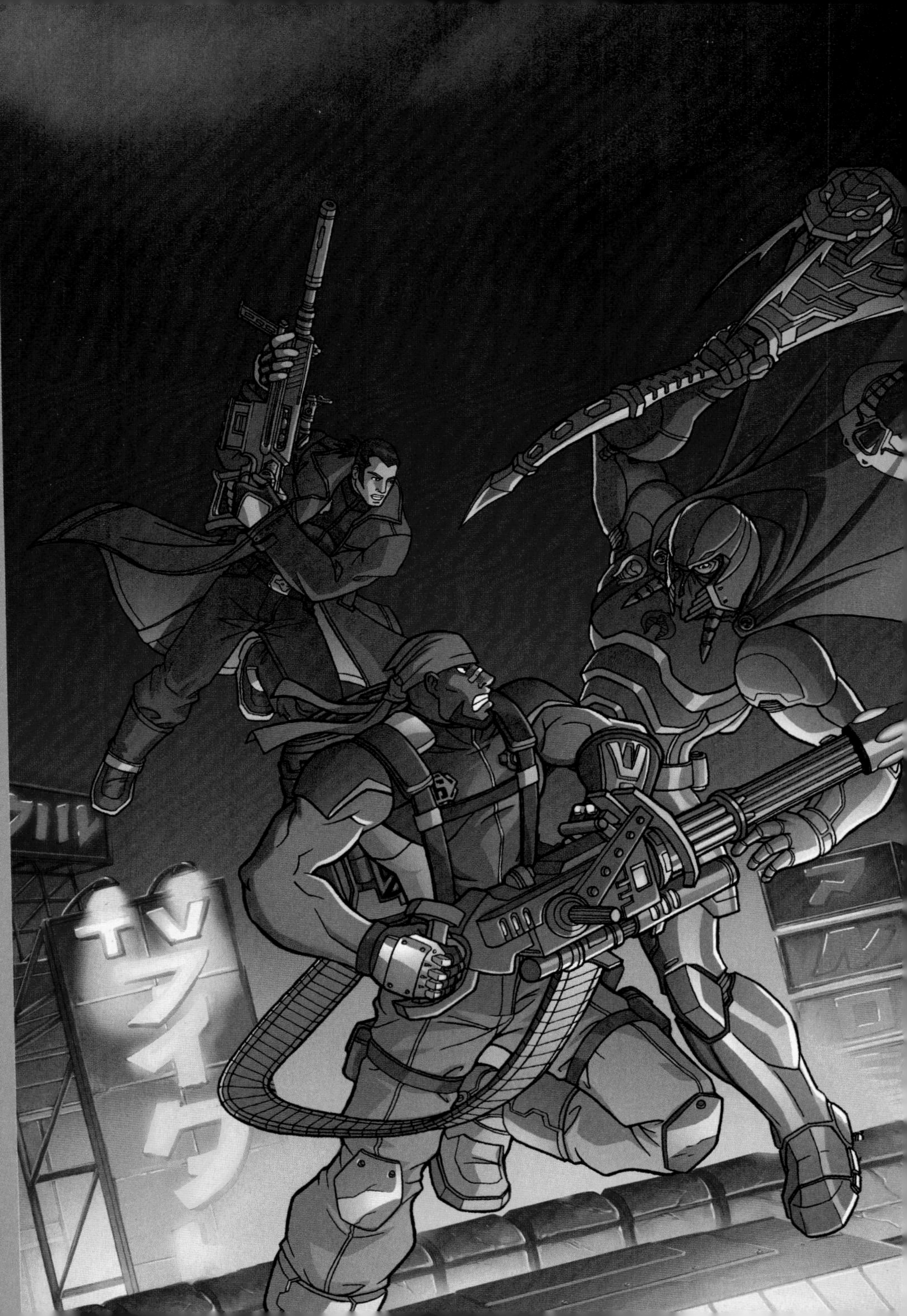
TV

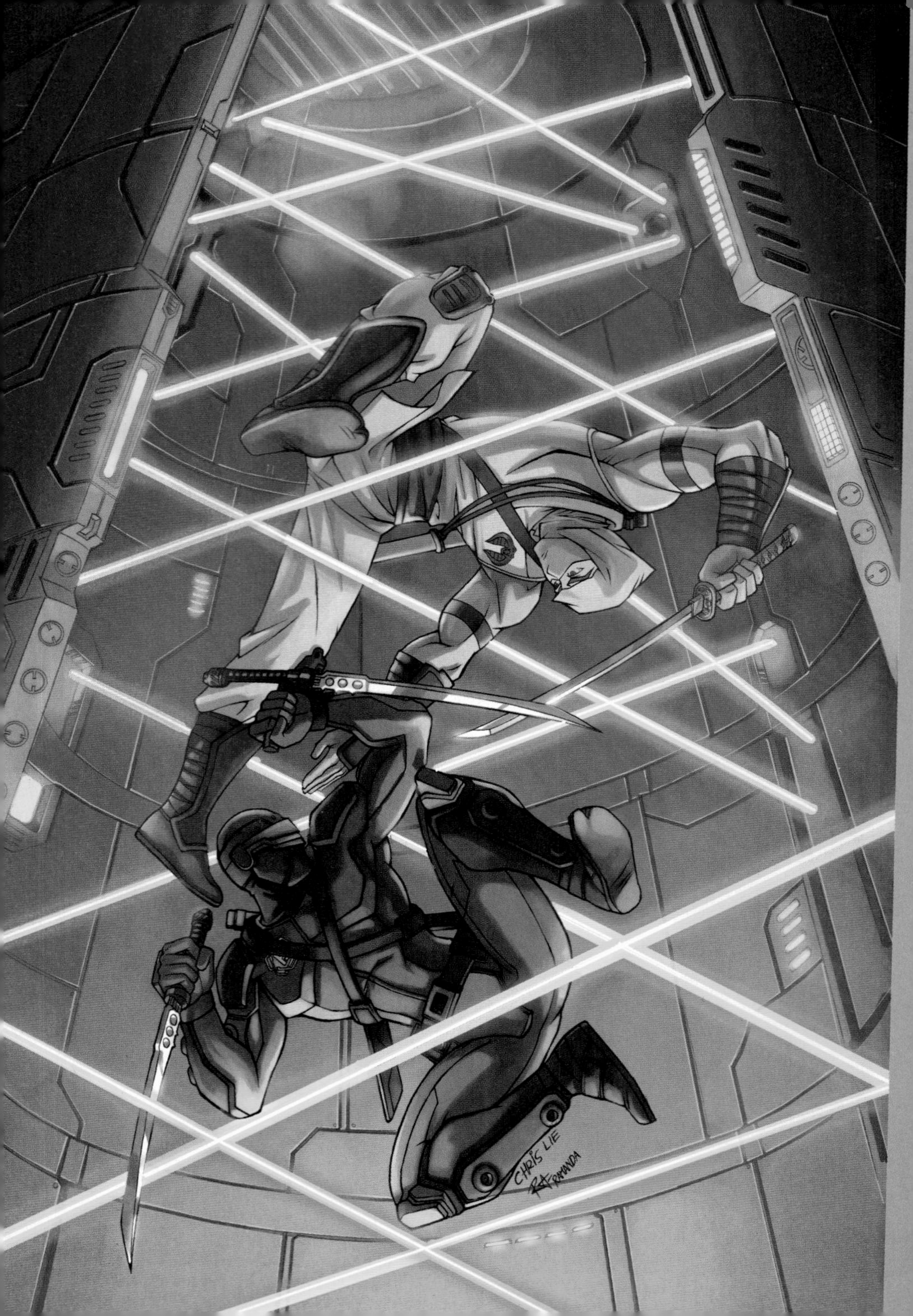
CHRIS LIE
RAMANDA

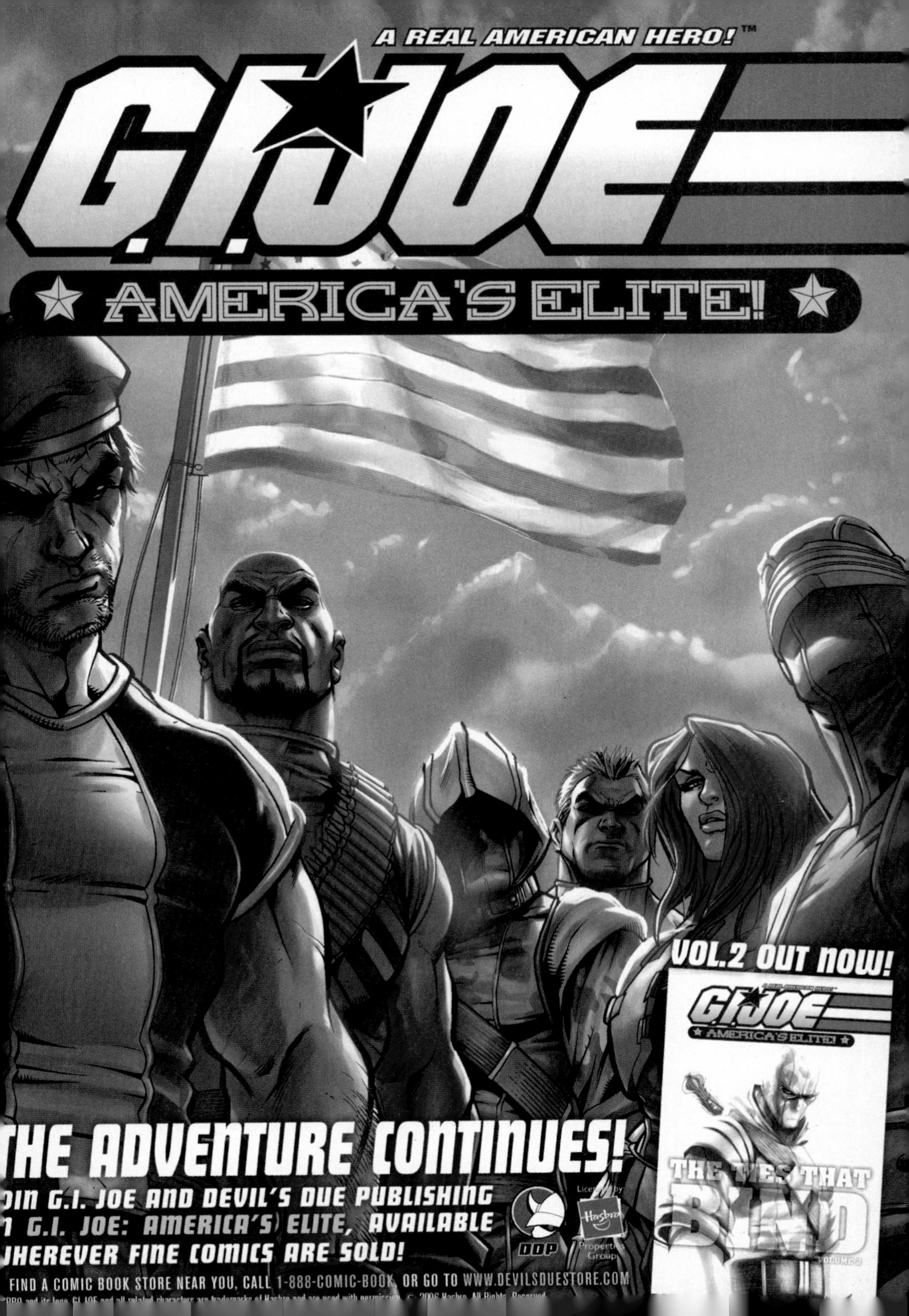

A REAL AMERICAN HERO!™
G.I. JOE
AMERICA'S ELITE!
VOL.2 OUT NOW!
THE TIES THAT BIND
THE ADVENTURE CONTINUES!
OIN G.I. JOE AND DEVIL'S DUE PUBLISHING
G.I. JOE: AMERICA'S ELITE, AVAILABLE
HEREVER FINE COMICS ARE SOLD!
DDP
Hasbro
Properties Group
FIND A COMIC BOOK STORE NEAR YOU, CALL 1-888-COMIC-BOOK, OR GO TO WWW.DEVILSDUESTORE.COM

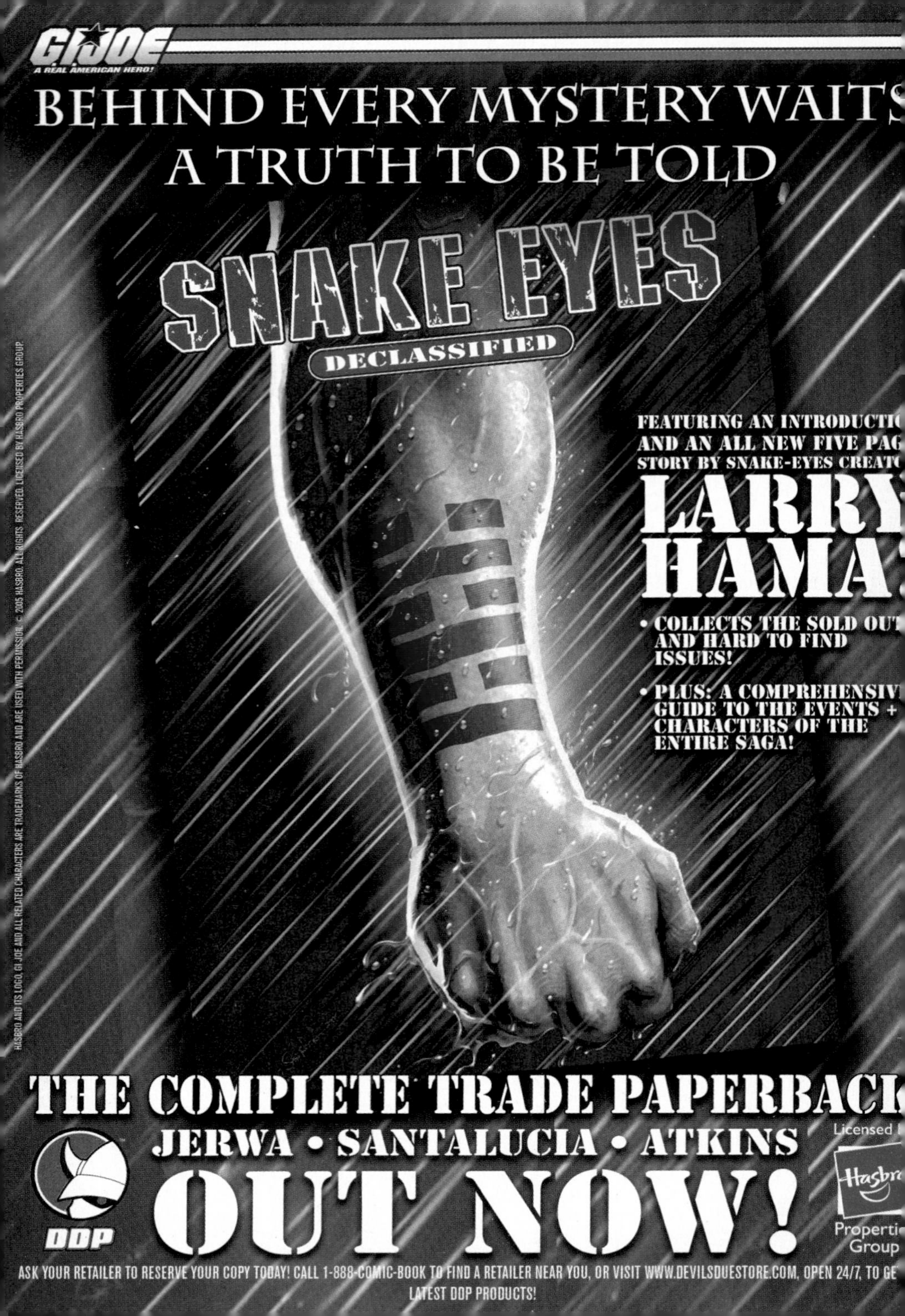
G.I. JOE
A REAL AMERICAN HERO!
BEHIND EVERY MYSTERY WAITS
A TRUTH TO BE TOLD
SNAKE EYES
DECLASSIFIED
FEATURING AN INTRODUCTI
AND AN ALL NEW FIVE PAG
STORY BY SNAKE-EYES CREATO
LARRY
HAMA
• COLLECTS THE SOLD OUT
AND HARD TO FIND
ISSUES!
• PLUS: A COMPREHENSIV
GUIDE TO THE EVENTS +
CHARACTERS OF THE
ENTIRE SAGA!
THE COMPLETE TRADE PAPERBACK
JERWA • SANTALUCIA • ATKINS
OUT NOW!
DDP
Licensed
Hasbro
Properti
Group
ASK YOUR RETAILER TO RESERVE YOUR COPY TODAY! CALL 1-888-COMIC-BOOK TO FIND A RETAILER NEAR YOU, OR VISIT WWW.DEVILSDUESTORE.COM, OPEN 24/7, TO GE
LATEST DDP PRODUCTS!
HASBRO AND ITS LOGO, GI JOE AND ALL RELATED CHARACTERS ARE TRADEMARKS OF HASBRO AND ARE USED WITH PERMISSION. © 2005 HASBRO. ALL RIGHTS RESERVED. LICENSED BY HASBRO PROPERTIES GROUP